THE WAY OF ST JAMES: VÍA DE LA PLATA
Seville to Santiago

About the Author

Alison Raju is a former teacher of French, German and Spanish to adults and the author of two other guides published by Cicerone Press: *The Way of St James: Le Puy to Santiago – A Walker's Guide* and *Via de la Plata: Seville to Santiago*.

THE WAY OF ST JAMES: VÍA DE LA PLATA

Seville to Santiago

by

Alison Raju

2 POLICE SQUARE, MILNTHORPE, CUMBRIA, LA7 7PY
www.cicerone.co.uk

© Alison Raju 2001
ISBN 1 85284 343 8
A catalogue record for this book is available from the British Library

For Jim

I would like to thank María-Jesús Vegas García de Blas (Seville), Bernhard Münzenmayer (Vienna) and Maurice and Marigold Fox for their assistance.
Photos, unless otherwise indicated, are by Maurice and Marigold Fox.
Maps: Harveys Maps

Advice to Readers

Readers are advised that while every effort is taken by the author to ensure the accuracy of this guidebook, changes can occur which may affect the contents. It is advisable to check locally on transport, accommodation, shops, etc, but even rights of way can be altered.

The publisher would welcome notes of any such changes.

Front cover: Statue of Santiago peregrino, church of Santa Marta de Tera (Zamora)

CONTENTS

INTRODUCTION

THE ROUTE

APPENDIXES

WAYS OF ST. JAMES IN SPAIN

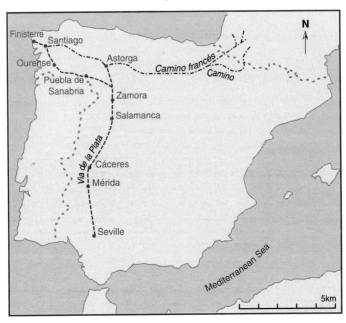

Legend

Pilgrim route on a road	═══════	County boundary	‑ ‑ ‑ ‑ ‑
Pilgrim route on a track	‑ ‑ ‑ ‑ ‑	Water	
Road	═══════	River	∿∿∿
Railway	┝┼┼┼┤	Church	⚲
Track	‑ ‑ ‑ ‑ ‑	Settlement	•

INTRODUCTION

History and Background

The Vía de la Plata, like the Camino francés (from the Pyrenees to Santiago), is a long-distance walk with a difference. For although the so-called 'French road' is the most well-known, well-travelled and well-documented of the pilgrim roads to Santiago de Compostela (and to such an extent that for many people it is the only one) it was, in fact, only one of several used in former times. Pilgrims in the past obviously did not travel to Roncesvalles by train or bus to begin their journey there, as do their modern counterparts, but set out on foot from their own front doors and as well as the northern coastal route, for example, the Camino aragonés over the Somport pass to Puenta la Reina, routes from the east of Spain and several roads through Portugal, there was also the Camino mozárabe or Vía de la Plata. This was so named, it is now thought, not because it followed the old Roman silver route from Huelva in the south to Astorga in the north but as a corruption of the Arabic *bal'latta*, used to describe wide, paved or public roads. This route, with its own network of tributaries, took pilgrims from Seville and other places, both along the way and adjacent to it, through Mérida, Cáceres and Salamanca to Zamora. From there many continued ahead via Benavente and La Bañeza to join the main flux of European pilgrims coming from the Pyrenees in Astorga. Others deviated via Puebla de Sanabria and Ourense to go directly to Santiago through Galicia. It is sometimes suggested that this was to avoid the Montes de León and the stiff climb up to Cebreiro but as the route through the western part of Zamora and the province of Ourense is extremely strenuous and necessitates climbing up (and down again) both the Puerto de Padornillo (1368m) and then the pass at A Canda (1268m) on two successive days this is not a very plausible explanation. There was also the option of going through northern Portugal, via Bragança and Chaves, to rejoin the route through Galicia again in Verín.

The original Vía de la Plata was a Roman road, running in more or less a straight line south–north from Mérida to Gijón, and anyone walking the Vía de la Plata today will be very much aware of being in Roman Spain. It was in two distinct parts: a paved section as far as Salamanca and a compressed earth track from there to Astorga and onwards. A section of the original paved road has been restored, about a kilometre leading uphill out of the small spa town of Baños de Montemayor on the boundary between Extremadura and Castille-León, and gives us an idea of the surface on the first part of the route. The Romans also built innumerable bridges along the way, many of which are still standing. Some of these are quite simple ones, like those at Casas de Don Antonio and Valdesalor (both south of Cáceres), the one over the Río Turienzo near Estación de Valderrey (shortly before you reach Astorga) or the much longer and more elaborate constructions such as the bridges over the Río Tormes in Salamanca, the Duero in Zamora and the Guadiana in Mérida, 792m long, with its 60 arches. (This is the way pilgrims enter the town. Mérida did not have just one Roman bridge as pilgrims left the town by another one too – over the Río Alberragas to the north.)

Typical small Roman bridge (author)

The entire Roman route was also divided into *mansiones* or stages of 20–25 Roman miles, with a *mansio* or place where travellers could rest overnight at the end of each one. The route was marked with miliarios, milestones, one every '1000 steps' or 1472m, and a number of them are still visible with their markings on them; these stood some 2ft 6in (76cm) high, like stone pillars, and were engraved with a Roman numeral. Several of them are still standing too, especially in the area near the Puente de la Magdelana, below Calzada de Béjar. Numbers CXLVIII (148) and CXLIXI (149) were repositioned in 1994 by the local 'Amigos' (south of Fuenterroble de Salvatierra, some 50km south of Salamanca) and relevant ayuntamientos (town halls) have plans to reinstate others along the route as well.

The Romans did not invent this route completely from scratch, any more than the pilgrims, whether on the Camino francés or the Vía de la Plata, created a completely new road to take them to Santiago, but they used and improved on existing paths and tracks instead. (A lot of research done on the Vía de la Plata has been carried out by people interested in Roman roads, rather than pilgrim routes.) The Romans who came to the south of Spain arrived by boat, from southern Italy, and could sail up the Guadalquivir river as at that time it was navigable not only as far as Seville but beyond as well. The road that became the Vía de la Plata originally started in Mérida, the town known as Augusta Emeritus, which they developed for their *emeritus* or pensioned-off soldiers from the fifth and tenth legions, and this road was used as a means of moving troops northwards. Later on it was extended as far south as Seville. There are an enormous number of Roman remains all along the Vía de la Plata, starting with the city of Italica on the outskirts of Seville, and especially in Mérida, with its theatre (still used for performances today) and which originally held 3000 spectators, an amphitheatre with seating for 14,000 and a circus which could accommodate 30,000 people. It also has a splendid Roman museum and the so-called Acueducto de los Milagros (a look at it will reveal why) and its two Roman reservoirs, one of which, the Embalse de Proserpina, nowadays used as a recreation area, is a few kilometres to the north on the route of the Vía de la Plata itself. Anyone who is interested in things Roman could follow the Vía de la Plata (in a car, for example) just for this reason. The Roman aspects are not limited to the Seville–Astorga section either – the *termas* (hot springs) in Ourense, for example, were also in use in Roman times and, as already indicated, there are several bridges of Roman origin in other places along the route too.

So much for the Roman aspects. The route they established forms the physical basis of the one that interests us, the route which pilgrims in future centuries would take. Pilgrims from the south of Spain and other parts of the Christian Mediterranean (who travelled to Seville by boat), as well as Arabs and Orientals, apparently, made use of the existing Roman road infrastructure to take them to Santiago. This *camino* (the Vía de la Plata) – a great Roman engineering feat – also had its own network of tributaries: from Córdoba, for example, and Granada, joining the route in Mérida, or from Toledo, where pilgrims joined it in Salamanca. It is often thought that pilgrims to Santiago only used the Vía de la Plata after the Reconquista (in 1492) but they actually began much earlier. The Vía de la Plata as a pilgrim artery began in the twelfth century, after the fall of Toledo in 1085, but especially after the political and religious annexation by Galicia of a large part of the western fringe of Spain through which the Vía de la Plata ran – the area around Salamanca, for example. Another important influence in 'getting the pilgrimage off the ground' along this route was the powerful Archbishop Gelmírez; it is already well known how he was responsible for promoting the Camino francés across the north of Spain but under his rule the diocese of Santiago de Compostela, which already reached to Salamanca, was extended as far south as Mérida in 1179. Spain was still under Muslim rule, of course, but during this period there was a degree of tolerance allowed to Christians – the Mozárabic ones, those living under Muslim rule (as opposed to the Mudéjar Muslims living later under Christian domination) – and the Vía de la Plata was the route these pilgrims took to Santiago, hence the name Camino mozárabe. The Vía de la Plata was also the route used in 1062 (under Fernando I) to take the body of St Isidore of Seville up to León and after the Reconquest of Córdoba the bells of Santiago cathedral, which had been taken to the mosque in Córdoba 200 years previously by Al-Mansur, were returned via this route to their rightful home in Galicia.

The movement of pilgrims along the Vía de la Plata was never as great as along the Camino francés but it too had its own infrastructure of pilgrim hospitals. The question is often raised as to the existence of

Jacobean churches or other influences along this route. Once again, there are not as many as there are on the Camino francés (one explanation that has been suggested is that the Mozárabic pilgrims were exiles/refugees and thus had no time to leave permanent traces of their passage) but there are certainly a significant number and the interested reader is referred to the summary in Appendix B. The other important factor to remember, when considering the historical aspects of the pilgrimage along the Vía de la Plata, is the role played by the Order of the Knights of Santiago, founded in Cáceres in 1170 and whose purpose was to protect pilgrims on their way.

Legend

Pilgrimages had been popular amongst Christians ever since Constantine the Great had the Church of the Holy Sepulchre built over the site of Christ's burial in Jerusalem, in AD 326, and the discovery, shortly afterwards, of the Holy Cross itself. Those journeying to this shrine were known as *palmeros* (palmers) whilst *romeros* went to Rome, the burial place of St Peter. But why did pilgrims want to go to Santiago? Those who have already walked or ridden the Camino francés will very likely know something about the discovery of the body of St James in Galicia but for those who do not, the story begins after the death of Christ, when his disciples dispersed to different parts of the then known world, to spread the Gospel as they had been bidden. St James (son of Zebedee, brother of John and Christ's first cousin) went to Spain, we are told, where he spent a couple of years evangelising, apparently without a great deal of success. He then returned to Jerusalem but was beheaded by Herod shortly afterwards, in AD 44. Immediately following his martyrdom, however, his followers are said to have taken his body to Jaffa, on the coast, where a ship was miraculously waiting for them, and they set off back to Spain. They landed in Iria Flavia on the coast of Galicia, present-day Padrón, some 20km from what is now Santiago de Compostela, after a journey (and in a stone boat!) which is purported to have taken only a week, thereby providing proof of angelic assistance. The body was then buried in a tomb on a hillside, along with, later on, two of his followers, and then forgotten for the next 750 years. The story is, in fact, considerably more complicated than this but these are the bare bones.

Early in the ninth century Pelagius, a hermit living in that part of Spain, had a vision (which he subsequently reported to Theodomir, bishop of Iria Flavia) in which he saw a very large bright star, surrounded by a ring of smaller ones, shining over a deserted spot in the hills. The matter was investigated and a tomb found there containing three bodies. They were immediately identified as those of St James and two of his followers and when Alfonso II, King of the Asturias (791–824), went there he declared St James the patron saint of Spain. He built a church and a small monastery over the tomb in the saint's honour, around which a town grew up. It was known as 'campus de la stella' or 'campus stellae', later shortened to 'compostela'. This is one explanation of the origin of the name. Another is that it derives from the Latin *componere* (to bury), as a Roman cemetery or early Christian necropolis is known to have existed under the site of the present-day cathedral in Santiago – and where the remains of St James are still believed to be housed today.

News of the discovery of the body of the saint soon spread, however, and led Santiago de Compostela to become the third great focus of Christian pilgrimage from the Middle Ages onwards. The spread of the news was encouraged, moreover, both by Archbishop Gelmírez and the cathedral authorities, who were anxious to promote the town as a pilgrimage centre, thus attracting money to the area, and later by the Order of the Knights of Santiago, who saw in it the opportunity to assist the Spanish church in its long struggle against the Moors. Both factions were also helped by the fact that the Turks had seized the Holy Sepulchre in 1078, thus putting a stop to pilgrimages to Jerusalem and because journeying to Rome had also become difficult, for political reasons. However, Santiago was attractive as a potential pilgrim 'venue' in other respects too, as it fulfilled the various criteria necessary to make a pilgrimage there worthy of merit. It was far away (from other parts of Europe, for example) and difficult to reach, thus requiring a good deal of hardship and endurance to get there (and back again too, of course). It was sufficiently dangerous (wolves, bandits, fever, rivers that were difficult to cross) as well as being in a Spain locked tight in struggle with the Moors, and for this reason pilgrims often travelled in quite large groups. The road itself was also well enough supplied with shrines, relics and other sights worth seeing and as traffic increased roads were improved and bridges and hospices were built. Churches were dedicated to St James, too, whilst others contain his statue or depictions in paintings or tilework. As Santiago Apóstol he is portrayed bareheaded, with halo and a book (open or closed) in hand, but he more frequently appears as Santiago Peregrino in pilgrim outfit, with hat, stick, cape, gourd and satchel and with shells on either hat, lapels or both. His other common representation is as Santiago Matamoros (the moor-slayer), riding on a charger, with sword, shield and often a dead Moor or two falling at his feet. It is not unusual, however, to see a mixture of the apostle and pilgrim versions, with halo, book, stick and cockle shells, whilst there are also bareheaded pilgrim occurrences. Depictions of the Santiago sword, with bent handle, like a shepherd's crook, are also found in places associated in some way with St James.

A number of very tiny chapels (*ermitas*) built along the way were also dedicated to St Roch (San Roque in Spanish), the pilgrim saint from Montpellier. After a pilgrimage to Rome St Roch devoted his life to caring for plague victims but withdrew to live in a forest when he contracted a disease which left him with an unsightly sore on his left thigh. For this reason he is depicted in art – and there are a number of St Roch representations along the Vía de la Plata – with the front flap of his coat turned back, to warn people to keep away from him, and is accompanied by the faithful dog, often with a loaf of bread in his mouth, who brought the saint his daily rations. Legend has confused him with Santiago Peregrino at times, and he not infrequently appears in a 'pilgrim version' as well, with added hat, staff and cockle shells on his clothing.

Why did people go on pilgrimages anyway? For a variety of reasons. As a profession of faith, as a form of punishment (a system of fixed penalties for certain crimes/sins was in operation during the Middle Ages), as a means of atonement, as a way of acquiring merit (and thus, for example, reducing or, in certain cases, cutting in half the amount of time spent in Purgatory) and as an opportunity to venerate the relics of saints available in shrines along the way. (Indulgences were also available from the cathedral authorities in Santiago to those who made the journey in Holy Years). No doubt, too, there were some who were just glad of the opportunity to escape their surroundings. Those with the means to do so went on horseback and some wealthy people made the pilgrimage along with a considerable retinue. The majority of pilgrims went on foot, however, and even amongst the rich there were some who preferred to walk, rather than ride, because of the greater 'merit' they would attain afterwards.

The pilgrim in former times was not at all sure that he would eventually reach his destination, let alone return home in one piece, so before setting out he took leave of his family and employer, made his will and generally put his affairs in order. He (or she) obtained his 'credentials' (pilgrim passport) from his bishop or church, which he could then present in order to obtain food and lodging in the many pilgrim 'hospitals' and other establishments along the way. This was both a precaution against the growing number of pseudo-pilgrims and as a means of providing proof of his journey: he had his papers stamped at different stages along the way so that once he arrived in Santiago he could obtain his *compostela* (certificate of pilgrimage) from the cathedral authorities there. This in turn entitled him to stay in the pilgrim shelters on his return journey as well as furnishing evidence, if needed, that he had actually made the pilgrimage successfully.

The pilgrim had his staff and scrip blessed in church before setting out and travelled light, carrying little else but a gourd for water and, on his return journey, his scallop shell. This singled him out as a pilgrim, rather than as any other type of traveller, and is the symbol embedded above doorways and in other places on the many and varied buildings that accommodated them along the different pilgrims roads. (Originally these were worn only by returning pilgrims but today they are common on hats, rucksacks and round the necks of those beginning their journey to Santiago, almost a required item of 'pilgrim uniform' for some.) Pilgrims with funds could obviously stay in inns and other publicly available lodgings (such as the *ventas* that lined the Vía de la Plata, often on the site of the former Roman *mansiones*) but there were also hospices and other facilities specially provided for them. Some of these were in towns, whether in the centre or outside the walls to cater both for latecomers and possibly contagious pilgrims, whilst others were in the middle of the countryside, often by bridges or at the crossing of important pilgrim feeder roads. Much of the pilgrim accommodation was provided by religious orders, by churches and civic authorities, as well as by benevolent individuals. The facilities offered varied considerably from one establishment to another and one or two such buildings are still standing, such as the one in Rionegro del Puente.

There are different explanations as to the origins of the scallop shell or 'coquille Saint Jacques' but one is that when the followers of St James arrived in the port of Iria Flavia with the apostle's body they saw a man riding along the beach (a bridegroom in some versions) whose horse took fright and then plunged into the sea. When they re-emerged both horse and rider were covered from head to foot in scallop shells (and even today the beaches in this part of Galicia are strewn with them). It was customary to set out in the springtime in order to reach Santiago for the feast of St James on July 25th and return home for the winter. This was especially true in Holy Years, those in which July 25th falls on a Sunday (the next ones are in 2004 and 2015), the only time the 'Puerta Santa' or Holy Door of the Cathedral of Santiago is open. This is sealed up at the end of each such year and then symbolically broken down again by the Archbishop in a special ceremony in the evening of December 31st preceding the new Holy Year, one during which special concessions and indulgences were, and still are, available to pilgrims. On returning home many joined confraternities of former pilgrims, such as the *cofradías* in Castilblanco de los Arroyos and Rionegro del Puente, the forerunners of the modern-day associations of 'Friends of St James' that now exist in several countries to support, promote and encourage the different routes to Santiago. Unlike the Camino francés, however, from which there are a number of extant accounts of pilgrim journeys from the twelfth century onwards, there are no surviving writings documenting individual pilgrim journeys to Santiago along the Vía de la Plata.

Solitude in the springtime   (author)

The Vía de la Plata today

The route from Seville to Astorga has been waymarked (very thoroughly and clearly) since 1991, when the late Andrés Muñoz Garde researched the route and painted yellow arrows, like those on the Camino francés, to guide a large group he was leading along this stretch of the Vía de la Plata. He was the one person who really set the route on its feet again in recent times. People living along the way are sometimes heard to remark 'Ah, yes, now there is a new route to Santiago,' assuming it must be something that has been invented recently, but although it has been waymarked for 10 years very few pilgrims used it in the early years. The other catalyst was the very active group of Amigos del Camino de Santiago in Seville, led by the late José Luis Salvador Salvador, who not only continued and maintained the waymarking but also visited all the villages along the way within reasonable walking distance of each other, talking to priests, *alcaldes* (mayors), the local police and so on to set up a network of very basic sleeping accommodation in parish halls, schools, sports centres and so on, so that nowadays, apart from large towns, there is always somewhere (usually very spartan, obviously) for pilgrims to sleep, apart from *hostales*, *fondas* and so on where these exist. The Seville 'Amigos' also produce a special *credencial*, a 'pilgrim passport' for the route (see below). There are also several other associations of 'Amigos de la Vía de la Plata' along the way (those in Fuenterroble de Salvatierra and Zamora are particularly active) and the group in Ourense played a big part in clearing and waymarking the route through Galicia.

In 1992 only about 50 people walked the route in a whole year (this author was one of them) and it was quite different then, not only from the well-travelled Camino francés but also from the route today. Nowadays people living along the route know who pilgrims are, where they are going, what the yellow arrows are for and that they are living along an important pilgrim road to Santiago. There are also many more pilgrims – relatively speaking, of course. In 1993, a Holy Year (when July 25th, St James's Day, falls on a Sunday) there were about 100 (compared to 99,000 on the Camino francés), some 450 in 1996 and what was often described by local people as *un montón* (a 'huge number') in the 1999 Holy Year – about 1500 altogether! This compares with over 150,000 on the Camino francés in 1999 and 55,000 in the year 2000. Many of these did not walk (or cycle) all the way from Seville but, like those who start in Sarria on foot on the Camino francés in order to walk the minimum 100km required to qualify for their *compostela*, many of them started in Ourense for the same reason. A lot of people also start either in or after A Gudiña because the Xunta de Galicia has set up a certain number of *refugios*, .which obviously makes it much easier to walk the route. In the past there were also no guidebooks; nobody, even priests and people with yellow arrows outside their doors, knew about the route or where it went, and anybody walking along with a rucksack bigger than a daysack was automatically either a 'hippie', a tramp or a *transeunte* (somebody walking from town to town theoretically in search of work) and looked at often very oddly by people in shops and places with accommodation. Unlike the Camino francés, where the numbers of pilgrims has risen and fallen in different periods but where there has always been at least a continuous trickle, the pilgrim route along the Vía de la Plata came to a complete halt for a long time, possibly one or two centuries, and in the public eye, at least, it had disappeared into oblivion.

Oak trees between Almadén and the Finca Mateos Arroyos

The walk from Seville to Santiago, whether via Astorga or Ourense, can be completed in six weeks by anyone who is fairly fit and who also likes to visit places of interest along the way. It can be undertaken in sections, too, by those who lack the time to do it all in one go or would just like to cover certain stretches, and indications are given in the text as to how to reach (or leave) the main towns along the way. Anyone in Britain who is thinking of walking any part of the route should certainly consider contacting the Confraternity of St James for advice and membership – their annually updated guide to accommodation and services is extremely useful.

The present guide is intended principally for walkers but as a large part of the route is suitable for mountain (but definitely NOT touring) bikes indications, with alternatives, are provided in the text for the stretches where it is unsuitable. (Cyclists may find it helpful to go through the text in advance and highlight aspects relevant to their needs.) Pilgrims on bikes should be aware, however, that they will not normally be able to travel very fast on the walker's route ('speed merchants' should stick firmly to the roads), that they may have to get off and push from time to time (and will therefore need suitable footwear) and that in Spain all types of cyclist are required by law to wear helmets. Details of bike repair shops are given where known.

Like the Camino francés, which many pilgrims on this route have already walked or cycled, people make the journey along the Vía de la Plata for a variety of reasons – historical, cultural, religious, as a(nother) significant action or event in their lives – and late twentieth and early twenty-first century pilgrims are people from all walks of life. Many are Spanish, of course, but there is also a significant proportion from Belgium, Netherlands, France and Germany, as well as from Britain and places much further afield. It is still, however, surprisingly uncommon for people who live along the Vía de la Plata itself to set out from their own front doors and make their first journey to Santiago along a route which would lead them there directly. For some reason, perhaps because of the massive publicity during the nineties about the Camino francés being THE Camino de Santiago rather than just one of many routes to the city of the *apóstol*, people seem to think that they should go to Roncesvalles (from Seville, for example!) to set out on the 'proper' Camino, though this is gradually changing. Others are misinformed, thinking that the route from Seville is not waymarked or that the Vía de la Plata is all road walking, since the N630, the main road which in fact follows the historical route taken by the Vía de la Plata, is confusingly also named Ruta de la Plata. Other people are unwilling to follow a route where 'there are no *refugios*' (specially provided facilities with beds and hot showers).

Many of those who make the journey along the Vía de la Plata travel alone, others in twos or threes, others in quite large groups, particularly those on foot. Many complete the entire route in one stretch; others, with more limited time, cover only a part of it or do it a section at a time over several years. Most who go to Santiago along the Camino mozárabe, and especially those who have been able to do the whole route in one go, would probably agree afterwards, however, that like their (probable) earlier journey along the Camino francés, it has changed their life in some way, even though they may never have set out with this intention at all.

Most long-distance footpaths avoid not only large towns but even quite small villages as well. The Camino de Santiago along the Vía de la Plata, on the other hand, because of its historic origins (much of the original *calzada romana* is subsumed under the N630) and the need for shelter, deliberately seeks them out. However, one of the differences between the modern pilgrim and his historical counterpart, whether he walks, goes by bike or on horseback, is that very few return home by the same means of transport. The modern pilgrim route has thus become a 'one-way street' and it is unusual, today, to encounter anyone with either enough time or inclination to return to his or her point of departure by the same means as he or she set out. Moreover, since the waymarking with yellow arrows is also 'one way only' it would be difficult to follow the Vía de la Plata backwards, though some sections are waymarked (in white, and somewhat patchily) in reverse for use as a revival of a *ruta de transhumancia* (see below).

The route is a varied one, in climate, scenery, history and architecture, and the pilgrim sees a big cross-section of Spain along it. The part from Seville to Astorga is not physically difficult to walk in that there are no stiff climbs but the distances between accommodation are often very long. It is also a solitary route, which some people obviously like, but quite a few people who have done the Vía de la Plata after the camino from Roncesvalles have said that they did not like it at all because they rarely met anyone else or any other pilgrims. The walking (or cycling) is almost all on old tracks and paths, very often the sort that are used for transporting animals or, if not, on extremely quiet minor roads. The pilgrim is normally far away from roads, sometimes never seeing anybody at all, or any villages, all day long. (This obviously needs a certain amount of organisation if you are not to get caught without anything to eat when you are hungry or short of water as there are hardly any public fountains until you reach Galicia.)

The Seville–Astorga section has also been used, in reverse, from Gijón to Cáceres, as a *ruta de transhumancia*, used for droving animals in large numbers, and in 1995 the practice was revived and huge numbers of cattle were moved on foot to try and help restore the tradition. Anybody walking the route who sees white waymarking in reverse may have wondered what the white arrows were for; these were painted to guide the people driving cattle on their way.

Those who decide to continue via Puebla de Sanabria and Ourense will find the route very strenuous, with a lot of stiff climbs and descents, but it is also very beautiful (in nice weather, of course). The route from Seville to Astorga is 742km (plus 250km more along the Camino francés for pilgrims who choose this alternative) while the route for those who go directly via Galicia to Santiago is 991km so there is virtually no difference between the two options, in terms of distance.

People who 'turn left' at Astorga often find it quite a shock, however, to be suddenly immersed in a sea of pilgrims after walking for so many weeks on their own or only with their companions whilst other people who have continued through Galicia have said that they found it something of a 'let-down' when they arrived in Santiago, unknown, amongst all the other pilgrims coming from the east who all knew each other by then.

Topography, economy and language

The Vía de la Plata leaves Seville, capital of the province of the same name and one of the eight that make up the autonomous *región* of Andalucia, crosses the Río Guadalquivir and leaves via the city's industrial suburbs to the northwest. To begin with the scenery is not particularly interesting: flattish landscape with scrubby vegetation and the ubiquitous *jara* (cistus) bushes that smell like church incense. You will also see very large cacti, interspersed with cotton fields, orange trees and, increasingly, plantations of cork trees with their bark often stripped bare, the more recently removed a bright red-brown, the others already regrowing their coats (it takes seven years before they are ready to harvest again) a dull grey colour. After passing through Guillena – the first of several small towns with their characteristic white-painted houses with thick walls and wrought-iron bars at the windows, many of them single storey, their white-painted churches, public buildings and *frontón* (pelota court) all huddled close together – the route continues through the Parque Natural de la Sierra Norte de Sevilla to Castilblanco de los Arroyos along one of the first of many *veredas*, *cordeles* and *cañadas*. These routes were the highways of old and the classification of the different categories (which you will encounter in the names of some of the tracks you will take further on) was laid down by Alfonso X in 1284. The largest was the *cañada real*, 90 *varas* (75m) wide, followed by the *cordel* or *ramal*, 45 *varas* (33m), and the narrower *vereda* or *cordón*, 25 *varas* (20m) wide. Nowadays these old pathways are used mainly for the movement of animals but some of them have also been cleared and waymarked as recreational walking routes. However, since there are many extremely large estates (*cortijos*) in this part of Spain there are often few tracks and paths to walk on, open to the public or not, and for this reason you will sometimes have to use minor tarred roads (such as the 16km stretch between

Castilblanco and El Berrocal, for example). The entrance gates to these *cortijos*, often quite elaborate white-painted constructions, are to be seen by the side of the road from time to time, though the farm buildings themselves are usually well out of sight.

Gradually the landscape becomes more undulating and the cork trees increase in number, as do the *encina* (holm oak) plantations. This is an evergreen relation of the *roble* (ordinary oak tree) and whose acorns provide food for the many hundreds of black, dark brown and grey pigs (the *cerdo ibérico*) that you will see grazing to either side of the walled lanes as you walk along – the 'source material' for the *embutidos* (sausage – literally 'stuffed' or 'packed in') for which Extremadura is so well known (along with its wines). However, while the landscape may have changed by now, the regional accents have not and the pilgrim will have to wait awhile before hearing the sort of Castilian he or she has probably been taught. One reason, apart from sheer speed of delivery, why local people you encounter may be difficult to understand is that in Andalucia and many parts of Extremadura all intervocalic and terminal 's's disappear so that *dos meses* (two months), for example, will sound like 'doh may'.

The Vía de la Plata enters the province of Badajoz (one of the two, together with Cáceres, that form the autonomous *región* of Extremadura) just south of Monesterio. Here the landscape becomes hillier, with mules working in the fields and mountains away in the distance, before opening out into the fields full of grass (and wild flowers in the springtime), vineyards and olive plantations that characterise the scenery between Fuente de Cantos and Mérida.

By the time the pilgrim approaches Cáceres (whose temperatures can rise to 50° C in the summer) the terrain becomes more barren, several castles are visible in the distance and the Vía de la Plata crosses the two big rivers (the Almonte and the Tajo) that combine to form the Embalse de Alcántara (a very large reservoir). The route continues to climb, up to the Puerto de Cañaveral and through the walled town of Galisteo, after which the landscape changes again for a while, a well-irrigated area planted with tobacco and sunflowers and with brick barns and farm buildings not encountered elsewhere. The Camino leaves the province of Cáceres just after the spa town of Baños de Montemayor with its traditional *balneario*. ('Taking the waters' is not, perhaps, a phenomenon the reader would initially associate with Spain but there are, in fact, many such places in the provinces of Salamanca, Ourense and parts of northern Portugal.)

After crossing the border between the autonomous *regiones* of Extremadura and Castille-León (this is one of the largest, with nine provinces), just below the Puerto de Béjar, the pilgrim will notice that the style of house-building has altered. The white-painted houses have disappeared, for the most part, and the adobe or stone constructions which replace them have wooden exterior balconies running along them at first floor level. It is here, too, that you will begin to encounter public fountains and *lavaderos* (places to launder clothes, often on two levels, the lower pool to wash, the upper to rinse) in the villages. You will see *cruceiros* (wayside stone crosses) there too and as you cross the wide, high, flattish plateau land between here and Salamanca (at nearly 1000m) you will see large herds of jet black and dark grey cattle, as well as brown ones, all with enormous horns, grazing to either side of the Camino. By this time, too, the linguistically-observant pilgrim will have noticed several placenames whose composition includes 'del Camino,' 'Calzada de' or 'Calzadilla de', indicating the passage of an important route and thus the line of Roman and pilgrim roads.

Cruceiro (wayside cross) typical of many in Galicia   (author)

After Salamanca the route passes through the area known as the Tierra del Vino which, as its name suggests, is reputed for its wine production. Beyond Zamora, after crossing the Duero, it enters the Tierra del Pan, with its seemingly endless undulating cornfields, reaching into infinity and beyond. However, those who continue north from here, via Benavente and La Bañeza to Astorga, will find, after crossing the Puente de la Vizana and entering the province of León, that the scenery changes dramatically, with its lush green fields well watered by an extensive system of irrigation canals. Those who opt to go via Puebla de Sanabria and Ourense, on the other hand, will not encounter much change until they reach Mombuey, when the oak and chestnut woods begin, the terrain becomes very hilly and they find themselves, in spirit if not yet in fact, in Galicia.

After the hilltop town of Puebla de Sanabria and the passes of Padornelo (1350m) and A Canda (1250m), the Vía de la Plata leaves the province of Zamora and the autonomous *región* of Castille-León and enters Galicia, comprised of the provinces of Lugo, Ourense (which you enter here), Pontevedra and La Coruña. It has its own language (not a dialect), related to Portuguese, and which together with *castellano* ('Spanish') is used as an official language in the *región*. As a result you will find that not only will people reply to you in *gallego* but that all road signs, official notices and so on appear in both languages. The spelling of placenames often varies between the two languages, however, and as at present the *castellano* forms have not yet been officially standardised, the names you see on maps and notices may differ from those you see on signposts and on entry to villages big enough to have placename boards. Some of the more common phonetic differences between the two languages, such as the interchange of e and ei and o and ue, are given in the glossary in Appendix D, together with other linguistic information the pilgrim may find useful.

Galicia is a very verdant area for the most part, with the highest rainfall in Spain. Unlike the south of Spain with its enormous *latifundios* (very large properties), the land in Galicia is divided (and subdivided) into tiny, often uneconomic individual holdings (*minifundios*), the result of centuries of sharing out land among its owner's descendants. As a result you will frequently see people working in the fields (many of whom are women) doing tasks by hand that would elsewhere be done more economically by machine. Unlike Andalucia, Extremadura and

Castille-León, where villages are often very far apart but whose buildings are tightly concentrated together, those in Galicia (the *aldea* or hamlet rather than a full-blown *pueblo*) are often tiny, not far from each other and much more spread out so that you are not usually very far from a building of some kind. The region is also crises-crossed with a veritable maze of old green lanes, which wend their way through fields separated from each other by dry stone walls or stone boundaries made of large slabs set on end, like rows of giant teeth, so that without some kind of waymarking system this Camino would be almost impossible to follow. Traditional vernacular architecture is also much more evident in Galicia than on the earlier part of the route and as well as innumerable fountains and *lavaderos* (not infrequently still in use) one of the characteristic features of its countryside is the *hórreo*.

This is a long rectangular granary, of stone or sometimes brick, raised up on pillars and used for storing potatoes and corncobs. They have slightly pitched roofs with a cross at one end and a decorative knob at the other. *Hórreos* vary greatly in length, from those that are only 3–4m long to enormous structures with two or three compartments and that stretch for 20–30m. You will also encounter innumerable *cruceiros* with sculptures on one or both sides on the cross itself and often other figures or decoration on the shaft, small stone bridges, houses with a *patín* (stone outside staircase with a landing halfway up to access the first-floor accommodation) and a number of *pazos* (large country manor houses; the Pazo de Oca near Bandeira – open to the public – is worth a visit). There are also villages which still retain their communal oven building, the occasional watermill in working order, a *galpón* (building used for holding local fairs under cover) and dozens of often very tiny granite Baroque-style churches. And in the area between Verín and Ourense you will also see the hilltop remains of several fifteenth and sixteenth-century fortified castles.

Due to its location Galicia remained isolated from the influence of much of what was happening to the rest of Spain in former centuries and as a result retains evidence of its Celtic origins. There were many *castri* in the area around Xinzo de Limia, traces of which can still be detected, while traditional Galician music uses the *gaita* (bagpipe). (Those interested in the architecture, working life and customs of Galicia should visit the Museo do Pobo Galego when they reach Santiago.)

Typical hórreo

Galicia is also a very heavily wooded area, many of the trees centuries old, and as a result is very pleasant to walk in, even in the height of summer. Unfortunately, however, in recent years, large areas of its forests have been devastated by an epidemic of huge fires, suspected to have been started deliberately but quite why or by whom no one seems to know. Those who continue on to Finisterre will also see something of the Galician coastline, with its *rías*, the fiord-like inlets along the Atlantic from the border of Portugal to the province of Asturias on the Costa Verde.

Before you go

a) Read up as much as you can about the route, its history, art, architecture and geography; a short bibliography is given in Appendix C.

b) Do not expect anybody – anybody at all! – to speak English. You will have to communicate in Spanish all the time, for everything you need, however complicated, so if you are not already fairly fluent consider a year's evening classes or home study with tapes in your preparations: you will find it extremely difficult if you are unable to carry out practical transactions as well as feeling very isolated on what is already a solitary route if you are also unable to converse with the Spanish pilgrims and other people you meet along the way.

c)   Decide what type of footwear you will be taking – for example, walking shoes, lightweight boots, heavy (thick-soled) trainers, and break them in before you go. Likewise, if you purchase a new rucksack for the journey, go out walking with it (fully laden) on as many occasions as you can before you set off.

Planning your schedule

As indicated, Seville to Santiago can be walked comfortably in six weeks by anyone who is fairly fit, leaving plenty of time to visit places of interest along the way. Allow plenty of time when planning your itinerary, especially if you are not an experienced walker. Those starting in Seville and who are not experienced walkers or are not very fit have the advantage of being able to find accommodation at 20–25km stages, more or less as far as Mérida, so that by then, when you need to walk longer distances, you will already be fit and into the swing of things.

Try not to plan too tight a schedule but allow plenty of time and flexibility to account for unforeseen circumstances (pleasant or otherwise). Where and how many rest days you take is up to you (though Seville, Mérida, Cáceres, Salamanca, Zamora and Ourense are 'musts'), as is also whether you include several short days' walking in your programme, arriving at your destination during the late morning so as to have the remainder of the day completely free. If you are extremely tired, or having trouble with your feet, a complete day off works wonders (particularly in a small place with no 'sights' to be visited) and is well worth the seeming disruption to your schedule. Allow at least three days to visit Santiago at the end – there is plenty to see – and, especially if you continued via Astorga, you will meet up again with other pilgrims you encountered along the way.

Equipment

1. **Rucksack**. At least 50 litres if carrying a sleeping bag.

2. **Footwear** – both to walk in and a spare pair of lightweight trainers/sandals.

3. **Waterproofs**. Even in summer it may rain, especially in Galicia. A 'poncho' (cape with a hood and space inside for a rucksack) is far more useful (and far less hot) than a cagoule or anorak.

4. **Pullover**. Much of the route is high up and as you go further north it can get cold at night, even in summer.

5. **First aid kit** (including a needle for draining blisters). The type of elastoplast sold by the metre is more useful than individual dressings. Scissors.

6. **High-factor sunscreen** if you burn easily.

7. **Large water bottle**. At least two litres if walking in hot weather.

8. **Sleeping bag**. Essential if staying in *refugios* or other very basic accommodation.

9. **Sleeping mat**. Also essential for basic accommodation where you will have to sleep on the floor and useful for siestas in the open air.

10. **Stick**. Useful for fending off/frightening dogs and testing boggy terrain.

11. **Guidebook**.

12. **Maps**.

13. **Compass**.

14. **Torch**.

15. **Sun hat** (preferably with wide brim).

16. **Small dictionary**.

17. **Mug, spoon and knife**.

18. If you are addicted to tea/coffee or can't get going in the morning without a hot drink a 'camping gaz' type **stove** is a great advantage, even though it will add extra weight to your luggage. This is especially useful in seasons when you will probably set out very early to avoid the heat, since although bars and cafés open early in Andalucía the further north you go the later they open, rarely before 8.30 or 9am except in big towns, and while in small places they

may in fact be open many do not serve hot drinks until the early afternoon. (A few of the *refugios* that exist have cooking facilities but not all.) If you do take a camping gaz stove make sure it uses the 200g cylinders – smaller ones are not readily available in Spain.

19. A **tent** is not worth the trouble as rooms are usually available (in bars, cafés) if you are not staying in the more basic accommodation, and campsites in Spain (of which there are few along the route anyway) can also be relatively expensive.

In general, travel as light as you can, not just for the weight but because of the long distances, the constant hills in Galicia and, according to the season, the heat.

San Roque in pilgrim attire, church of Santa María del Valle,
Villafrance de los Barros

There and Back

How to get there

Seville and Madrid: by air direct from London; by train from London via Paris; by coach direct from London. Seville can also be reached by bus from Madrid and other parts of Spain.

Other places along the Way (for those who are only doing a section) such as Mérida, Cáceres, Salamanca and Zamora are most easily reached by bus via Madrid.

How to get back from Santiago

Air: there are scheduled Iberia flights from Santiago to Heathrow (expensive). Otherwise go to Madrid or Bilbao by coach or train and fly from there.

Train: to Paris. Leaves at 9am every day, arriving Hendaye late evening, in time for the connection overnight for Paris, arriving early the following morning.

Coach: to Paris, direct, two to three times a week, depending on the time of year. Cheaper, comfortable and slightly shorter than the train journey. The journey takes 24 hours and arrives at the Porte de Bagnolet bus station from where you can continue to London. There is also a weekly service direct from Santiago to London in summer.

Finally, a very pleasant but slower way to return (and with more time to 'come back down to earth') is to take the FEVE narrow-gauge railway along the north coast from El Ferrol to Bilbao; you can get more information about this from the tourist office in Santiago (note that the FEVE is not part of the RENFE network).

Being there

Accommodation

Various types of accommodation are available along the way, ranging from luxurious five-star hotels (such as the state-run *paradores* established in redundant historic buildings) down to very basic accommodation provided on the floor in community centres, former schools, sports halls and so on. As the availability of accommodation changes rapidly, however, it is suggested that you either contact the

'Amigos' in Seville for the latest information, particularly about the very basic variety (available only to those with a *credencial* – see below) or obtain the Confraternity of St James's annually revised guides to (all types of) accommodation on this route: see Appendix C for addresses.

Hotel usually implies a higher standard of accommodation than that found in a *hostal* which, in turn, normally offers more facilities than a *fonda* (*hospedaje* in Galicia) and a *casa huéspedes* and, going down the scale, a *posada*. (*Residencia* after either *hotel* or *hostal* means it only provides accommodation: neither meals nor breakfast are available.) A number of bars also provide rooms (*habitaciones*) – *camas* means 'beds') so it is worth asking about these, even if there is no sign or notice to say so. However, a word of warning if you intend to stay in any of these and want to leave early in the morning to avoid walking in the heat: make sure you arrange to pay the previous evening and retain your passport as well as checking how you will actually get out of the building the following morning (which doors or entrances will be locked and how they can be opened), otherwise you may find yourself unable to leave until at least 9am. Note too that you will find it difficult to find accommodation during the *semana santa* (the week before Easter Sunday), not only in places like Seville and Zamora, which are well known for these celebrations, but elsewhere as well. (It is also almost impossible to find anywhere to stay in Zafra during the *feria,* which lasts for the whole of September and the first week in October.) In general, the commercially available accommodation listed in this guide is at the middle to lower end of the market, especially where there is plenty of choice.

A *refugio* is simple accommodation set up especially for pilgrims on foot or by bike (but not for those accompanied by a back-up vehicle) and is only for those holding a *credencial* (see below). (This is to ensure that these facilities are not used by 'pseudo-pilgrims,' backpackers or other travellers.) *Refugios* are provided by churches, religious orders and *ayuntamientos* (town halls or local authorities) and are gradually being set up in different places along the route, and there are several in operation in the province of Ourense, as indicated, established by the Xunta de Galicia along the route that goes directly to Santiago through their autonomous *región*. Others are located, at present, in Castilblanco de los Arroyos, Zafra, Casar de Cáceres, Fuenterroble de

Salvatierra and La Bañeza and another is in preparation in Fuente de Cantos. Note, however, that *refugios* are not provided as cheap substitutes for hotels but as alternatives to sleeping rough, places to shelter pilgrims from the elements, so you cannot expect anything more than that they are clean and that the plumbing works. Unlike hotels and *fondas*, however, you will not encounter any difficulty in leaving *refugios* early and will find too that other people are doing the same.

Planning the day

Long-distance walkers in Britain usually operate on a 'nine-to-five' basis, leaving their accommodation shortly after breakfast and returning in time for an early evening meal. There may be few, if any, places of historical, religious or cultural interest directly on the path, such as churches, cathedrals or stately homes that require a detailed indoor visit (as opposed to historic bridges, fortifications, market crosses and so on that can be inspected fairly quickly from the outside) and those that do normally work 'nine-to-five' as well so that combining walking and sightseeing is usually incompatible. Walkers in Britain, in the main, tend just to walk. In Spain, however, not only are there an enormous number of places well worth visiting along the Vía de la Plata, of outstanding artistic, architectural, cultural or religious interest, but they are also open at convenient times for the walker: as well as 10am to 1pm in the mornings they normally open again in the evenings from 4 or 5pm to 8pm or later. Churches in big towns are usually open all day but elsewhere those in small villages are nearly always locked, unless there is a service in progress. However, it is often possible to visit during Saturday afternoons when they are being cleaned in preparation for Sunday.

   In July and August it is extremely hot during the day along the Vía de la Plata and there is very little shade at all apart from many areas of Galicia. When walking in hot weather it is important to avoid becoming dehydrated by drinking plenty of water before you set out as once you realise you have not had enough to drink it is too late to do anything about it, even if you have supplies with you. It is difficult to do but if you can drink at least half a litre of water as soon as you get up (as well as any tea/coffee you may have) you will find the hot weather affects you much less. The best way to avoid walking in the heat is to get up before it is light and set out at daybreak (though not before or you will not be able to see the way). At this time of day it is cool and pleasant, with the advantage of being able to enjoy the scenery in the early morning light. It is also a good idea, in large towns and other places of any size, to go for a walk in the evening and check how you will leave, so as not to waste time or get lost the following morning.

OTHER PRACTICAL INFORMATION

Shops (for food)

These are usually open from 9 to 10am and 2pm and then again between 5 and 8pm or later. In small villages they may be unmarked and you will have to ask where they are (though in such places bars often double up as shops) and in parts of Galicia, in particular, you will encounter mobile food shops as well as the bakers' vans found in most other parts of the route, all of which honk their horns loudly to announce their arrival in the village centre. Except for large supermarkets in some big towns food shops close on Saturday afternoons and all day Sunday though bakers are often open on Sunday mornings if you can find them: there is usually only one in each village or district, they may not always be marked and may only have a small entrance on the street leading to the large baking area behind. The (mauve and yellow) *tabaco* logo on a building in a small place usually indicates that there is also a food and possibly general store inside as well.

Public holidays

There are more of these (*días festivos*) than in Britain: January 1st, Good Friday, August 15th, November 1st, December 5th, 6th and 25th. There are also three others which are taken locally and therefore vary from one area to another as well as (especially in August) the *fiestas* in honour of a town or village's own patron saint and which can last up to a week in some places. Shops, including those for food (but not bars or bakeries), will be closed on these occasions or open only in the mornings.

Meals

These are available between 2 and 3.30 or 4pm for lunch and 9 till 11pm for evening dinner. However, as many bars in Spain also provide *tapas* (different kinds of snack, both hot and cold) as well as *bocadillos* (sandwiches) you need not go hungry if you are feeling ravenous outside regular mealtimes (such places are referred to in the text as 'bar with simple food'). Breakfast in hotels and similar accommodation is rarely available before 9am though in bars in Andalucía you can usually find *tostadas* and other things to eat as early as 6.30am.

Cafés and bars

These often close very late but do not normally open before 8.30 or 9am and in small villages do not always serve hot drinks all day. Remember that in Spain a *cafetería* is not a self-service restaurant but a bar that also serves things to eat for breakfast, such as cake, *tostadas* (toast with olive oil, jam or dripping, for example), sandwiches or hot *tapas*. And if you are wondering why the *hogar del pensionista* (old people's day centre) is indicated in a book of this nature, this is because, in small places, it may be the only place to get a drink and/or a snack: even if they have very few facilities for their clients there will always be a bar inside.

Water fountains

If left running permanently, these are usually safe to drink from (watch out for local people filling jugs and other containers at mealtimes as this tastes better than the chlorinated tapwater). *Agua (non) potable* means that it is (isn't) safe to drink and *agua non tratada* indicates that it is chlorine-free. Petrol stations on main roads are indicated in the text as they usually sell cold drinks and chilled (bottled) water.

Changing money

Banks are only open from 8.30am till 2pm and only on Saturday mornings in large towns. However, there are cash dispensers (*cajeros automáticos*) in most places of any size and which accept a wide selection of cards (though there are none at all anywhere along the route between Zamora and Puebla de Sanabria). It is also possible to change money in post offices displaying the Deutsche Bank sign.

Post offices

Correos are usually open in the mornings only but stamps (as well as single envelopes) can also be bought in *estancos* (tobacconists).

Poste restante

If you want to send things to yourself further along the route (such as maps and guides) or have people write to you, you can do this via the poste restante system whereby you collect your mail (on presentation of your passport) at the post office. This service is called Lista de Correos, is free, and items are kept for you for a month before returning them to the sender. Address the letter/parcel to yourself, Lista de Correos, postal code and name of town and province. (The most likely places you will need will be Seville, Mérida, Cáceres, Salamanca, Zamora, Ourense and Santiago de Compostela.) If you decide (while in Spain) that you have too much in your rucksack it is considerably cheaper to post it to yourself this way in Santiago than to send a parcel home to Britain. Make sure, however, when collecting such items, that the clerk looks not only under your surname (*apellido*) but also under your first name (*nombre*); as the Spanish system of surnames is different you may find your mail has been filed in the wrong place.

Telephones

In Spain (which has one of the most expensive telephone systems in Europe) phone boxes usually take both coins as well as phone cards (available in newsagents in denominations of 1000 and 2000 pesetas). Most Spanish area codes begin with a 9, which is included when calling from abroad. The emergency number for the Guardia Civil is 062. Telephone books (*guía telefonica*) are by province (white and yellow pages in separate books) and entries are then arranged by town or population centre so that it is easy to locate, for example, hotels and *fondas* in a specific place. Postcodes are also included.

Stamps for pilgrim passports

Modern pilgrims who seek proof of their pilgrimage also carry a *credencial* (pilgrim 'passport') which they have stamped at regular intervals along the Way (such as churches, town halls) and which they then present to the cathedral authorities in Santiago to help them obtain their *compostela* or certificate. More information about this is available from the Confraternity of St James or from the 'Amigos' in Seville.

Church services

Masses are usually held at 12 noon or 1pm on Sundays, as well as on Saturday evening for Sunday. During the week there will normally be one at 8pm in places of any size and often at 8.30 or 9am too.

Dogs

Their owners nearly always tell you, 'he won't hurt you', though this is often hard to believe. They may tell you, too, that it is the rucksack that bothers them (and as dogs are reputed to see only in black and white there may be some truth in this, faced with mysterious humpback monsters on two legs) but it is not much comfort when faced with an aggressive one. They live all along the route from Seville to Santiago, usually running around loose, hear you ages before you have any idea where they are and are often enormous (though the small ones are, in fact, a greater nuisance, as they have a nasty habit of letting you pass quietly by and then attacking from behind, nipping you in the back of your ankles). A **stick** is very useful, even though you might not normally want to walk with one – not to hit them with but to threaten. When you do meet them keep on walking at a steady pace (but do not run) and if you see flocks of sheep apparently alone give them a wide berth as they will be accompanied if not by two then certainly by four-legged guardians.

Fording streams

If you come to a river/stream with no bridge and no stepping stones you will have to wade across. This is not a very common occurrence but if you do need to, remember to keep your shoes/boots on as you may not always be able to see sharp objects or detect how clean the water is.

Road walking

In the short stretches that require walking on busy roads remember to walk on the left, facing the oncoming traffic, though you will have to use your discretion if you encounter sharp bends that could obscure you from view.

Road signs

Brown for natural features (rivers, reservoirs) and purple for historic monuments.

Spectacles

If you wear glasses it may be a good idea to carry a spare pair or at least your prescription with you in case you lose/break them.

Using this guide

Waymarking

The route described in this book starts at the cathedral in Seville and ends at the one in Santiago de Compostela, nearly 1000km and six weeks later, in the direction of the (modern) pilgrimage. It is therefore described in one direction only. Those who would like to walk the route in reverse or return on foot will therefore find it extremely difficult, although the white waymarking in reverse, mentioned above, will help, as well as indications in the text such as 'track joins from back L', redundant for those walking only towards Santiago but helpful for the person going in reverse and faced with a choice of paths to select. Waymarking (*señalización*) is in the form of yellow arrows (*flechas*), familiar to those who have walked the Camino francés, painted on tree trunks, walls, road signs, rocks, the ground, sides of buildings and so on, and are normally extremely easy to spot. They appear at frequent intervals and the walker will not usually encounter any difficulty following them. If, at any time, they seem to have disappeared, wherever you may be, this will normally be because you have inadvertently taken a wrong turning: retrace your steps to the last one you saw and start again from there, checking carefully. (Sections where it is known that waymarking is poor are indicated in the text.) In the province of Zamora the Fundación Ramos de Castro has placed terracotta information boards in villages along the way, all in the same general style but each one explaining details about the history of the route in that particular area. In Galicia, in addition, there are standardised concrete marker stones, about the size of old-fashioned milestones, bearing an embossed conch-shell design and positioned at places where you make a manoeuvre from the path you are already on, while in the province of Ourense there are also special carved slabs made by the local artist Carballo, with the stylised figure of a pilgrim indicating changes of direction; there are over a hundred of these but although each one is slightly different they are all in the same general style.

Maps

Maps are a problem in Spain. It would be possible to follow the Vía de la Plata just with the waymarks and this guide but that would be very limiting. Maps are useful not merely as a means of finding the way when lost but also for situating the walk in the context of its surroundings and for making any diversions the walker might wish to make to visit places of interest within striking distance of the route. At present there are no comprehensive, up-to-date Spanish equivalents of the Ordnance Survey maps of Britain available for the whole country and it is for this reason that sketch maps of the route are included with this text. To situate yourself generally, however (though not to walk from), two maps in the Michelin 1:400,000 (1cm to 4km) orange series are recommended: 441 North West Spain and 444 Central. These cover the entire route from just south of El Berrocal to Santiago but miss out the first 50km from Seville; if you want to include that section as well you will need 446 Southern Spain too. Such Spanish maps as are available in Britain can be purchased from, for example, Stanford's map shop in London, The Map Shop in Upton-upon-Severn, or from some of the larger general bookshops.

Textual description

Each section begins with the distance walked from the previous one, a description of the facilities available, a brief history, where applicable, and an indication of the places of interest to visit. (Pilgrims wishing to spend time in any of the larger towns should obtain information leaflets and a street plan from the tourist office there.) The text is not divided up into stages as in this way the walker (or cyclist) can decide for him or herself the distances he or she would like to cover each day. The figures after each placename heading indicate the height in metres where known and, in parentheses, the distance in kilometres from both Seville and Santiago via Ourense; the continuation from Granja de Moreruela to Astorga has just the totals going forwards – not in reverse. Thus, for example, Santiponce is 10km from Seville and 981km from Santiago. In the case of large towns (Mérida, Cáceres, Salamanca, for example) the distances to/from them start/end in their centres, normally at the cathedral. When a series of manoeuvres is given in quick succession this means that there is little space between them and for this reason distances are not given.

Placenames

Placenames and other names that help in wayfinding (street names, prominent buildings, rivers) appear in the text in bold type. Introductory and more descriptive text is in italic type. Note that 'river' in Spain rarely implies a wide, deep, fast-flowing stretch of navigable water such as the Guadalquivir or the Duero: most, if not actually dried up, are no more than narrow trickles at the bottom of a wide riverbed and may be non-existent at certain times of the year. The word Camino refers to the Camino de Santiago. Some vernacular terms indicating features passed along the way (such as hórreo, lavadero, cruceiro, ermita) have been retained in the original since translation of such vocabulary is cumbersome and an English word does not always convey the exact equivalent.

In Galicia spellings of placenames may vary: in Galician on signposts, for example, and/or in Castilian on maps. If versions given in this guide appear inconsistent at times, this is because they are based on those seen on street and placename boards and signposts encountered along the way, not on those found on maps or in other guidebooks (and for this reason the Galician term is often the one provided).

Abbreviations

These have been kept to a minimum. **L** *indicates that you should turn/fork left,* **R** *that you should turn/fork right,* **(L)** *and* **(R)** *mean that something you pass is to your left or right,* **LH** *= left hand,* **RH** *= right hand,* **KSO** *= keep straight on,* **rte** *= restaurante,* **CD** *= cash dispenser,* **HT** *= high tension,* **//** *= parallel,* **km** *= kilometre,* **KM** *= kilometre marker (found on the sides of all main roads),* **FP** *= footpath,* **N** *followed by a number (such as N630) refers to the number of a main road,* **C** *(or the first two initials of the province you are in, such as ZA = Zamora) to a local road,* **RENFE** *is the abbreviation for the Spanish national railway network,* **s/n** *after a street name in an address means sin número (establishment in question does not have a number, either because the street is very short or because the building – bank, museum, big hotel, for example – is extremely large).*

Appendixes

For those who feel that their pilgrimage would be incomplete unless they continued to Finisterre a description of this route is given in Appendix A. Other appendixes contain a summary of Santiago and pilgrim references in places along the way (B), a bibliography with a list of suggestions for further reading (C), a glossary of geographical and other frequently encountered terms (D) and an index of principal placenames (E).

Unlike pilgrimages to Lourdes, Fatima or other locations where miracles are sought and help for specific problems requested and where being in the pilgrim destination itself is the most important factor, on the Vía de la Plata/Camino mozárabe it is the making of the journey itself that is the pilgrim's principal concern, the arrival in Santiago being only a conclusion to the rest of the undertaking. Timings have not been given from place to place but 4km per hour, exclusive of stops, is often considered average, especially when carrying a heavy rucksack. However, a comfortable pace may often be more than this – a fit walker may well be able to maintain a speed of 5–6km or 3 miles per hour.

The route is practicable, though not necessarily recommended, all through the year (and definitely not in July and August if you are starting in Seville, when the temperatures will be well up into the nineties Fahrenheit and beyond). In winter the days are short, it is often very windy on the southern part of the route and it rains a lot in Galicia. The weather may be dry over much of the route through Extremadura and Castille and León but as a lot of it is quite high up (Salamanca, for instance, is at over 760m though the area around it is more or less flat) it gets very cold, with a biting wind. If you are not restricted to a particular time of year the end of April to the middle of June or the autumn are best – dry, but not as hot as in summer, and accommodation is also much less crowded. Traditionally, as many people as possible have aimed to arrive in Santiago for the festivities on July 25th, St James's day, particularly in Holy Years. Many still do.

¡Ultreya!

THE ROUTE

SEVILLE 12m, 650,000 (0/991)

The fourth-largest city in Spain, the Hispalis of Roman times, situated on the Río Guadalquivir. All facilities; international airport, RENFE, buses to all parts of Spain. Accommodation in all price brackets but no refugio or other specifically pilgrim facilities. Tourist office at Avenida de la Constitución 21.

The Asociación de Amigos del Camino de Santiago, who issue the special Vía de la Plata credenciales ('pilgrim passports' – their address can be found in Appendix C) have information sessions on Tuesdays and Fridays, 7–9pm, at the Casa Civico de las Columnas, Calle Pureza 79 (in the Triana district on the west side of the river). You can obtain the first stamp for this 'passport' from the cathedral office, entering by the Puerta de los Palos (marked 'praying only' – there is another entrance for tourist visits).

Try to spend at least one whole day here. The major monuments include the cathedral, the Giralda, the alcázar and gardens, Pilate's House, the Santa Cruz quarter, and the best way to see Seville is on foot (ask at tourist office for map with walking tour and for details of combined ticket giving entry to principal monuments). Santiago and pilgrim references include a painting of St James (Juan de Roelas) in Capilla de Santiago in Cathedral Santa María de la Sede (north aisle), statue of San Roque in chapel of Hospital de la Caridad and statue of St James the Pilgrim in the frame of the cathedral's west portal (where you will also find the first waymark).

A word of warning: Seville is notorious for its thieves and pickpockets.

On your first day there are two possibilities:

a) you can walk from Seville to Santiponce (10km) in the late afternoon/early evening, with time to visit the Roman city of Italica without your rucksack and then return by bus (very frequent service) to Seville (Plaza de Armas bus station, by river) to sleep. This section is very industrial, not very scenic,

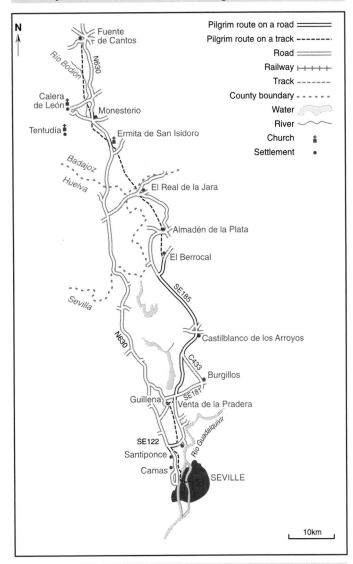

and this option would enable you to walk on to Castilblanco de los Arroyos (33km from Seville) the following day.

b)   you can leave Seville in the morning and walk to Guillena (23km), a short day with time to visit Italica en route.

Starting from the cathedral and with your back to it cross the **Avenida de la Constitución**, go down **Calle García Vinuesa** and turn first R into **Calle Jimios**, forking L. Continue ahead on **Calle Zaragoza** (veering slightly L) to the end (*well waymarked*). Turn L into the **Avenida de los Reyes Católicos** to the end. Cross the **Paseo de Cristóbal Colón** and continue over **Puente Isabel II**, crossing the **Río Guadalquivir** into the Triana district (*note* azulejos – *blue ceramic tiles* – *on buildings*).

Turn first R on the other side into **Calle Jorge**, R into **Plaza del Callao** and L into **Calle Castilla**, a very long street, passing to the L of the church of the **Virgen del Patrocinio**. At the end, before a LH bend, cross a slabbed area (**Plaza Hermanos Cruz Solis**) and turn R up a flight of steps. Turn L on the other side, cross both sides of **Avenida Carlos III** (*signposted 'Aeropuerto' and 'NIV Córdoba'*) and turn R on the other side. 100m later turn L to a car park office and continue diagonally R towards an electricity pylon and then past floodlights in order to turn L onto a minor road and cross a bridge over the other half of **the Río Guadalquivir**.

On the other side you have two options (*both waymarked*):

a)   The original Camino went through **Camas**, now a suburb of Seville, 5km away *(but apart from the Hostal Cruce on the N630 and despite its name it has nowhere to sleep!)*. If you want to go there (*shops, bars, banks*) continue ahead along a track, go under the E803 and KSO(L) on a bike/pedestrian track which leads you directly to its centre. Turn R (**Calle José Payan**) and KSO past a supermarket. Fork L at the church of **Santa María de Gracia** (opposite the *ayuntamiento*). Continue on the road to **Santiponce** and then proceed as in b) below. *(Hostal El Madera is midway between Camas and Santiponce, on LH side of road.)*

b)   There is also a variant, however, quieter but neither more scenic nor any shorter, which takes you away from the road and nearer to the river. For this option fork R down the slope, immediately after crossing the bridge, past a building marked 'Aljarafesa Ebar Camas', go over a bridge over a canal and continue on a wide earth track //

to the river. *No shade at all in this section. Former wasteland now planted with cotton fields.*

Continue // to the river for 1km and then turn L and then diagonally R to pass to RH side of a *finca* on to an untarred road. Continue on it (*suburb of Camas ahead to L*).

Go under the motorway and KSO ahead, veering slightly R, passing a *galería de tiro* (rifle range) and go under a railway bridge. KSO on other side (road now tarmacked) – *more cotton fields on either side* – towards **Monasterio de San Isidro** (now visible ahead, 1km).

Continue for 1km, pass a house on L called 'Mi Ranchito' and reach a junction with the N630. Turn L, go under the N630 (signposted 'Italica') and cross a slip road to the N630. KSO ahead to a roundabout and petrol station (at entrance to Santiponce). Turn R (signposted 'Italica' – monastery is now on your R) and enter

10km Santiponce 16m (10/981)

Shops, bars, bank (+CD), Hotel Ventorillo Canario opposite entrance to Italica. Site of Roman city of Italica, founded in AD 206, with Roman theatre on outskirts (city buses from Seville terminate here). Monasterio de San Isidoro closed for repairs at time of writing.

Continue past the monastery (R) and public garden. Turn R at a T-junction (**Avenida de Extremadura**) and follow it, passing the ruins of **Italica** on L. KSO to the junction (800m) with the N630, veering R. Cross it (carefully) and continue ahead in the direction of 'La Alcaba, 3'. 300m later, at a group of 10 tall trees, fork L off the road and then turn L, just before an old bridge, onto a *camino de tierra* and KSO (literally) along a wide track between fields, undulating slightly, for 5km, passing a large concrete tower after 2km.

After 5km reach a T-junction and turn R (*Guillena visible ahead*). 400m later turn L alongside a fenced-in plantation of new trees on a track leading to a (nearly dried-up) river. Cross it via stepping stones (*cyclists dismount*), turn L on the other side and continue on a wide track between plantations of trees and under electric cables, leading past a cemetery (R) and along **Calle Portugalete** into

13km Guillena 22m (23/968)

All facilities, hotel. Bar Hostal Francés has rooms. Fifteenth-century church of Nuestra Señora de la Granada.

Continue ahead (**Calle Real**), passing **Plaza de España** and the *ayuntamiento*, to a church. Continue ahead to its RH side. Continue ahead, passing a sports centre and at the end of the football pitch turn R to a river (*Río Rivera de Huelva – the original crossing place for the Camino de Santiago*).

In dry weather (walkers only) cross the river and then veer L, on a track leading you to the road just before the **Venta de la Pradera** (3km). Otherwise, continue on LH bank of river and turn R over road bridge and continue to roundabout at the

3km Venta la Casa de Pradera (26/965)

Bar/mesón (open early).

From here to Castilblanco cyclists need to dismount in some sections. Otherwise they should continue on SE181 to Burgillos then turn L there onto C433.

If you forded the river cross the SE181 (road to Burgillos) and then turn R up a track. If you came over the road bridge fork L after the roundabout, in both cases onto a track along the perimeter fence of a factory. 200m later turn L down an unpaved road. Turn L onto a tarmac road and then immediately turn **hard R** (not waymarked) onto the *camino de tierra* along the perimeter fence of an orange tree plantation. Pass a noticeboard telling you about the *Cañada Real – 16km to Castilblanco, 6km to El Chaparral. No shade at all. Undulating countryside, continuing through olive plantations. This area is part of the Parque Natural de la Sierra Norte de Sevilla.*

At the top of the hill, by a pylon and cables, turn L at a T-junction. Go through a *cledo* (the first of many gates made of wire and wooden palings) with a cattle grid. *More cotton fields.* Continue ahead // to but a little away from the fence. Pass another information board, with a useful map to situate yourself. *This is now El Cortijo de Chaparral; white arrows on brown posts are waymarks for a local* ruta de senderismo.

KSO ahead when the fence veers R, descending gradually through *encina* trees. KSO(R) at a fork, KSO(R) at a second fork and then KSO(R) at a LH turn, forking R onto a path close to a fence when the track goes steeply uphill to L. KSO(R) at the next fork, following a line of fence most of the time.

Go through a second *cledo* (some 4km after the first). 1km later go through two *cledos* 10m apart and KSO. 800m later (after the double *cledo*) join the unpaved road coming from back L and KSO. 1km later reach the Castilblanco–Burgillos road. Turn L along it for 4km to the entrance to Castilblanco (*it is possible to walk on the RH verge in part, varying widths*).

After passing the Hotel Castilblanco (on your R) fork L by the fountain and sitting area downhill, veering R into the centre of town, along **Avenida de España**.

17km Castilblanco de los Arroyos 329m (43/948)

Small town with all facilities. Hotel Castilblanco, Pensión Salvadora (unmarked, 43 Avenida España). Bar Isidoro, Avenida de la Paz, does food, as does Bar Reina on main road. Refugio located behind petrol station on main road at entrance to village (ask at Policía Local for key and pilgrim stamp). Sixteenth-century Iglesia del Divino Salvador.

Pastureland in the springtime, near Castilblanco de los Arroyos

Continue down **Avenida de España** then along **Calle Costanillas** and **Calle Pilar Nuevo** and reach **Carretera de Almadén de la Plata**, opposite a large water trough marked 'Agua non potable'. Turn L onto the SE185, the **Carretera de Almadén**, and KSO for 16km(!), *undulating, but more up than down till you reach a TV transmitter on L, just after road KM14; little shade to walk in and few places to sit down. Cortijos to either side, often with elaborate entrance gates, so no other FPs or alternative paths.* After 16km reach the entrance to

16km El Berrocal (59/932)

A provincial nature reserve, dedicated to replanting of trees. The Camino (waymarked with usual yellow arrows) takes you through 13km of undulating woods, with no prominent features apart from three ruined houses though several herds of deer are visible if you are attentive. However, the 'reward' comes at the end when, after climbing a very steep hill, you suddenly arrive at two miradores (viewpoints) with splendid views in all directions. It is then only 1.5km down into Almadén de la Plata.

Cyclists, however, may prefer to continue on the road to Almadén de la Plata though before making up their minds they should read through the next section carefully. The ride through El Berrocal is very quiet and pleasant, most of it on easily rideable tracks, but for the last kilometre up to the two miradores you will have to get off and push your bike VERY steeply uphill. The view from the top is probably worth it though the descent the other side (1.5km) is also steep and you will need to walk part of the way down too. Alternatively, if you feel like walking up to see the view you can do so from Almadén – the path is signposted from the town.

Turn R through the entrance gates and continue ahead on a small road. Pass a watch tower (L) and the turn-off to **El Berrocal III** (on R) and continue ahead, downhill, through cork plantations. 800m later go through the gates of **Casa Forestal** and veer L towards large modern farm buildings. Pass to LH side of them, stay on the tarmac road and go through some gates with an information board at the side (*about the Senda de Las Cuqueras, a waymarked FP leading to the Pantano del Lanchor*).

Continue on the road, ignoring turns, for 2.5km to the valley bottom. Cross a causeway with concrete bollards, after which you start to climb again slightly. *(Waymarking is somewhat faded and needs repainting.)*

500m later turn L onto another causeway towards a deserted white concrete house on the hillside. Veer round to R, passing behind animal enclosures and continue ahead on a wide earth road, climbing steadily. 1km later the spruce plantations on the L give way to eucalyptus trees and you begin to descend again (gradually). 500m later go through some very tall gates (kept open) onto open heathland with cistus bushes *(the ones that smell like church incense)*.

Continue ahead, climbing gradually, ignoring the first LH and RH forks. 1km later, at a fork of two equal paths, fork R ahead *(the L one leads downhill)*. 400m later reach a junction with several paths and a gate some 3m high: go through and take the LH (grassy) path ahead. KSO, following the line of fence to your R all the time, climbing gradually *(cyclists may find this part a bit bumpy)*. Continue for 1.5km, after which the track becomes a path and begins to climb much more steeply *(cyclists dismount here)*, still following the line of the fence *(good views to rear)*.

Veer L, uphill all the time, away from the fence, and 800m later turn L along side of the hill, continuing to climb but not quite as steeply. 100m later turn **hard R** onto a path coming from below L and 100m later reach the two

9.5km Miradores del Cerro del Calvario 550m (58.5/932.5)

Two viewpoints, like brick pulpits, with plunging view of Almadén de la Plata and the blue marble quarries (of Roman origin) to the north and the Sierra del Norte de Sevilla, that you have just come through, to the south. Splendid views in all directions. Cerro del Calvario was also, formerly, a place of religious cult.

Continue straight ahead, downhill on the other side, veering L. Follow the track down, go through *cledos* and turn R down a concrete lane continuing as a *camino de tierra*. Turn R at the bottom then immediately L. Turn R at the end to **Plaza del Pilar** in

1.5km Almadén de la Plata 449m (72/919)

Small town with all facilities. Bar Casa Concha has rooms, as does Bar Las Macias. Church of Nuestra Señora de Gracia; the ayuntamiento, with its clocktower, was built in early twentieth century behind façade of the former ermita of Nuestra Señora de los Angeles. Here, as in many other small towns in the south, (bitter) orange trees line the streets, much as plane trees do in Britain. Almadén formerly had a church dedicated to Santiago.

From here you have two options. You can either continue all the way to El Real de la Jara on a quiet, undulating and fairly shady road with little traffic (cyclists will find this an easier alternative) or go on paths, very hilly but quiet, through the Cortijo Arroyo Mateos, a private estate; the owner is quite willing to allow pilgrims to walk through it (the route is well waymarked) but requests them to telephone the estate office the evening before (for example, if you are sleeping in Almadén) so that the gates can be opened and you can both enter and leave without any problem (tel: 95.473.50.49).

a) **Cortijo Arroyo Mateos**. From the church in Almadén cross **Plaza del Reloj**, take the street to R of the shop at end, turn R and go uphill past a bullring (to your R). You enter the *finca* 6km after Almadén and leave it 5km later; at the exit turn sharp R downhill to a track for an easy 4km walk on a quiet road to El Real de la Jara; *at KM1 look out for a memorial to the late José Luis Salvador Salvador, one of the two people to really revive the use of the Vía de la Plata as a pilgrim route in the late twentieth century.*

b) Road option. Turn R in the centre of Almadén past **Plaza del Pilar** and KSO to end of town, passing a cemetery (on R). KSO on SE177 (= A463). After 10km KSO past a turn-off (on R) to **Cazalla de la Sierra** and enter El Real de la Jara via **Calle La Paz**.

16km El Real de la Jara 460m (88/903)

Small town with all facilities (bank+CD). Unmarked Pensión Salvadora next door (on L) to top of two houses which are both(!) no. 70 on main road (Calle Real) just down from Guardia Civil.

Continue along the street to the centre of town by the *ayuntamiento*. (Turn L at the end for the church of **San Bartolomé**: *Meson Cochero opposite does meals*). Continue ahead along **Calle José María Pedrero** to the end, where it becomes a *camino de tierra* (*the Vía Pecuaria Cordel del Monesterio*). Or, from the church, take **Calle San Bartolomé** then turn L to **Calle José-María Pedrero**. *(If you want to visit the Castillo*

Real, with a mirador, up on the hill 300m to the east of the town you can do so via a FP.)

KSO along a walled lane. Pass the remains of another *castillo* (to R) 1km later and KSO through undulating countryside with cork trees, *encinas* and dark brown pigs grazing underneath them.

7km later pass the entrance gates to **Dehesa Romeral** (a *finca*) and KSO. 2km later pass the entrance gates to **Dehesa La Mimbre** and KSO. 3km later, when you reach a couple of white buildings (a riding school?), one of which looks like a small chapel, go up the bank ahead of you, cross a minor road and KSO ahead along a *cañada*. KSO for 400m to the N630 and turn R alongside it for 100m to the

12.5km Ermita de San Isidoro (100.5/890.5)

You have now left the province of Sevilla and the autonomous region of Andalucía (shortly after El Real) and have entered the province of Badajoz in the autonomous región of Extremadura.

Chapel on site where the retinue transporting the body of Saint Isidore up the Vía de la Plata from Seville to León stopped en route to his final resting place in the Basilica de San Isidro in León. After this the landscape begins to change, the cortijos disappear and there are a lot of walled lanes. You will also see many mules in this area, still used to work the land.

Ruined castle, leaving El Real de la Jara (author)

Continue on a path uphill to RH side of the road for 1km until you reach a section of the old main road. At the end of it cross the N630 and continue on the hard shoulder of LH side. 500m later, at a junction, turn SECOND L onto a section of old road, veering R. Return to the N630 opposite gates to a *finca* called 'Las Navas' and continue on a FP and then track to LH side of the N630.

NB: In this area there are also other waymarked long-distance walks (with yellow AND WHITE markers): be careful not to follow these as only in places (not all the time) do they coincide with those of the Vía de la Plata. Similarly 'VP' on marker stones (confusingly) refers not to the Vía de la Plata but to the 'Vía Pecuaria', a route waymarked in white from Almadén to Monesterio.

Pass a second set of gates marked 'Las Navas' (on LH side this time) and continue uphill on a *camino de tierra* // to the road, passing a large, shiny corrugated-iron building (L). Continue uphill to the top at the

8km Cruz del Puerto 753m (108.5/882.5)

Large picnic area, wayside shrine, fountain (not always working). KSO on road for 1.5km down to

1.5km Monesterio 752m (110/881)

Small town with all facilities (bank+CD) and plenty of accommodation of all types, including Hostal D.P. El Pilar on main road (tel: 941.51.67.56). Pilgrim stamp and mini-refugio for those with credencial at Cruz Roja on LH side of main road at entry to town (open 24/24).

7km west of here, at Calera de León, there is the medieval monastery of the Order of Santiago, with Gothic church and two-storied cloister (worth visiting): you can walk there by deviating from the Camino – see *** below.

***However, if you do want to go to **Calera de León** cross over the river here and follow the yellow and white flashes but once you arrive in the town (*shops, bars*) they stop. If you are not retracing your steps to Monesterio you can return to the Vía de la Plata by taking the local road signposted 'N630 6km' for 3km. At the top of the hill turn L at the THIRD white gate post with cattle grid* (wide track with no gates on RH side of road here).

Another side trip (8km) to the monastery of Tentudía is also recommended. (The name is a corruption of 'hold the day', as the Virgin Mary extended the daylight so that the Christians could complete their defeat of the Moors here.) It contains the courtyard of a mosque, Mozárabic, Mudéjar, late Romanesque and Classical elements, a Capilla de Santiago and fine Italian tile-work, including a splendid tile Santiago Matamoros in the chapel. Open 10.15am to 5.25pm, free, closed Mondays. To walk there from Monesterio follow the signs to Calera de León and Tentudía west off the N630 up Calle Primero de Mayo and Avenida Ramón y Cajal. 500m beyond the modern Ermita de Nuestra Señora de Tentudía turn R along waymarked path (yellow and white flashes) for 8km to monastery. Retrace your steps for the return journey.

NB: There is hardly any shade, no water and no villages between Monesterio and Fuente de Cantos, 22km away.

To leave Monesterio: continue along the main road (**Paseo de Extremadura**) to the very end of the town (1.5km), turning L after the football ground (by town exit boards) onto a *camino de tierra* downhill alongside **Arroyo de la Dehesa**. Pass a concrete bridge on L and KSO.

After 1km you reach a place to ford the river (stepping stones) and a large water trough on the other side. Do NOT cross here: *the path (marked with yellow AND WHITE flashes) from here leads to Calera de León (the Camino to Fuente de Cantos is marked with yellow arrows).*

Otherwise, KSO alongside the river for 300m more to a proper, solid concrete bridge (*suitable for vehicles*). Cross over, turn R and then L up a wide walled lane, veering L at the top then R at a T-junction, passing (on L) a brick building with two round rooms and no windows. KSO for 2km until you reach a minor road, 5.5km from Monesterio. *(Calera de León visible on hill top to L.)*

Cross over and go through gates (cattle grid*). Continue ahead, veering L and following the line of the wall. 1.5km later go through another gate and continue on a walled lane ahead. KSO(R) at a fork along the line of the wall and 800m later reach two gates in the corner of a field. Go through LH (double) set and continue ahead on a grassy track gently downhill, through an area planted with scrubby broom trees, veering R alongside the line of a wire fence. *(Watch out carefully for waymarks in this section as there are not many places to put them.)*

At the bottom veer L alongside a fence, keeping close to it and following it round to the R uphill when it curves round. 500m later go through some gates and continue alongside a fence, through another (double) gate and KSO in a straight line ahead on a clear track when the fence stops. *This area is a paradise of wild flowers in the springtime, 'wall-to-wall' to the horizon, with wild orchids later in the year, on the track and elsewhere. Fuente de Cantos is suddenly visible, though still a long way away, when you get over the brow of the hill.*

Continue gently downhill, the track veering R, L, R and L again to the valley bottom. Cross the river via stepping stones, turn R towards a wall, L in front of it and continue on the track veering L, R, L and R. KSO(R) ahead at a fork (*leading to a semi-ruined farm on L*).

When a track joins from back L do NOT go ahead over a cattle grid but fork L between fields. KSO, following the road round. Approximately 1km before you reach the main road veer R over a bridge over the (probably dry) river. KSO. When you see the road ahead and a factory marked 'Fábrica de Material ganadero' fork L, // to the road, and KSO. This brings you out at the end of the town, by the road. Cross over and enter

22km Fuente de Cantos 583m (132/859)

Small town with all facilities. Casa Vicente on main road has rooms; refugio in preparation in old hospital building on outskirts of town. One of the town's two churches is another Iglesia de Nuestra Señora de la Granada, containing a) statue of Santiago Apóstol on main altar (with shells on each lapel) and b) statue of San Roque on RH side of church (when facing altar). Fuente de Cantos was also the birthplace of the painter Zurbarán (the Casa can be visited).

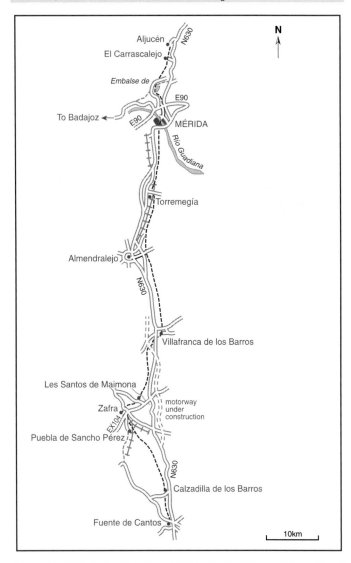

Approaching Fuente de Cantos in the springtime

NB: There is no shade at all between here and Zafra.

Continue ahead up **Calle Julián,** turn R into **Calle Santo Cristóbal,** L into **Calle Misericordia** and leading to the **Plaza de la Constitución** (*church and* ayuntamiento). Continue (out of the square) along **Calle Pizarro, Calle Olmo** (*not marked at start*) and KSO down **Calle San Juan** to **Ermita de San Juan** (*1515 but restored in 1999*). Cross the main road and continue ahead up an earth road between walls; this is the old road leading out of town, with the original *calzada romana* underneath it. KSO, ignoring turns, for 6km.

Cross a minor road and enter the village of

6.km Calzadilla de los Barros 556m (138/853)

Shops, bars, farmácia, bank. YH, Hostal Rodríguez (on N630).

Large ceramic tile plaque on wall at entry, with map and indication of the town's monuments. These include the sixteenth-century Ermita de Nuestra Señora de la Encarnación, the Ermita de San Isidro and the fortress-style parish church of the Divino Salvador (fourteenth–sixteenth centuries); this is a national monument, as is also its main altarpiece (fifteenth–sixteenth centuries) by Antón de

Madrid, with 23 sections depicting scenes from the life of Christ.
Town coat of arms contains scallop shell and sword of Santiago.

Cross the village from S to N by going down the main street (**Calle Fuente de Cantos**), turn first R, first L and then KSO (behind the *ayuntamiento* arch) into **Calle Zafra**, out into open country, and KSO. Fork L near two pig farms (one on each side) and KSO, ignoring turns till you reach the N630 at road KM693, behind the crash barrier at a sharp bend (*3km from Calzadilla; stork's nest on telegraph pole at side of road, formerly useful to orient yourself, is no longer there so watch out carefully in this section as waymarking is poor*). Continue ahead, on a section of old road, cross a bridge over **Río Atarje** and 100m later turn L onto an earth track between fields, running // to the river.

After 1km veer R, cross a small river via stepping stones and KSO(R) uphill with fences to either side. 1.5km later KSO at a crossing by a large pig farm (over to L) and KSO, the track becoming grassy along the shallow valley bottom. At an unmarked junction 400m later (no waymark) KSO(L) ahead. 3km later reach a junction with pink tarmac.

KSO, ignoring turns till you reach a level crossing (2km before Puebla de Sancho Pérez). Cross the railway line, KSO ahead and enter the main street (**Calle Sancho Pérez**), continue along **Calle Belén** and follow it down to the **Plaza de España** and church of **Santa Lucía** in

Vacant premises… (now demoloshed) (author)

15km Puebla de Sancho Pérez 522m (153/838)

Three shops (one at entry on L), bars (though all seem to shut down in the afternoons except Bar Galea on main road at end of village). Iglesia de Santa Lucía, Ermita de Nuestra Señora de Belén.

Cross the **Plaza de España**, go down **Paseo de Extremadura** and then the **Calle Obispo Soto** to the end. Cross the road (to Zafra) and go along a track to RH side of a dried-up river, veering round to R onto a minor road. Cross a bridge over a railway line and 500m later reach a level crossing. Do NOT cross the tracks but turn L alongside them to Zafra railway station. Go past an old station building and turn L along **Avenida de la Estación** for a further 2km into the town centre. *(Bike repairs: in Calle Juan Ramón Jiménez, off Avenida de la Estación to L.)*

4km Zafra 509m pop. 15,900 (157/834)

All facilities, RENFE, buses to Madrid, Seville, Mérida, Salamanca and other parts of Spain. Tourist office in the Plaza de España. Hostal Carmen, Avenida de la Estación 9, has two restaurants (Rogelio and Nuevo Rogelio) and rooms (tel: 924.55.14.39). Hostal Arias (tel: 924.55.48.55) by petrol station on the Badajoz road (200m off Camino) plus several others. For pilgrim stamp and spartan refugio facility organised by the 'Amigos' in Zafra (not available during September or early October) ask at Policía Local in centre of town.

Warning: as indicated in the Introduction, during the Feria de Zafra (agricultural fair) which takes place during the whole of September and the first week in October it will be IMPOSSIBLE to find anywhere to stay, either in Zafra or in the pensión in Los Santos de Maimona. During this period it is suggested (pilgrims with credencial only, however) that you continue to Los Santos and sleep in the albergue there (access via Policía Local in Casas Consistoriales).

Zafra is a historic town (often described as a 'mini Seville') with castle of the Dukes of Feria (now a parador), Colegiata de Nuestra Señora de la Candelaria (contains an altarpiece with painted panels by Zurbarán in a south lateral chapel and a Santiago Apóstol on main Baroque altarpiece; church is kept locked except at service times so best time to visit is just before evening mass). Former Hospital de Santiago still standing.

In the city centre turn L opposite **Parque de la Paz** and then turn R down **Glorieta Comercial** to the **Plaza de España** (*tourist office in building on corner*), cross it diagonally and then turn R down the **Calle Sevilla**. At the end turn L into the **Plaza Grande** and KSO into the **Calle Tetuán**, R up the side of the church of the **Candelaria**, along the **Calle Conde de la Corte** and into the square in front of the *ayuntamiento*. KSO along **Plaza del Pilar Redondo**, cross a street and go up a very wide tree-lined avenue (the **Calle Ancha**, but no name at start), straight across the **Plazuela San Benito** at the end and up **Calle San Francisco** to the top. Cross the main road and KSO past a group of eight blocks of modern flats on R with a medieval church tower 'growing' in the middle of them, up a minor road into open country. *This is the route (waymarked) which takes you on a tour of the town and past all the main 'sights' in Zafra.*

However, for a simpler route to leave: go through the park when you reach the town centre and turn R at the end, past Biblioteca Municipal (on L) with fountain behind it. Turn L into the main road to Badajoz, pass bus station and then you will see the blocks of flats on R surrounding the medieval church tower. Turn R up this old road and continue ahead. *Shortly before you reach it you will have a splendid 'balcony' view over the small town of*

5km Los Santos de Maimona 528m, pop. 8100 (162/829)

Shops, bars, banks. Pensión Sanse II (tel: 924.54.42.10) near main road at other end of town. Albergue (like a youth hostel, with bunks, kitchen) accessible via local police.

Maimona was a Moorish king and the 'Santos' not saints but merely 'altos', high-placed, important people, and there are several large historic houses in the town. The building which is now the town hall ('Casas Consistoriales') was once the Palacio de la Encomienda (Command HQ) of the Order of the Knights of Santiago and Los Santos formerly had a pilgrim hospital as well. Municipal coat of arms has cross of Santiago and two scallop shells and church has a Puerta del Perdón (where pilgrims who were too weak or ill to continue were granted the same remission of their sins and the same indulgences as those who completed the journey to Santiago; lion with sword of Santiago above door).

Go down the main street to the square in front of the church, pass to L of it, KSO down the street (*bar on R, no name but with a lot of old photos on walls; also has pilgrim stamp*) and cross the **Calle Sevilla**. Continue ahead down **Calle Teniente Blanco Marín** and **Calle Obispo Luna**, turn L and then R and cross the local road by house no. 38. Continue down **Calle Valmoreno** and then turn L, diagonally, into **Calle Maestrazgo**. Turn R then L then R again (**Calle Santísima**) down to cross **Río Robledillo**.

Continue ahead on a road lined with recently planted trees. 100m later turn R onto a *camino de tierra* and then turn L at a fork onto a walled lane, veering L when it levels out. KSO ahead at a crossing alongside a farm wall and then continue on an untarred road joining from back L.

KSO(L) at a fork 500m later (*N630 is over to your R*) and KSO on a clear *camino de tierra* with vines to either side and olive trees. At the next fork, 1.5km later, KSO(R) ahead. 1km later KSO at a crossing on a track between fences.

When the fencing ends some 2km later (*view of Villafranca de los Barros ahead here*) KSO(L) through olive plantations towards an industrial metal tower ahead (7km from Los Santos). Pass the ruined **Ermita San Isidro** (on R), with a very large fig tree beside it – *shady place to sit down* – and KSO through more olive groves.

At a crossing with a well on RH side (*motorway nearby ahead*) turn R. When you reach a railway line go over the level crossing and turn L under the motorway. Turn **hard R** on the other side, veering L towards the N630 (*no arrows here at present*).

Cross the N630 carefully and KSO ahead on a *camino de tierra*, KSO at a crossing and then turn L at a junction (with well on L). KSO until you reach the town, entering by the **Calle de los Caballeros**.

15km Villafranca de los Barros 450m (177/814)

Town with all facilities. Hostal Horizonte (tel: 924.52.56.99, not open all year), Pensión Mancera Lara, Bar/Rte La Marina (corner of Avenida F. Aranguén and N630) has rooms, Hotel Romero 1km away on main road. Pilgrim stamp in ayuntamiento.

Church of Santa María (much shell decoration inside, San Roque in south porch and Santiago Apóstol with book and shell in main altarpiece) and a number of interesting old houses.

Turn R into **Calle Zurburán** downhill. Cross the 'river,' continue ahead and turn L into **Calle Larga** and the **Plaza de España** (church and *ayuntamiento*). Cross it diagonally and take the top LH street (**Calle Santa Joaquina de Vedrona**) into a triangular 'square' (a *plaza*) with trees. Fork L up **Calle Calvario**, cross **Plaza de la Coronada** diagonally *(second church – San Francisco – on L)* and turn L along **Calle San Ignacio** past **Colegio de los Jesuitas*** out into open country (**ask for this as a landmark if you get lost*).

350m after the last buildings reach a local road. Cross over and KSO ahead on a wide *camino de tierra* between vines. *No shade at all from here to Torremegía.* After approximately 5km the road joins from R *(small white farm over to R)*. Fork L here onto a smaller *camino de tierra*, the old Roman road, straight as a die. 4–5km later the track veers L and joins an unpaved wide road coming from back R. KSO along it. 1km later, after a bridge over the river, the road bends R, along a line of electric pylons. 350m after a group of buildings on R (2km after bend) the Camino crosses a minor road. Here you can either:

a)   cross over and continue ahead to Torremegía or

b)   *(to sleep in Almendralejo, a deviation of 4km in each direction)* turn L and KSO for 3km. Turn L at end of road *(used as a popular local paseo, both morning and evening)*, cross the railway line (station to R) and reach the N630 in

19km Almendralejo 337m, pop. 23,600 (196/795)

Medium-sized town with all facilities, wine production centre. Several hotels, hostales, pensiones and restaurants. The town itself is not on the Vía de la Plata as it dates only from 1536 and was therefore not on the calzada romana. Ermita de Santiago (in outer suburb, 2km to west). If you stay in Almendralejo you can either return to detour point before continuing or rejoin the Camino (turning L onto it) 3km to north by taking road to Alange marked 'Don Benito' at crossing on leaving town.

From the turn-off to Almendralejo continue ahead through more vines and KSO. 3km before Torremegía reach a five-point junction *(old bridge to R with large tree is a good place for rest)* and KSO ahead (north) all the time. The Camino gets gradually nearer to the railway line and then turns L under it. Veer R, keeping on RH side of the 'river,' and continue on a track between fields, leading into the village along the **Calle de la Calzada Romana** (*unnamed at start*).

16km Torremegía 302m (212/779)

Shops, bars, rte. Hostal La Moheda (tel: 927.34.01.74, expensive) but no other accommodation. Iglesia de la Concepción, Palacio de los Megía (with shells in the door).

Cross **Calle Gabriel y Galán**, **Calle Almendralejo** and turn L along **Calle El Castuo** to the main road if you want shops, bars or rte. Otherwise: KSO ahead to very end of the village (*last part of street has tall trees and seats, good for a sit-down*) then continue ahead on a *camino de tierra* into open countryside, forking L in the direction of a cemetery and brick water tower, both on the other (LH) side of the N630.

Continue alongside the main road on the *camino de tierra* for 3km, passing **Viveros Castaño** (*supplier of swimming pools and garden ornaments*). Cross a small river and the local road to Alange and Don Benito and fork slightly R away from the N630 onto a section of old road, passing some very tall eucalyptus trees (*shady but very dirty*).

Continue ahead on an old road till you reach a black and white bar (a barrier) in front of the railway line. Continue ahead, crossing the line carefully (*goods trains still use it*) and then KSO ahead on an old tarred road until it rejoins the N630. Continue along its RH side (or in field if mown) for 1km and at the top of the hill, when the N630 bends L, pass to RH side of the crash barrier and continue on a section of old road, veering L. At another group of eucalyptus trees (just below road) – *shady, view of Mérida ahead* – turn R down the FP through fields, leading in a more or less straight line towards the town.

4km later KSO(R) at a fork and KSO ahead at a crossing almost immediately afterwards. KSO(L) at the next fork, veering L then R downhill. At a T-junction some 2km later, under electric cables, turn R and continue until you reach the end, between two factories near the Río Guadiana.

Turn L, go under the road bridge and continue on an unpaved road // to the river until you reach the Roman bridge (pedestrianised). Turn R over it and cross the **Río Guadiana** into

16km Mérida 218m, 51,600 (228/763)

All facilities, RENFE, buses to Madrid, Seville, Cáceres, Salamanca. Capital of the autonomous region of Extremadura. No pilgrim-only accommodation but several hotels and hostales, including Hostal Senero (Calle Holguín 12, tel: 924.31.72.07), Hostal Nueva España (Avenida de Extremadura 6, tel: 924.31.33.56) and Pensión El Arco (Calle Cervantes 16, tel: 924.31.83.21). Tourist office: Calle Saenz de Burnaga s/n (near Roman theatre).

Mérida was founded in 23 BC as a settlement for veterans of the Iberian wars (hence its name: Augusta Emerita). It contains more important remains of Roman antiquity than any other town in Spain and it is worth spending a whole day here. Roman amphitheatre, theatre (still used), bridge over the River Guadiana (one of the longest of its kind), National Museum of Roman Art (free at certain times), Visigothic Museum (free), Trajan's Arch, Alcazaba, church of Santa Eulalia (the city's patron), church of Santa María. Note, however, that to visit the major Roman and Christian monuments you have to buy a combined ticket for all of them; individual tickets are not available.

Roman amphitheatre, Mérida

After crossing a Roman bridge over the **Río Guadiana** continue ahead past **Puerta del Puente** and a small public garden (R) and then fork L up a narrow street to **Plaza de España** (*Cathedral of Santa María to L,* ayuntamiento *opposite)*. Leave by the top LH corner along **Calle Santa Julia**, veering R and then turn L into **Calle Trajana**, passing under **Trajan's Arch** (Arco de Trajano). Turn R and then immediately L into **Plaza de la Constitución**, in front of the post office, and continue ahead into **Travesia de Almendralejo**. Turn L into **Calle Almendralejo** in front of the police station and then turn R into **Calle Calvario**. Continue to very end (*bar on L opens early)*, turn L and go under the railway line, then turn R and immediately L to cross the **Río Albarregas** via Mérida's other bridge of Roman origin. *The Acueducto de los Milagros is now on your R, built by the Romans to bring water into the city via an underground channel coming from the reservoir (*Proserpina*) 5km away. The aqueduct was originally 838m long and 25m tall at its highest point. The area around it has now been landscaped as a public park but is not, unfortunately, well maintained.*

Continue on **Avenida Vía de la Plata** for 100m on the other side then fork (not turn) L up a one-way street (with a 'no entry' sign) leading past the **Pan Emerita** bread factory.

The waymarking here has 'EP'– Embalse de Proserpina – in yellow, one of the two reservoirs of Roman origin (the other, Cornado, is to the north-east of the town) as there are, in fact, two pilgrim routes out of Mérida. The one described here is the EP route; the other, marked 'CR' and following a section of the calzada romana*, has to return to the N630 a lot of the time, due to new road construction, including coming back to El Carrasceljo via the road. The route via the Embalse de Proserpina is much quieter and, after the reservoir itself, goes through beautiful countryside with* encina *and cork plantations. Here, as earlier on, you will find the black, brown and grey* cerdos ibéricos *grazing on the fallen acorns below.*

KSO at the roundabout (*the Mérida-Badajoz road crosses R to L)*. KSO. Cross the motorway and continue ahead on a minor road leading downhill (*note cross on* rollo *to L at top of hill)*. KSO at a small roundabout (*RH turn leads to* urbanización) and continue by the side of the Roman embankment of the

Roman Acueducto de los Milagros in evening light, Mérida

6km Embalse de Proserpinà (234/757)

Now a tourist attraction with water sports, several cafés, chiringuitos (open-air snack bars) and campsite (open April 1st to September 15th) the reservoir supplied Mérida with its drinking and other water in Roman times.

At the end of the wall leave the road and continue along the shore (*NB: bars not open early*) and then return to the road to cross the bridge. Pass a Red Cross post (R) and KSO on the road (*very quiet, very little traffic*), undulating between fields with *encinas*, becoming increasingly rocky. 4km after the reservoir and 300m after an isolated white house on L, turn L off the road onto a *camino de tierra* undulating through trees.

KSO(R) at the first fork, KSO(L) at the second and then continue between fences. 1km later cross a cattle grid and KSO alongside the wall, then cross another and KSO. Go through a gate and veer R up into the village. Turn R along the main street to the church in

Statue of Santiago Peregrino, cathedral chancel, Zamora

Church of Nuestra Señora de Gracia, Almadén de la Plata

7.5km El Carrascalejo 308m (241.5/749.5)

Fountain, church of Nuestra Señora de la Consolación but no other facilities of any kind.

Turn L downhill after the church, veering L behind it down to cross a bridge over a small river. Pass the base of a former wayside cross (L), cross another track at right angles and KSO(R) ahead on the other side, through undulating vines, till you reach the street leading into

2.5km Aljucén 270m (244/747)

Two bars, shop, farmácia, fountain, simple meals available in 'Kiosco Parque' by arrangement. Church of San Andrés has Santiago crosses on all its pedestals (inside the building).

Make sure you have enough water before you leave Aljucén.

Continue down the main village street and follow the road round to R at the end, leading to the N630. Cross a bridge over **Río Aljucén** and just before the petrol station (*2.5km from Aljucén, bar/café*) and opposite a turning to 'Las Navas de Santiago, 17' turn R onto a path leading through trees, following to L of the fence.

Between here and Alcuéscar you leave the province of Badajoz and enter Cáceres. For the next 15km you will not pass a single building and are unlikely to meet anyone at all. This section is well-enough waymarked but watch out carefully for the yellow arrows as the route is not always as straightforward as you might expect. Like many other areas of the Vía de la Plata this one is a paradise of wild flowers in the springtime.

After 1.5km KSO(L) ahead at a fork, still following the line of fence to L. 300m later go through a wide gate (or cattle grid to L of it) and continue ahead on a track with fencing posts to RH side at first, then veering L, and KSO(R) ahead at a fork. 500m later the path continues alongside a drystone wall and 500m after that you reach another wide gate. Fork L on other side, slightly uphill, and continue ahead at the top, on the level.

500m later (after a gate) reach a crossing and KSO ahead, descending, with fence to your R. 200m later fork L and 200m after that fork R. 100m later turn L and then R, veering R to turn L at a fork

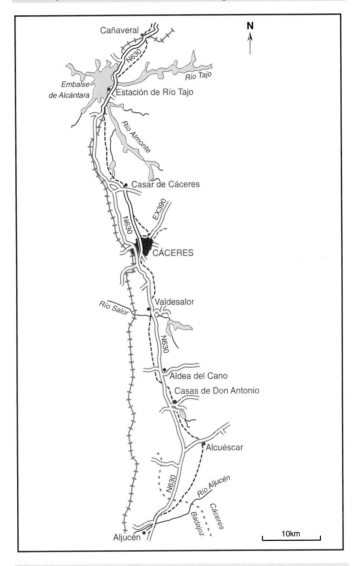

with a track you are now on (*there are a lot of cistus bushes in this section*).

500m later go through a *cledo* and KSO. 1km later KSO(R) ahead at a fork and 300m later go through a gate. Some 9km after leaving the N630 reach a junction marked 'fin de recorrido' (*referring to a local ruta de senderismo, the Cordel del Gato*) and KSO(R) ahead and then 400m later KSO(R) again at a fork. Continue uphill.

KSO for 3km, with a fence over to your L all the time, and reach a fence with a large, wide open level space behind. Go through it on a track. 2km later (at end) fork R and KSO. 2km after that reach the

15km Cruz de San Juan/Cruz del Niño Muerto (259/732)

Stone wayside cross, so named because on one such feast day (June 24th, Midsummer's Day, celebrating the anniversary of St John the Baptist) a young shepherd boy coming to the fiesta from the Valle de la Zarza was eaten by a wolf.

Continue ahead but watch out carefully as 3km before Alcuéscar, because of pipe-laying, the turning to the R by a house called 'Campo' is not waymarked as the arrows are missing at time of writing; this path brings you out in the upper part of the town, after which you veer L down to the lower part and the **Residencia**. However, if you KSO here you will arrive at the Montánchez road 1.5km later, after forking L when you get close to it; turn R along it and enter

6km Alcuéscar 489m (265/726)

Shops, bars. Casa Alejandro in upper part of village and Bar El Trio lower down both do meals. Accommodation (for pilgrims with credencial only) at the Residencia for handicapped men run by the Hermanos Esclavos de María y de los Pobres at the bottom of the village on the way out. (Note, however, that they do not charge and that you should consider leaving a donation.) Hostal Canuto, another hostal and a hotel are located at KM249 on the N630 at the junction with the local road to Alcúescar, 3km to west.

If you would like to visit the isolated Visigothic church of Santa Lucía de Trampal you can do so by following the well-signed track, out of the Plaza de España in Alcuéscar, 2.5km each way.

Leave by turning R (*if you have come from the top of the village*) in front of the **Residencia**. 500m later fork R then at the next fork KSO(L) ahead and at the next KSO(R) along a walled lane between fields.

After 1.5km pass between two sets of gates and KSO. KSO(R) at the next two forks and KSO(L) at the next one after that. 800m later reach a crossing and KSO ahead. 500m later KSO(R) at a crossing and KSO(R) at the next.

Approximately 1km before the village (*visible ahead*) the track becomes asphalted. 200m later turn R onto a *camino de tierra* leading to the village, crossing a Roman bridge over the **Río Ayuela** (*three central arches and five square ones. Note two defunct telegraph poles nearby, with stork's nests on top*).

9km Casas de Don Antonio 413m (274/717)

Bar in village and another on N630 at exit. No accommodation. Ermita de la Virgen del Pilar (with statue of Santiago Matamoros) at exit.

To visit the village: cross the local road and go uphill, veering L (*bar in centre*). Follow the main street down to a second church to rejoin the local road.

To continue without visiting the village: turn L on the local road and continue to the N630 (*bar opposite*) and turn R on a track on its RH side, // to it. KSO for 2km. *300m after road KM580 (castle behind road is the Castillo Arquijuelas de Arriba) there is a Roman* miliario, *still standing and in good condition except that its inscription is now very faint.*

800m later, just past a large wrought-iron gateway on the other side of the road (**Criadero Santa María**) veer slightly R to cross a small Roman bridge over the **Arroyo de la Zafrilla** (*one curved central arch and one square one to either side of it, three in all*). 200m later the track returns to the road; cross over and continue on a similar track on LH side.

300m later, near a field of large trees (and when you can see Aldea del Cano) the Camino veers L away from the road. Pass another *miliario* just after crossing a dried-up river bed and 150m before a group of six eucalyptus trees.

(If you want to go into Aldea del Cano – for example to eat – you can make your way to the N630 from here along the LH edge of a field

opposite or otherwise go 200m further and turn R down an unpaved road opposite a large barn, 300m in each direction, emerging on the road between cemetery and Centro Cultural. To return to the Camino, though, you can fork R partway up this road on your way back and turn R beyond the barn.)

7km Aldea del Cano 396m (281/710)

Fountain, shops, bars in centre of village on other side of road. Bar/rte 'Las Vegas' on N630. Church of San Martín.

KSO, cross a minor road and KSO towards *encina* plantations (*not much shade to walk in though plenty to sit in*). KSO(R) at a fork and then again at a second fork and KSO ahead. Fork L at a junction (*view of another castle ahead over to R, the Castillo de Arquijuelas de Abajo*) and continue uphill. At the top, when it levels out, KSO(R) at a fork and continue ahead in the direction of a tall red and white pole on the horizon.

Reach **Cáceres air club** then continue to climb gently for 1km more, then cross a track at a crossing and begin to descend. KSO at a crossing (*Castillo de Mayoralgo visible over to R*) and continue ahead.

When you get near the village veer R to cross a Roman bridge over the **Río Salor** (*14 arches though not all are visible*) and turn R to the main road in

15km Valdesalor 380m (293/698)

Shop, bars, bar/rte by petrol station. Church of San Pedro.

Cross the N630 and continue on a track // to it. KSO for 3km till you reach a minor tarred road coming from R. Turn L along it to the N630 just before the road KM562. Cross over and continue on a FP on the other side, below the road, widening out to a track after a while.

Continue up to the top of the hill, passing a wooded area on the L and crossing the entrance road to a property on your L and then continue // to the main road when it bends L. Just after road KM560 (2km from the bottom of the hill) the track veers R to the main road.

Cross over and KSO diagonally on the other side, down the track alongside a wire fence on LH side, marked 'Zona militar, no pasar'. KSO, keeping // to the fence on your RIGHT. 700m later, near some farm buildings over to your L, the track divides. KSO(R) ahead on a smaller track between fields. Pass the *finca* 'San Antonio' and 300m later, at a fork, KSO(R) ahead alongside fencing on RH side. 200m later cross a track coming from R and fork R down **Calle Océano Atlántico** at the start of an industrial area (*where all the streets are named after seas*).

KSO until you reach some traffic lights after the local road (**C520, Carretera de Don Benito**) joins from the back R by a petrol station (*bar/rte on L*). Cross over to RH side and fork R down the **Ronda San Francisco**, a very long road, passing a large hospital (on L) before you reach, abruptly, the foot of the old part of the town in front of you.

12km Cáceres 464m, pop. 69,193 (305/686)

All facilities, RENFE, buses to Madrid and places on the Gijón–Seville service. Accommodation in all price brackets, including Hostal Almonte (Calle Gil Cordero 6, tel: 927.24.09.25) and Pensión Carretero (Plaza Mayor 22, tel: 927.24.74.82) but no pilgrim-only facilities. Tourist office: Plaza Mayor 33. Bike repairs: Bicicletas Cáceres, Calle de Badajoz 10. Sello: church of Santiago, ayuntamiento (entrance at rear).

City founded in Roman times with the old town, dating from the thirteenth century onwards, completely self-contained within the modern one. Surrounded by its walls with gates and towers it has many monuments worth visiting, whether churches, palaces or other imposing houses (two-hour guided walking tour of the historic quarter available from tourist office in the mornings). Church of Santiago (just outside the old city centre, like those in Salamanca and Zamora and as was often customary for pilgrim churches) has a bas-relief of a pilgrim with staff, scrip, hat and shell and a Santiago Matamoros in the main altarpiece (see Appendix B for other Santiago references in Cáceres). Another place worth spending a whole day.

When you get to the very end of the **Ronda San Francisco** arrows point you to pass to RH side of a bridge and then KSO ahead, up the **Calle San Ildefonso**, veering L up to **the Plaza Las Candelas** and then veering L again up **Calle de la Consolación** (*not marked at start*) to the **Plaza de Santa Clara** (*with stone crucifix in centre*).

Leave by the top RH corner, turn L into **Calle Puerta de Mérida** and continue along the **Calle Adarve del Padre Rosalio**. Turn L at end under the THIRD archway, down a short flight of steps, into the **Plaza**

Mayor (*tourist office,* ayuntamiento). Then, to continue, there are two options, though b) is 3km longer, is not waymarked and is not suitable for cyclists:

Pilgrim bas-relief above north portal, church of Santiago, Cáceres

a) From the **Plaza Mayor**, with your back to the tourist office and the old town, turn R (opposite the *ayuntamiento*) into **Calle Gabriel y Galán**, with the **Plaza Duque** at the end, then L into **Calle Sancti Espiritu**, continuing on **Calle Margallo** to the **Plaza Argel** and the **Plaza de Toros** *(bullring)*. Cross over and continue down LH side of the bullring on the road signposted 'Casar de Cáceres', veering L to the **Calle Carretera de Casar** (*not marked at start*) and then R down the central reservation (*seats*) of **Calle Brunete**. When the buildings end KSO on the road.
NO SHADE AT ALL in this section, either to walk or sit in. From time to time you can leave the road itself to walk on sections of old road and from about 1km before the petrol station (3km from Casar de Cáceres) you can walk off-road on a wide track to its LH side.

b) Leave the **Plaza Mayor** by the **Calle Gabriel y Galán** but then continue ahead along the **Calle Muñoz Chavez**, **Calle Peñas**, **Avenida de San Blas**, pass the church of **San Blas** (L) and continue along **Calle Lope de Vega**. Cross the N521 at traffic lights (Red Cross station opposite) and continue ahead on **Avenida de Heroés de Baler** (marked 'Torrejón El Rubio'). After this you turn L into an industrial estate and when the tarmac stops continue in roughly a straight line, passing through several gates and emerging on the road to Casar de Cáceres 1km before the petrol station. *It is doubtful, however, whether this route holds any advantages over the other option as it is no more scenic and no shadier.*

11km Casar de Cáceres 369m (316/675)

Shops, bars, bank. New refugio in square opposite the ayuntamiento (20 beds, showers, kitchen; contact Policía Local for key). Hostal Las Encinas 3km away on N630, near KM542 (tel: 927. 29.02.01); if you stay here you will have to return to the village to continue on the Camino, picking up arrows again near the Ermita de Santiago (on the northern outskirts of the village).

Iglesia de la Asunción (parish church, in centre of village) has a Baroque wood painted Santiago on LH side of main altarpiece with fine Santiago Peregrino complete with staff, gourd, hat and scallop and modern but inverted black scallop in grille of SW chapel. The town also has four ermitas, one each to its north, south, east and west; Santiago, to the north, has modern Santiago Matamoros with a giant sword above the altar while those to the south, east and west are dedicated, respectively, to San Bartolomé, Los Mártires and La Soledad.

At the entrance to Casar de Cáceres continue down the walkways of the public garden *(Paseo de Extremadura – well kept, various sorts of trees)*. At the very end cross the road and KSO ahead down **Calle Larga Alta** to the **Plaza de España** and *ayuntamiento*.

Turn L into **Avenida Constitución** and then R into **Calle Santiago** to the end. Turn R then L to the **Ermita de Santiago**. Pass to its LH side and KSO on an untarred road out into open country.

KSO for 2–3km then KSO(R) at a fork by a farm. *NO SHADE AT ALL but a very nice walk in the early morning if you like being 'on the roof of the world' in wide open spaces. More miliarios in this area.* KSO for several kilometres. *(Cañaveral visible ahead on mountainside in distance.)*

50m after the entrance to the **Finca La Higuera** (*9km from Casar de Cáceres*) reach a fork, both options with gates. Go through LH set of gates and then KSO(R) ahead on the other side, veering L uphill. 500m later go through more gates and KSO ahead alongside a fence. *(Landscape becomes increasingly rockier, some very large, with unusual formations.)*

700m later, near a farm on R, go through more gates and KSO straight ahead on the other side in a straight line. DO NOT go through the gates on L but continue ahead on the track and 500m later go through more gates. KSO, go through some more gates and continue on a walled lane, then continue between gate posts out into open heathland, passing in front of an isolated house on L.

Shortly afterwards (*5km from the Finca La Higuera*) you reach a single concrete gate with TWO sets of waymarks. *Here you can either continue ahead, joining the road and continuing on a FP to its RH side until the bridge over the Río Almonte or turn R and use a section of the* calzada romana *whose course has been passing to the R of the track you have been on till now but is overgrown and impassable up to here. This option is waymarked, though not all that well; it is NOT suitable for bikes and is not described here. Both options meet up before the road bridge (the only means of crossing the two rivers). View of the Embalse de Alcántara ahead from here.*

KSO ahead, veering L and cross a cattle grid. Then: cyclists: KSO here and continue north on the N630 (turn R onto it) until the **Hostal Miraltajo**. Walkers: immediately after crossing the cattle grid turn **hard R** towards the N630 (at road KM527) and continue on a FP, clear, that goes // to the road below to your L, up and down, undulating, clearly marked (*good views*).

Rejoin the N630 just before road KM525 (2km later). Cross over to LH side (*VERY carefully – there is a huge amount of very heavy traffic*) and cross a road (and rail) bridge (nearly 1km long) over the **Río Almonte**. *(Over to your L you can see the Torreón de Floripes, the only remains of the village of Alconeter after it was flooded to make the reservoir.)*

On the other side of the river you will see arrows leading you off to the L, below the road onto a narrow and not very clear (though well-waymarked) FP. This is a new option and not yet very well trodden; it may also be very slippery in wet weather and it only lasts for 500m anyway, before returning you to the road.

Unfortunately the only way to cross the two rivers (*until some enterprising person sets up a pilgrim ferry service, at least*) is via the N630 and the road/rail bridges – a total of 5km.

After crossing the **Río Almonte** KSO for 3km and then cross the **Río Tajo**. KSO on the other side for 1.5km to the

22km Hostal Miraltajo 250m (338/653)

Bar, rte, rooms (tel: 927.19.20.04).

[Pilgrims interested in Roman bridges may like to make a 4km detour from here to the huge, imposing Puente Mantible/Puente Alconétar which was re-sited in a valley beside the N630 when the reservoir flooded its original position. Take the gravel path to the north end of the Hostal terrace and follow it down to the banks of the reservoir and then nearly all the way to the bridge: you may need to scramble up to the N630 for a short distance to avoid cliffs.]

Turn R off the road opposite the Hostal onto a *camino de tierra*, climbing gradually all the time (*good views as you go*). Cross a cattle grid and KSO on a level track, isolated and high up. About 2km before you get level with Cañaveral KSO(L) at a fork and then KSO(R) at the next. KSO.

a) When you come level with Cañaveral at a big junction (*with information board*) you can turn L, marked 'Cañaveral', downhill, on a path which will take you into the town. Go through a gate, continue on the *camino de tierra* and go over the restored fourteenth-century **Puente de San Benito** and KSO uphill, following the sign for 'Cañaveral' up to the N630. Turn R onto the pavement.

b) However, if you do not want to go into Cañaveral (to eat or sleep) continue straight ahead here, passing Cañaveral railway station and the industrial estate, veering L to join the N630 2km beyond the town near the **Ermita San Cristóbal**.

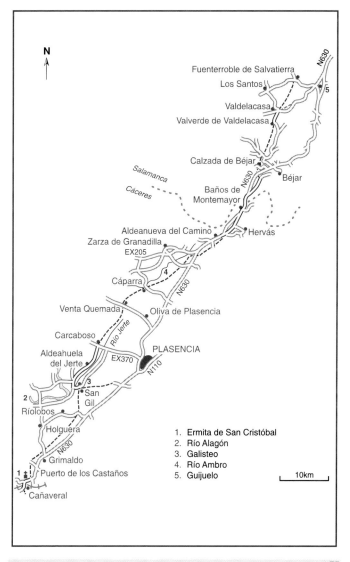

1. Ermita de San Cristóbal
2. Río Alagón
3. Galisteo
4. Río Ambro
5. Guijuelo

15km Cañaveral 362m, pop. 2100 (353/638)

Bars, shops, bank (+CD), Hostal/Rte Málaga (tel: 927.30.00.67) on main road. Fourteenth–sixteenth-century Iglesia de Santa María, sixteenth-century Ermita de San Roque.

After turning R onto the pavement you can either KSO on the N630 (**Calle San Benito**) or, quieter, fork L on the other side up **Calle de Monrobel** (fountain on L). KSO to the square in front of the church and then turn R, passing to RH side of the *ayuntamiento* up **Calle de Centro**. Turn L and then R into a long unmarked street leading to the N630. Turn L.

Continue on the N630 out of town for 1.5km (road KM508), pass a turning (on R) to Cañaveral railway station and 500m later reach the

2km Ermita de San Cristóbal (355/636)

Cyclists may prefer to continue on the road here, although there is no hard shoulder till you reach the pass, as the path, short-cutting many of the bends, is steep and will be bumpy.

Turn L off the road but do NOT take the more obvious road to its L but pass to RH side of a fountain (*not working but with seats*) alongside a wall and which you will see over to your R. Pass to RH side of the fountain alongside the wall at first, picking up a clear track coming from L and go under some electricity cables uphill.

At a junction 700–800m later KSO(L) ahead uphill and 80m later turn R, veering L to a fork R (do NOT follow a wall to L) uphill up a steep *cortafuego* (firebreak) (*good views to rear as you climb*) in the direction of a TV transmitter mast at the top of a hill ahead. The track winds its way (mainly) uphill till you reach a minor road (leading to the TV mast on L). Turn R along it (*extensive views ahead on a clear day*), join the local road coming from your L and 600m later reach the

4km Puerto de los Castaños 500m (359/632)

No facilities at all. The next section (as far as Galisteo) is NOT suitable for cyclists, even on mountain bikes. They should continue on the main road for 3km more, until just after Grimaldo (bar) and then turn L on a minor road to Holguero. KSO at a crossroads with the Torrejoncillo–Riolobos road and then turn R at the next crossroads along another minor road more or less following the Río Alagón to Galisteo.

The Camino leaves through the woods on the north side of the former hotel, through a *cledo/cancela* to the LH side of the N630. *Watch waymarks carefully, as at first they seem confusing but they become more straightforward as you go: follow the line of either the barbed wire or the walls, in more or less a straight line, on what are, in fact, old tracks but which are now hard to recognise.*

Follow the path alongside the wall on your L, keeping fairly close to it. 2.5km later, 100m after going under (more) electric cables turn L through a gate. Veer R downhill and 150m later cross a stream via stepping stones. *Several big trees – nice shady place for a rest.*

KSO alongside the line of wall. 100m later a FP is signposted to 'Grimaldo, 500m' (*bar, castillo*). Continue alongside the line of fence, reach a road by a gate (*you may see foxes in this section*) and cross over, going through the gate on the other side too, and KSO to L of the fence.

Go through a gate and then immediately through a second one next to entrance gates next to a large private property on L with big metal tanks on the horizon and then go through another gate. KSO, to RH side of the fence this time.

1.5km later go through a gate and continue straight ahead on a path with fences on both sides. At the end go through another gate and continue alongside a fence on (your) RH side. Go through a gate and KSO.

1km later, after you have gone quite a long way downhill and the ground to your L opens out (*an area known as the 'cuatro terminos'*) watch out carefully for waymarks indicating a RH turn* through a gateway in fencing to your R. Continue downhill on a small FP on the other side alongside a fence on L. Go through a gate and then, 1km later, another, keeping straight on ahead all the time alongside the fence on your LH side. 1km later reach TWO gates and go through the RH one and KSO ahead by the fence all the time. When you reach a FOURTH gate in front of you (*3–4km from where you turned R through fencing**) go through the one on its LEFT and continue alongside the wall that is now on your RH side. (*The walled town of Galisteo – still some three hours away – is visible ahead to L.*)

KSO and 500m later go through a gate on R and continue alongside the wall on your LH side. 1km later, when you see a small reservoir below to R, arrows indicate that you should stick close to the wall but you can in fact (and less complicated) continue on the track you were already on as they meet up anyway 50m later and keep veering L, sticking close to the wall/fence all the time. 1km after you saw the reservoir, reach a gate, go through it, turn L onto a *camino de tierra*, cross a small river (stepping stones if needed), turn L again and then go up a bank (by a large drain) onto the local (tarred) road ahead.

Turn R along it for 600m then turn L up a track to a white gateway and cattle grid, set well back from road, to the *finca* **Valparaíso** and continue uphill. At a junction at the top KSO ahead, veering L alongside a fence downhill. *Here the landscape changes abruptly, becoming much greener and giving way to fields full of tobacco, beetroot, sunflowers, and irrigated by a system of canals.* Fork R at a junction at the bottom.

Cross a canal and turn R along its LH bank (go through a gate by a ruined house) for 1km. Just before a bridge turn L, passing to L of some deserted farm buildings, passing close to them and picking up a track with an irrigation channel to its LH side. Go through three sets of gates, after which the track becomes an unsurfaced (non-tarred) road and on L, at a bend, there are some willow trees and a seat (*nice place for a rest*).

Go downhill past a barn, cross a bridge and after passing between irrigation channels on both sides of the road turn L, then R 100m later, uphill between fields on an unsurfaced road. KSO at a crossing (Camino becomes a *camino de tierra*).

1km later (after turning L through irrigation channels) reach a road. Cross over, turning L in front of Bar/Rte 'Los Emigrantes' and then turn R under an archway (the **Puerta del Rey**) into the walled town of

24km Galisteo 308m (383/608)

Small town with shops, bars, bank, Hogar del Pensionista (in main square, does simple food). Bar/Rte 'Los Emigrantes' at entrance does meals and has rooms but these are nearly always full. Small refugio in Calle Cuchifejos. Camping Merendero by old bridge leaving town also serves food when open.

The town has a complete set of walls, with a paseo both along the top and round the outside, an alcázar and church of Santa María with Mudéjar apse and scallops in groups of five in decorative ironwork in north portal. Take a walk round the ramparts (several access points) to get a good view of the town and its surrounding area. Most of the town is inside its walls, now being restored to form a paseo. Its three puertas are still intact: Puerta del Rey, Puerta de Santa María and Puerta de la Villa. Walkway outside the town walls too.

Walled town of Galisteo

Turn L (after going through an archway) and then R into **Travesia del Rey**, leading to the square with the *ayuntamiento*, and then turn L into **Calle Gabriel y Galán** and leave the town by the **Puerta de la Villa**. Fork R into **Calle Huerto de los Olivos**. Go downhill to the bottom, turn R onto a local road, pass **Camping Merendero** (on R) and cross a bridge over **Río Jerte** (*note stork's nest on memorial in middle of bridge*). 200m later turn R onto a slightly bigger local road. KSO(R) at a junction and KSO for another 5km. *Style of farm buildings begins to change, with a lot of brick barns (often decorative).*

6km Aldeahuela del Jerte (389/602)

Bar, shop, farmácia.

Continue ahead through the village road and KSO to

5km Carcaboso 271m (394/597)

Bars, shops, bank (no CD), Rte 'Los Golondrinas.' Bar Pacense (on main road) has rooms. Modern church of Santiago Apóstol with glass roundel of Santiago Matamoros above west door.

Make sure you have enough water before you leave here.

Plasencia (11km to the east, all facilities) is not on the route of the Roman Vía de la Plata, as explained in the Introduction, but is well worth a visit. Hotel Rincón Extremadura, Bar Micasa, Pensión Blanco and Hostal Muralla all have rooms. Its casco antiguo *contains the old and new cathedrals, several churches and historic houses and the town had seven pilgrim hospitals in medieval times.*

Cyclists: should continue on the local road to **Valdeobispo** and then turn R onto another one leading to the **Venta Quemada** (*marked *** below*). Please note that the walkers' route is NOT suitable for bikes, of any sort.

Walkers: cross the **Carretera de Plasencia** and fork R up **Calle de la Iglesia**, passing the (modern) church of Santiago Apóstol (on R). Turn L at the end into **Calle Real** and then R into **Calle Pozo** then KSO(R) at a fork out of the village. KSO(R) at a fork by three modern concrete wayside crosses (on L), cross a river and follow a lane as it veers L, alongside stepped sections of an irrigation canal on R.

At a junction (marked 'Bombay'!) and opposite a small *finca* on your L two routes are waymarked. The option straight ahead is a short-cut, following the canal and joining the other route at ** below. Otherwise, turn R here down a lane and KSO for 1km to a junction with three very large barns. Turn L uphill, passing through a gate. KSO on a track skirting the edge of a field, go through another gate uphill, pass between a gap in the irrigation channel and KSO ahead to a *cledo*. On other side follow a track through *encinas* and some 700m later, when the track bends R to a gate (pond over to R), KSO ahead on a grassy track alongside a field.

Go through another *cledo* and follow a fence down to a pair of stone gate posts with the passageway blocked off with brushwood to keep cattle in: climb over (low) a stone wall to L (*not difficult if you take your rucksack off first*). Continue ahead a few metres then pass through a gap in a hedge to R, into a field, and go along its LH edge for 100m to a small gate onto a minor road.**

Cross over and go through a *cledo* on other side of a bridge over the irrigation canal. Turn L when you get inside, alongside the road, veering R uphill 200m later, at the top of which you will come to a wall. Continue alongside it for 350m more then cross over the wall onto the clear track on its other side. *(For some reason best known to the waymarker you were not able to do this much earlier.)* KSO on this track.

Go through some metal gates and 150m later, when the track bends L, veer R over towards a wall and KSO alongside it. 1km later, when you reach another wall (in front of you) go through some gates on your R and continue ahead on the other side, with the wall on your L now (KSO NORTH all the time). KSO for 3km then cross another wall (in front of you).

When you see a cattle pen made of pink breeze blocks (500m later) go R to skirt it and then KSO alongside a wall on L again on the other side. Cross two more walls *(fairly tumbledown)* and then, after climbing a final wall, reach a minor road at the

13km Venta Quemada (407/584)

Isolated house at side of road. No facilities of any kind. The next stretch of the Camino is very beautiful, quiet and peaceful, along a very wide walled lane, with a fair amount of shade and good views into the distance (the Embalse de Gabriel y Galán and a national park are over to the west).

Cross the road and KSO ahead down a very wide walled lane for 6km. Pass houses on R and the lane becomes narrower, reaching the Roman arch at

6.5km Cáparra 400m (413.5/577.5)

Remains of ancient Roman city with four-square triumphal arch; this is no mere museum piece, and the Camino actually passes underneath it, surrounded by fields. It has now become more 'touristy', though this means that you can now get into the meagre ruins of the adjacent town.

KSO down the road ahead and 350m later fork R down a walled lane. KSO for 2km (gate halfway down) and at the end go through a gate into open rocky countryside with *encinas*. KSO ahead.

1.5km later reach more gates. 200m later cross the end of a gravel road and KSO alongside the wall on R. 700m later cross a river (*some stepping stones*). Pass the end of another gravel road and KSO. Cross a river (*bed may be dry*) and then go through a *cledo*. 500m later go through another and turn L onto a minor road. KSO (literally) for 5km.

Turn R onto a local road and 800m later KSO(L) at a fork (*'No Entry' sign – 'excepto servidumbres'*). 1.5km later the tarmac ends. Veer L, cross a river (*bed probably dry*) and then arrows direct you under a road bridge under the N630. *The mountains of the Sierra de Gredos are over to the R in the distance.*

a)   Walkers: on the other side, on your L, is a set of gates (always locked) with arrows indicating that you should go through them. Climb over a wall to their R, cross a field diagonally R and then pick up the *calzada romana* – a wide walled lane coming from your R.

b)   Cyclists: do not go under the bridge but continue ahead on a *camino de tierra* and then turn R onto a local road leading to the N630. 1km later, at the side of bar/rte, Casa Basilio, go up the *camino de tierra* to pick up the *calzada romana* 1km later and turn L along it.

KSO along the (usually) wide walled lane. *(Undulating, a very nice, quiet section, with quite a lot of shade – to rest in, at least. Very easy to follow.)* Shortly before Aldeanueva reach a precast concrete factory (on L) and the tarmac starts. Cross the road to **Gargantilla** and see the first ceramic map (*of the route*) on L. KSO down **Avenida de la Olivas** into **Plaza del Mercado** in the centre of

18.5km Aldeanueva del Camino 529m (432/559)

Shops, bars. Hostal/Rte Montesol at end of village has inexpensive rooms (tel: 927.48.43.35). Fountain with good (chlorine-free) drinking water (**hard L** on entry). San Servando, one of the town's two parish churches, has modern·tiled Santiago panel above high altar.

Triumphal Arch, Cáparra   (author)

Continue straight ahead, over a bridge (*dried-up river, second ceramic map to R*) and continue ahead past the *ayuntamiento*. KSO(L) ahead down a long street with first floor balconies, passing a church (on L), to the very end, where you join the N630 at road KM438. *The section to Baños de Montemayor is basically on the road, though you can walk on the verge on its RH side for quite a lot of the time.*

After 4.5km you pass the first turning to Hervás (pop. 3500, accommodation available), which is worth a detour (total 8km). Apart from the Palacio de los Dávilas, the Convento Trinitario and the church of Santa María it contains the best-preserved judería *(Jewish quarter) in Spain. To return to the Vía de la Plata do not retrace your steps to the N630 the way you came but rejoin it further to the north by taking the SECOND turning.*

At road KM434 the porch at the entrance gates to El Salgural (a finca used for environmental courses) is a good place for shelter (if raining, or from sun).

After the second turning to **Hervás** (*bar/rte opposite*) walkers can use a small FP on RH side of the road (*cyclists: stick to road*), joining a wider lane for a while before returning you to the road. Cross over and continue on LH side for 350m then, shortly before road KM430, fork L down a lane // to the road. This returns you to the road 800m later.

Cross over to RH side, go back a few steps to cross a ditch and then turn L to pass BEHIND the **Ermita Santísimo Cristo de la Misericordia** (*so as not to walk on road at dangerous bend*). Seats, cruceiro. *In use but kept locked: you can see inside through the windows. (The 'dip' in the skyline ahead is the Puerto de Béjar, where you will be going after leaving Baños.)*

10km Baños de Montemayor 708m (442/549)

Small spa town with shops, bars, banks, and plenty of accommodation for its size (one hotel, five hostales and four fondas). Campsite 'Las Cañadas' (Cat.1) at KM432 on N630. Tourist office in the ayuntamiento.

A rather 'touristy' place where people still go to 'take the waters' and a lot of basketwork (cestería) is on sale. Thermal baths of Roman origin (with small museum), famous for the cure of respiratory and muscular complaints. Church of Santa María.

Continue on the pavement then fork R off the N630 (*fountain on R*) near the former church of **Santa Catalina** (*now a municipal auditorium*), passing to its LH side (*this is the Calle Mayor: another fountain partway up on R*). Continue to the top then fork L to a square with the *ayuntamiento* (*and tourist office inside*).

Pass in front of the *ayuntamiento* (it is on your R), turn L into **Calle Castillejos** and then turn first R, veering L steeply uphill (*this is still Calle Castillejos*), joining the **Carretera de la Estación** (coming from back R). 100m later, at a 'hairpin' in the N630, fork R ahead up a restored section of the *calzada romana*, which short-cuts many of the zigzags in the N630 that you can see over to your L. *(Cyclists: worth pushing up this section.)*

The *calzada* stops after 1.5km, reaching the N630 100m before the border between the autonomous regions of Extremadura and Castille-León and the provinces of Cáceres and Salamanca. Cross over and:

a) Walkers only: fork L down a FP, cross a stream, continue alongside the wall of a field on L, go round some very big rocks to R and cross a wall and exit at the end of a second field onto the main road again. This avoids a dangerous bend but is not waymarked and may be boggy.

b) Cyclists or walkers: continue on road up to the

3.5km Puerto de Béjar 870m (445.5/545.5)

Bar/rte on L. Refugio in preparation in old school.

300m past the petrol station (*with café*) fork L down a lane next to the *finca* 'Coto de Nuestra Señora del Carmen' (*sello at house on R*). *NB: be careful to keep following the yellow arrows and not the red and white French-style* balises *of the GR10 and GR100 (Ruta de la Plata) in this area, which coincides only in part with the Camino de Santiago along the Vía de la Plata.*

Cross a minor road and KSO downhill on a walled lane, ignoring any turns to R, to the valley bottom and cross the **Río Cuerpo de Hombre** by the

4km Puente de la Magdalena (Malena) 650m (449.5/541.5)

Many miliarios nearby in this section.

Turn R on the other side along a sandy lane (the *calzada romana*) that continues // to a small tarmac road on its L for some 3km, climbing gently all the time. Join the road shortly after the **Colonia San Francisco** (*a former farm*) and continue along it for 250m to a sharp RH bend by some houses. KSO ahead here up a stony lane (*GR100 continues here, GR10 turns R on road*) that zigzags its way fairly steeply uphill at the start and then more gently. Pass a cemetery and chapel (*sign says 'Humilladero', indicating a devotional place, normally marked by either a cross or some other type of image*) and enter the village of

5.5km Calzada de Béjar 796m (455/536)

Bar, fountain, Church of Nuestra Señora de la Asunción.

Enter the village by **Calle Baños** and KSO along the main street and then along **Calle Salas Pombo** to the end of the village (*fountain and* lavadero *on R*). KSO ahead on a minor road then 500m later, at RH bend, KSO ahead down a grassy walled lane, straight as a die.

Arcaded village street with balconies

1km later cross a minor road and KSO ahead. *Grass gives way to sandy/stony lane, in a wide plateau with walled cornfields to either side and mountains in the distance. Gradually the landscape becomes more rocky. (The steel-grey cows you see in this area are not a cross between black and white ones but a breed of their own.) 3–4km further on are two partial* miliarios *on L, with markings.*

Cross a dried-up river bed and shortly afterwards reach a minor tarred road. Turn L along it for 150m then turn L up a sandy track. KSO for 2km, KSO at a crossing over a (dry) river bed, pass a wayside cross (R), take RH option at a fork and enter

7.5km Valverde de Valdelacasa (463.5/527.5)

Fountain, bar at end of village in Hogar del Pensionista (unmarked, in former school). Church of Santiago. Former pilgrim hospital in house with 1704 over the door and Santiago sword in coat of arms.

Enter the village via **Calle Salas Pombos** (*RH fork after wayside cross*), pass another wayside cross (R) and the church of **Apóstol Santiago** (R) and KSO ahead to L of the church (**Calle Iglesia**), turn R at end (**Calle Altozano**) and then immediately L (unnamed street) and L again at the end then turn SECOND R behind an old school into **Calle las Eras** and continue ahead into **Carretera de Valdelacasa**, climbing gradually all the time. Stay on the road to

3.5km Valdelacasa 964m (467/524)

Two bars, shop behind church. Originally there was only one house here – hence the village's name.

Cyclists may wish to make a 10km detour here to Guijelo for accommodation (shops, banks, Hotel Torres – tel: 923.58.14.51, Pensión Comercial). If so you can return to the Camino the following day by taking the minor road to Fuenterroble de Salvatierra: from the N630 cross the railway line, turn R and follow its windings for 6km to Fuenterroble.

Turn L at an entry on the road marked '10 Guijelo' and then immediately R into the **Calle Camino Real de la Plata** out of the village. Continue on the road for some 2km and then, at a junction with two *caminos de tierra* to L, turn (not fork) L onto a sandy *camino de tierra* veering R. *Large information board about the Vía de la Plata here and very large boulders on RH side of road; this is the* termino *(boundary) of Fuenterroble de Salvatierra –* milias *(Roman miles) 147–151, measured from Mérida.*

 KSO, ignoring turns and climbing gradually all the time. *(Look out for more* miliarios.) When the track levels out KSO at a crossing (with gates to either side of the track). KSO, climbing gradually again, and when you level out reach a crossing of similar tracks. Turn R and then L onto a minor road (*Fuenterroble is now visible 1km ahead, over to R*). Continue downhill and enter the village via the **Calle Larga**.

8km Fuenterroble de Salvatierra 955m (475/516)

Shop in Bar Ultramarinos, second bar (both do hot meals if requested in advance). Refugio in Casa Parroquial, run by Don Blas, the very helpful parish priest; the ashes of the late José Luis Salvador Salvador, former president of the Seville 'Amigos', are buried in the front wall of the building.

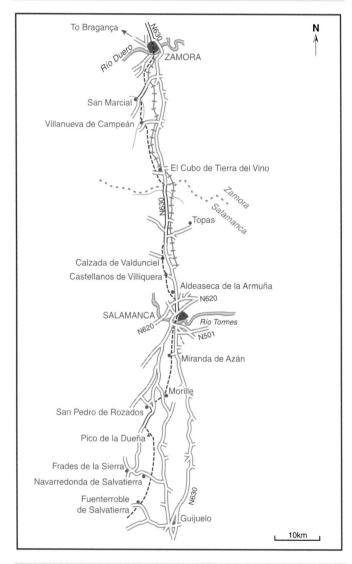

Fortress church of Santa María la Blanca has been impressively restored and is now in use again as the parish church, after being closed for decades, and is worth a visit. Inside there is an enormous modern statue (in wood) of Christ risen from the dead which was taken on a pilgrimage around nearby villages before being placed in situ. (Useful information board near church and parque temático showing the construction of Roman roads and explaining Roman burial customs, miliarios, and the Vía de la Plata.) Ermita del Santo Cristo.

Pass the *ermita* (on L) and continue to a junction with Casa Parroquial on the opposite RH corner (*very large freestanding wooden cross outside*) and turn L (signposted 'Liñares'), L, R and L again. KSO for 1.5km (*this is the road to Casafranca*) then turn R onto a *camino de tierra* at a crossing with another one on LH side of the road. KSO along a wide walled lane, ignoring turnings, for 5–6km. *The Camino goes through gates and* cledos *from time to time but it is well waymarked.*

Reach an area with scrubby trees and then a track crossing diagonally. Go through a gate, fork L and 100m later turn R alongside a fence then turn L 20m later alongside a fence on L. 1km later, at a break in the fencing when a wide track joins from back L, KSO and 100m later go through a gate and KSO ahead (*track turns L here but do not take this*).

*There are a lot of roaming cattle in this area (*ganadero suelto*). You will also notice, if you have not already, that the route appears to be waymarked (in white) in reverse in this area and elsewhere; as explained in the Introduction, this is not, in fact, done for pilgrims' return journeys (though cyclists in particular make use of them) but was prepared in the mid-nineties when the old drover's route from Asturias to Cáceres was reopened (and used) for the transfer of large numbers of animals from one area to another in search of new pastureland.*

After a while you join a gravelled track and then cross a minor gravelled road leading (L) to **Navarredonda de Salvatierra**. Cyclists: turn L here, continue to **Frades de la Sierra** and then turn R onto another minor road which will take you all the way to a turn-off 2km before **San Pedro de Rozados**. Alternatively, you can continue to the cattle grid* and deviate from the walker's route from there.

Walkers: KSO ahead then 300m later KSO(R) at a fork (or short-cut the bend by walking on the grass to L) and 300m later on, when the road bends R, KSO(L) ahead on a grassy track which veers L and then picks up another track coming from back R, which leads you to a wall and a cattle grid.*

Turn L here uphill alongside a wall. Keep as close to it as is practicable, deviating to L to go through a gate in the fencing. Continue uphill for 3km till you reach the

5km Pico de la Dueña 1140m (490.5/500.5)

Highest point on the route with spectacular views on a clear day. The 'pico' itself is now surmounted by a modern cross of the Order of Santiago and forms a sort of 'Cruz de Ferro' for the Vía de la Plata, though it is at present cordoned off behind a wire fence.

Continue ahead, gradually downhill, keeping the wall to your R, passing a large wooden wayside cross (some 3m high). Reach a local road 700m later and turn R along it (*very little traffic and a lot of the time you can walk on its very wide verges*). KSO on the road for 6km to

6.5km Calzadilla de Mendigos 950m (497/494)

A large pig farm on the road (it has its name on it). For pilgrims going all the way to Santiago from Seville this is roughly the halfway point on their journey.

Continue on the road for 6km to a junction. If you want to go into San Pedro de Rozados (2km, to eat or sleep) turn L here. Otherwise, KSO on the road and take the next turning on R (opposite non-tarred road on L) to Morille.

8km San Pedro de Rozados 505/486 (980m)

Two bars, panadería, shop but no fountain. Pensión Casa Milario (tel: 923.34.40.75) – ask in Bar Morena, which also does hot meals on request and has a pilgrim stamp and book.

Enter the village via **Calle Eras Viejas** then turn third R (**Calle Oriente**). Turn R at the end (or turn L to visit the church) and KSO, the street becoming a sandy *camino de tierra*. Cross the road to Salamanca and KSO ahead down another sandy *camino de tierra* then turn L 150m later on a similar track // to the road.

KSO for 3km, veering R at the end to a T-junction. Turn R, veering L immediately and then turn L to **Calle San Pedro**. KSO to the end (some 'kinks' in it) and turn R to a *plaza* in front of the *ayuntamiento* (the building with a clock) and Consultorio Médico in

4.5km Morille (509.5/481.5)

Fountain, bar (opens late).

Continue up the street to LH side of the *ayuntamiento* (**Calle Mayor**) and KSO to the end, uphill (L after bridge) out into open countryside, passing a cemetery and a large pond (on R). KSO. Go through a *cledo*, two sets of gates and at the next gate, by a farm, cross a minor untarred road and KSO ahead through the middle of three sets of gates, ahead downhill, through a narrow field with walls on both sides. At the end continue ahead on a lane walled to one side then go through a *cledo* and turn L, alongside a line of fencing on your R, uphill.

Continue alongside the wall on L for a while then continue straight ahead. Go through a *cledo* into a lane with fencing to either side. Go uphill and at the top you get your first view of Salamanca. Continue downhill on the other side, veering L to pass to R of a farm ahead.

KSO, ignoring turnings. Pass **Miranda de Azán** (*on your R; turn R for bar, 300m on* camino de tierra *in each direction, simple food available*). KSO. At a crossing after turning to Miranda de Azán KSO ahead over a bridge and continue for 3km towards the cliffs of the Alto de Zuerguén (*good views of Salamanca in the distance*). Go uphill to rocks (*cyclists: dismount briefly – nice place for a rest if not too hot*) and continue ahead towards cathedral towers in front of you.

When you reach a T-junction by a ruined building (2km later) turn R then L onto a track coming from R and KSO. (*The N630 is getting closer all the time, over to your R.*) 150m before you reach the N630 fork L ahead alongside electricity cables towards blocks of flats and cross the **Avenida Virgen del Cueto** and continue ahead down **Calle Villar del Profeta** (*pedestrianised*) // to the N630, to the end. Fork R over a railway line and KSO on **Calle Camino de Miranda**. At the end turn R and then L (in front of the *parador*) to a roundabout with a fountain at the bottom of the hill. Bear L here alongside **Río Tormes** and cross it by the Roman bridge. Turn R on the other side, past the church of Santiago, and then L, up **Calle Tentenecio** to the cathedral. Continue along the **Rúa Maior** (*sic*) to **Plaza Mayor**.

20.5km Salamanca 808m, pop. 167,000 (530/461)

All facilities, RENFE, buses to Madrid, Zamora, León and other parts of Spain. Accommodation in all price brackets, including Hostal Peña de Francia (Calle de San Pablo 96, tel: 923.21.66.87), Fonda Barez (Calle Melendez) and Pensión Estefania (Calle, Jesús 3–5). Campsite 2.5km out of town towards Zamora. No pilgrim-only accommodation. Bike repairs: Bicicletas Palacios, Avenida de los Reyes de España 6, Bicicletas Gilfer, Calle Bólivar 43 and La Cadena, Calle Vitigudin 17. Stamp for pilgrim passport: the various parishes have their 'despachos' but a sello can be obtained from the office of the church of San Marcos, 12.30 to 1.30pm, Calle San Marcos (small street at back of church); the cathedral sello is available from Iglesia de San Sebastián, across Plaza de Anaya.

Another place to spend a whole day. Tourist office: Gran Vía 11 and a second office in arch in Plaza Mayor (ask for leaflet with walking tour of city). Two cathedrals (Old and New), university (founded by Alfonso IX in 1218), Plaza Mayor, Patio de las Escuelas, Casa de las Conchas, and many churches and convents, including church of San Tomás de Canterbury. Capilla de Santiago (twelfth-century Romanesque-Mudéjar style) outside historic quarter, by river. Museum in Old Cathedral (fee) has statue of St James.

To leave Salamanca: from the **Plaza Mayor** leave by the big arch and go up the **Calle Zamora**. Pass the **Iglesia San Marcos** (L) and KSO. When you see the **Plaza de Toros** ahead of you veer L onto the main road (N630) to Zamora. *The arrows start again on the R, just before the city boundary*. KSO and pass the **El Helmántico** football stadium on the R (*bar/rte on opposite side of road has rooms*). At the road junction just after the stadium cross carefully, watching out for arrows and KSO on the N630. *NB: In the section between Salamanca and Zamora there is VERY LITTLE SHADE.*

Just before road KM335 fork L onto a *camino de tierra //* to the road and KSO into the village of

Astronaut sculpture in north portal, Salamanca New Cathedral

6km Aldeaseca de la Armuña 820m (536/455)

Bars, shop, farmácia, bank (+CD), fountain in public garden.

Enter the village via **Calzada de Zamora**, continue to **Plaza Mayor**, continue ahead and then turn SECOND L (**Calle Iglesia**) to the church, passing behind it. KSO and take the SECOND *camino de tierra* on R, the **Camino Mozodiel**. 1km later, at a junction of similar tracks, turn R, passing a large walled enclosure and KSO. 1km later reach the crossroads of similar *caminos de tierra*, KSO but then 200m later turn R, veering L (*trees over to R*) and KSO to

5km Castellanos de Villiquera 830m (541/450)

Two bars, shop, farmácia.

Enter past the cemetery along **Calle de los Santos** (*small* cruceiro *at start*). Turn R at the end and then L to the church, pass in front of its entrance and then turn R down **Calle Calzada** between the Casa Consistorial and the church. Continue right to the end, cross a minor road and continue ahead on a *camino de tierra* into open countryside. KSO for 3km, cross a local road and enter

4.5km Calzada de Valdunciel 807m (545.5/445.5)

Bar, shop, bank (no CD), fountain in square. Hostal/Rte El Pozo 500m to east on N630 (tel: 923.31.00.16). Church of Santa Elena contains altar to Santiago Peregrino.

From here cyclists will find it easier to turn R to the N630 and continue on it until El Cubo de Tierra del Vino.

KSO to a square with a *frontón* (*turn R here for church, bars, shops*), pass in front of Casa Consistorial (*sello*) and KSO ahead, over the river and out into open countryside again. KSO. 800m later fork R at a junction and KSO, getting closer to the N630 over to your R. When a track comes to an end in a field turn R alongside a fence to the road (N630) at KM323. Turn L along a rough track, first below and then above the road, for 2km, returning to the N630 at a turning to **Topas** (*big grain silo over to R*).

Continue ahead on the road (*though it is possible to continue below it, to L*), cross **Río Ribera de Cadoña** (probably dry). Continue on the road to KM318 (*bascula pública* – public weighbridge) and then cross over to RH side to walk on a track alongside a railway line on your R.

KSO for 2.5km, till just before you reach the high-security **Topas prison** (*its watchtower is visible well ahead*). Go down to the road at the end of the section with a crash barrier, cross over to LH side then turn L up a track which goes // to the road but inside a field. This then veers R, passing between fields in the direction of some houses ahead.

Pass these, KSO(R) at a fork and go through the gates into some woods (*not well waymarked at time of writing*). Go through a second set of gates and KSO. Go through a *cledo*, cross a lane leading to the N630 (to your R) then a second one and continue on the lane between fencing. Cross an area of open ground and at the end, at a T-junction, turn R to return (over a cattle grid) to the N630, just past road KM311. Turn L and KSO for 2km. Turn L into

19.5km El Cubo de Tierra del Vino 846m (565)

Three bars, shop, farmácia. The village takes its name from the fact that this area, south of the Río Duero, is rich in vines, whereas the region to its north, the Tierra del Pan, is mainly cornfields. You are now in the province of Zamora.

Enter the village via **Calle Mayor** to a square with the *ayuntamiento*. Continue L ahead, passing a church *(on L, picnic area on R)*, cross a bridge and turn L onto a wide *camino de tierra* that continues // to the railway line.

When the railway line bends sharp L KSO on a sandy *camino de tierra* // to the railway all the time. KSO for 5km till you reach a T-junction with a bigger *camino de tierra* and where the railway bends sharp R. Turn L and then 100m later turn R. KSO for 2km to a T-junction on a ridge, with woods to L and R in front ahead and KSO(R). *Good plunging views of plain ahead on a clear day.*

Continue on the ridge, passing a fenced-in enclosure on L, ignore LH turn and KSO ahead, veering L downhill. KSO, ignoring turns. At a fork by trees KSO(R) and then KSO(L) at the next and continue between fields, ignoring turns to L and R, undulating then descending into

13.5km Villanueva de Campeán 765m (578.5/412.5)

Fountain in main square, shop. Bar Jambarina (Calle del Señor 12) does meals and is very 'pilgrim-friendly'. Very small refugio with bunks and hot shower. Note first of a series of decorative terracotta plaques in main street, indicating position of the village on the Vía de la Plata. As explained previously, these have been placed in the prominent places of any size along the route in the province of Zamora by the Fundación Ramos de Castro. They are all in the same general style but each one provides information and references specific to its situation and local history.

Enter the village by the cemetery (R). *(Ruined building over to R is the former Monasterio de Nuestra Señora del Soto)*. Continue along **Calle Calzada** *(for church and bar/shop turn second R into Calle El Señor)*. Continue along it to the end of the village, cross a minor road and continue out into open countryside, straight ahead on a *camino de tierra*. *(Flat everywhere around, on all sides.)* Shortly afterwards fork R and KSO.

There are two waymarked routes after Villanueva: one that by-passes the village of San Marcial, the other (cyclists will find this easier) that leads directly to it.

a)   Go over several crossings and KSO all the time, reaching the village of **San Marcial** (4km) *(bar at entry, on road, does simple food)*. Turn R onto the road *(ZA313, Carretera de Ledesma)* and KSO for 2.5km

(*Zamora visible ahead at top of hill*) and at a bend after KM7 (and just before the turn-off to **Tardobispo**) KSO(L) ahead on a *camino de tierra* towards Zamora ahead (*group of trees to L*).

b) Watch out for a waymark indicating a RH turn at one of these crossings, leading you to a small river and bringing you up to the top of a hill with a view of Zamora ahead. Turn L here and 20m later when you reach the ZA313 proceed as above (1km to a bend from here).

KSO, ignoring turnings and crossings, for 2.5km, passing farm buildings (on L). 300m after this turn L onto a minor untarred road then 300m later, at a crossing after a water pump and stone drinking troughs (on L), turn R along another *camino de tierra*. At the next crossing, 600m later (*fenced-in enclosure ahead*) turn R, veering L and then R towards (gradually) the railway line coming from R. When you get close to it it veers off to R. KSO.

Cross a new road (*under construction at time of writing, leading to industrial complex to L*) and continue ahead on a track leading towards a line of tall trees ahead on R, turning R at a T-junction to pass to L of them and then between farm buildings uphill. Turn R at another T-junction and KSO till you reach the C527 (a by-pass).

Cross over, KSO ahead and enter the former pilgrim district of **San Frontis** (*bar, shop, church of San Frontis*). Turn R along the **Río Duero** to cross it by the **Puente de Piedra**. Turn R into the **Calle del Puente** and then into the Plaza Santa Lucía, turn R behind the church (a few steps) and then second L into Calle Herreros, which will lead you up to the **Plaza Mayor** and the *ayuntamiento*.

19.5km Zamora 658m, pop. 57,734 (598/393)

All facilities, RENFE, buses to León, Ourense, Madrid and other parts of Spain. Plenty of accommodation: 6 hotels, 10 hostales and 14 pensiones, including Rte/Pensión La Alistan (Calle Libertad, near Tres Cruces), Bar Jarame (outside city walls), Bar El Jardín (near church of San Torcuato) and Hostal la Reina (Plaza Mayor) but no pilgrim-only accommodation. Sello: Policía Local or parish churches (such as San Ildefonso). Bike repairs: La Madrileña, Calle San Andrés 19.

NB: There are NO CASH DISPENSERS between here and Puebla de Sanabria if you are taking that route and none before Benavente if you are going to Santiago via Astorga.

Tiled Santiago Matamoros in Capilla de Santiago, Monasterio de Tentudía

Virgen de Macarena in Basilica, Seville

Town situated on north bank of Río Duero, developed and expanded by the Romans on the site of an existing centre of population. Cathedral and 19 Romanesque churches: Santiago del Burgo (Santiagos Matamoros and Peregrino on main altar reredos), San Juan de Puerta Nueva, Santa María la Nueva, San Cipriano, San Ildefonso, La Magdalena, Santa María de la Horta and Santo Tomé, as well as the cathedral, are all open to the public daily except Mondays, from 10am to 1pm and 5 to 8pm; San Claudio de Olivares (contains statue of San Roque as a pilgrim) and Santiago de los Caballeros, both on the western outskirts, are open the same hours but July–September only. San Esteban is now the Museo Baltasar Lobo, exhibiting the sculptures and drawings of the internationally renowned Zamoran artist who died in 1993.

Zamora is also well known for its week-long Semana Santa (Holy Week) processions (accommodation very difficult during this period) and many of the floats used, both modern and historic, are in the Museo de la Semana Santa (others are located in different churches). Castillo, ramparts, Palacio Episcopal, Palacio del Id, Parador de Truism in former palace of Dukes of Conde and Allots, Hospital de la Incarnation (now headquarters of regional government). Tourist office, Calle de Santa Clara 20 (tel: 980.52.69.53) does guided walking tours of the town (in Spanish) every morning in summer except Mondays. Worth spending a whole day here.

Cyclists: can use the walker's route from here as far as Tábara (on the route via Ourense) or Brachial del Brace if going via Benavente.

Leaving Zamora: from **Plaza Mayor** go down **Calle Costanilla** (to R of the *ayuntamiento*), continue, veering L, into **Calle Feria** and cross Ronda de Feria. Continue up **Cuesta de la Morana** (*church of San Lázaro on R; first yellow arrow after this*). KSO(R) at a fork up **Avenida de Galicia** (N122), leading to a roundabout and the N630 at KM275 (*hostal/rte by petrol station*). KSO along the N630 – the Vía de la Plata coincides with it for 5km more, as far as

6.5km Roales de Pan 700m (604.5/386.5)

Farmácia, bar, rte on N630.

Fork L onto a minor road // to the N630 by a factory just before entry to the village, opposite a road sign (pointing R) to 'Valcabado'. KSO

(**Calle General Franco**) to the *ayuntamiento* and church (*seats, another decorative waymark*).

Head of Santiago Peregrino, predella of the altarpiece
of San Ildefonso, Cathedral museum, Zamora

Do NOT turn L here but KSO ahead on the main street to the end of the village. Then KSO ahead along a *camino de tierra*, with a main road over to R but at a distance. Turn R at the next junction and 200m later turn L // to the road again. KSO, *through undulating cornfields (and occasional sunflowers) stretching to infinity. No shade at all (this area is the Tierra del Pan)*.

NB: As there is often nowhere else to paint arrows watch out for them on the concrete slabs that end the drain pipes of the irrigation system at junctions of caminos.

KSO for 3km, in a straight line all the time. Then KSO ahead, very slightly L, at a prominent junction.

KSO for 4km. When Montemarta comes in sight in the distance (*buildings, groups of isolated trees*) the Camino begins to veer L (west), away from the road. At the next junction after this turn R and KSO.

1.5km later (*with road and petrol station over to R*) KSO ahead at a junction. *(However, to eat or sleep in bar/rte Hostal El Asturiano at road KM289 on main road turn RIGHT here.)* Otherwise, KSO.

Turn SECOND L after a farm (on your R) and then veer L at a fork towards a *depósito de aqua* (*water tower on legs*). Continue along the street (**Calle Adrial**) and at a junction with a grassed area you will see another of the plaques put up by the Fundación Ramos de Castro explaining the history of the Vía de la Plata and its associations with the place in question.

KSO then turn second R down **Calle de Reblo** (*passing shop, R*) to a junction with a church in

12.5km Montemarta 690m (617/374)

Bar, shop and farmácia in village, near church, and others on main road. Bar/Rte El Asturiano (tel: 980.55.01.82) at KM289 on main road has rooms (this is the one you passed earlier, near the petrol station).

Turn L here past the *farmácia* and then R along the side of the *frontón* (pelota court) and then L behind it. Cross a causeway through a reservoir if it is dry and go up a FP to **Ermita de la Virgen del Castillo**, on the hill ahead of you. *(Cyclists dismount or continue to road and back-track.)* However, if it has water in it you will have to go round to the church via the road bridge opposite and then fork L uphill. *The ermita is a good place for a shady rest (outside entrance door) with good views and stone seating.*

Continue past the cemetery (on L) and then turn L uphill on the middle of three tracks, joining the RH one at the top of the hill and passing concrete building on L surrounded by barbed wire (marked 'Exco. Ayuntamiento 25.4.1994'). KSO ahead.

KSO for 3.5km, ignoring turns. Two TV masts (*repetidores*) can be seen over to L on the skyline. The path then begins to go uphill into an area of scrubby trees and cistus bushes. When it starts to veer sharply to L, just before a line of telegraph wires, at right angles to you, turn R onto another track (// to wires now), leading gently downhill to a road by a noticeboard explaining the division of the main road into the N630 and N631.

Cross over, go down a local road ahead, veering L and when it veers hard R KSO ahead along a *camino de tierra*, // to the main road and alongside more cables.

700m later return to the N630, cross it (*carefully) and continue ahead on a similar track. *(Cyclists, however, may find it easier to continue on the road from here to Fontanillos de Castro.)* KSO at a crossing and fork R past a small concrete hut, slightly uphill. When you get to the top you will see the **Embalse de Ricobayo** ahead of you below, with bright blue water if full, and on a hill at the end of it the ruins of Castrotarafe.

The arrows, in fact, lead you into the water, in order to take you (on the other side) to the ruins of Castrotorafe, but unless the water is low enough to walk/wade across you will have to take the upper of two tracks which leads you past some houses and then to the main road, where you can cross the dam by the bridge. *(Remnant of building sticking up by water's edge is an old mill.)*

Continue for 100m on the other side of the bridge and then, just after road KM253, turn L down a track, passing to R of two buildings. This takes you round the side of the *embalse*, // to it but slightly above, and leads you, round a small hill, to the ruins of **Castrotarafe**. *The route is well-enough waymarked but the paths are not always very distinct and cyclists will find it easier to continue on the road for 1.3km more and then turn L down a wide track, signposted in purple (as for historic monuments). Ruins are not very far (200–300m) from there and are clearly visible.*

10.5km Castrotarafe (627.5/363.5)

Remains of a town, possibly dating from Roman times, and inhabited until the eighteenth century, controlling the traffic crossing the Esla. Its castillo was the seat of the Knights of the Order of Santiago.

From the ruins (with them on your L) you can either continue by path to the village of **Fontanillos de Castro** or (*if you are hungry, for example*) go back to the road and turn L, where there is a bar/rte on L, next to a petrol station, 700m before the entrance to

2km Fontanillas de Castro 725m (629.5/361.5)

Bar/rte by petrol station, fountain.

Turn L into village (*first street on L is Travesia del Cemeterio*) then R at the water tower down **Calle Cementario** past the church (*with another decorative plaque, explaining local history and the historical importance of the* castro). Turn L (staggered) downhill and L at the bottom opposite house no. 12 (*fountain opposite no. 14*). KSO to the end of the village (this is **Calle la Barca**) and then turn R down a *camino de tierra* at a junction. *(Riego del Camino is visible ahead.)*

KSO, KSO at the next junction (1km later) and fork R after a large group of trees. Fork R again at a large isolated tree and by the first building cross a *camino de tierra* coming from R diagonally. Continue ahead on a small but clear FP between fields, alongside the wall of a building along **Calle Ferrabal** to the main road in

6km Riego del Camino 705m (635.5/355.5)

Bar on main road (with simple food).

Turn L and then fork second R between buildings and KSO on a *camino de tierra* again. Turn R up the *camino de tierra* after the last house towards a white silo and KSO at a fork, // to the road (N630) over to your R.

KSO (quite literally) for 6km. At the end turn R at a T-junction to the village. Veer L over a bridge and turn R on a concrete lane leading to a main road. Turn L and continue to the church in

6.5km Granja de Moreruela 708m (643/348)

Four bars on main road (Bar Cle-bis, last one on L of road facing north, does sandwiches and has pilgrim book, sello and key for very basic accommodation in the Casa de la Cultura), shop.

This is where the two Caminos divide, one continuing ahead (north) to Astorga, the other turning left (west) to go directly to Santiago via Puebla de Sanabria and Ourense. For the second option see 'Route via Puebla de Sanabria and Ourense' p.115. To continue via Benavente and La Bañeza to Astorga proceed as described here.

From here a detour to the west is suggested to visit the ruins of the Convento de Moreruela, the first Cistercian convent in Spain, founded in 1158, with a pilgrim hospital added in the sixteenth century. To do so turn L off N630 (signposted) just before entry to village, which takes you directly there, 3.7km each way. The convent is on private land and is being restored at the time of writing but it is usually accessible and worth the detour.

Cyclists: to avoid the fairly long section on the N630 you can follow the walker's route for the next 2.5km as far as the ZA123 (to Tábara), turn L along it and then, shortly after crossing the bridge over the Esla, turn R along a local road through Bretocino, Olmillos de Valverde, Burganes de Valverde, cross the Tera in Mozar de Valverde and turn R to Santa Cristina de Polvorosa and enter Benavente from the west. This route is slightly longer but very much quieter that the N630.

Turn L by the church (*decorative plaque explains the separation of ways*) into **Calle Dr González Galindo** and then first R up **Calle San Juan** (*waymarked 'Astorga'*). Fork second L uphill to the village square and make for the prominent grain tower and TV mast, where you take a *camino de tierra* // to the main road. KSO on this, ignoring turns, for 2.5km, till you reach a local road, the ZA123 to Tábara. Turn R and then just before the road junction with the N630 turn L onto a *camino de tierra* which veers round to R, // to the road.

Continue on this track, // to the road (some 15m away). (*Bar/Rte Hostal Oviedo, tel: 980.58.60.80, meals and rooms, on R just after junction at road KM237/238.*) KSO, returning to the road at KM236. Continue for a while on the hard shoulder then on a track beside the road for 6km. 2km before Santovenia there is a proper track and you get your first view of Benavente over in the distance to the northwest.

You will continue to see it away to your left until you reach it, though you often appear to be going east, away from it – this is because there is no bridge over the Río Esla until you reach the outskirts of the town itself.

9km Santovenia 715m (652)

Bar/Rte Esla (tel: 980.64.70.14) has rooms, another bar, two shops. Fountain at end of village on R. The 'Santovenia' of the village's name refers to Santa Eugenia la Mozárabe (see plaque on church about her).

Continue on the main road past the church *(seats – nice place for a rest)*. Stay on the road for 1km to a cemetery at the top of the hill then continue on a *cañada* to RH side of the N630. *This section is not very interesting as you walk between the irrigation channel and the road as far as*

5.5km Villaveza del Agua 700m (657.5)

Two bars, one in centre, one at end on L (with rte).

Continue through the village on the road and fork L just before **Bar/Rte La Huerta** and pass behind it, KSO ahead (staggered) at a junction towards **Barcial del Barco** *(church with its octagonal tower visible on hill ahead)* and when you reach the road again at a crash barrier at the bottom of the hill KSO(L) ahead underneath the church, turning R uphill just after you have passed it. Veer R and at the top turn L along the main road into

2.5km Barcial del Barco 717m (660)

Three bars.

Continue to the end of the village and when you are on the level of a large grain silo fork R (**Calle Toro**) in front of a café-bar and continue to a level crossing.

Walkers: fork L here, along the disused Zamora–Astorga railway line (tracks still there so you can walk on the sleepers); it is 8km to Benavente from here by this route. Cyclists: should continue ahead on the old road via Castropepe to cross the bridge over the Esla at the entrance to Benavente (12km).

Walkers: KSO along the railway track and after 1km cross a metal bridge over a tributary (probably dry) of the Río Esla. Here you can either KSO on the railway line *(very tedious, especially if your stride and the spacing of the sleepers do not coincide, and it also gets increasingly overgrown as you proceed)* or go down an embankment on LH side immediately after crossing a bridge and take the *camino de tierra* that follows the railway line to its L all the time. 2km later you will see a black water tower to RH side of the railway line (on its level) and a dilapidated white building on LH side on field level: go up a bank to a metal 'box' bridge and use it to cross the **Río Esla**.

Immediately after crossing the bridge turn R down a FP and KSO(R) along a track through a poplar plantation and on a shady path beside the river. Take the second R turn along a *camino de tierra* with concrete irrigation channel alongside it and then turn L 500m later, cross a road and enter the village of

6km Villanueva del Azoague (666)

Bar in Plaza Mayor.

KSO, following the street (**Calle Huerta**) as it veers L, turn R into **Calle Mayor** which becomes **Calle de Benavente** – a very long street with a large *azucareria* (sugar factory) on the LH side (*the Museo del Azúcar is located inside*). At the end (2km) cross the main road (N525) – *carefully* – and KSO ahead on the other side past a large bathroom fittings showroom (L) to another junction (with the Vía del Canal) and then to a third (*not waymarked at the start*) with the **Avenida General Primo de Rivera**; turn R along it into

3km Benavente 747m, pop. 12,500 (669)

All facilities. Accommodation in all price brackets (three hotels, eight hostales, five pensiones), including Hostal Raúl (Calle Ancha 15, tel: 980.63.10.42), Fonda California (Primo de Rivera 32, tel: 980.63.38.34), Hostal Ría de Vigo (Primo de Rivera 27, tel: 980.63.17.79) and Hostal Paraíso (Calle Obispo Regueras 64, tel: 980.63.33.81). Sello: ayuntamiento, between 8am and 3pm. Tourist office in Calle Fortaleza 17.

Old town has churches of Santa María del Azoque and San Juan del Mercado (both open for visits 10am to 1pm and 5 to 8pm), Hospital de la Piedad (former pilgrim hospice with cloister and pilgrim door knocker in early sixteenth-century entrance) and Ermita de la Soledad. Castillo de la Mora (only tower remains of original building) is now the parador. Modern octagonal church of Santiago in northern suburbs.

Pilgrim knocker on hospital door, Benavente

Turn L (off **Avenida Primo de Rivera**) up **Calle Aquero** (middle of three streets) at a prominent junction. Turn R up **Calle Ancha**, passing (R) the church of **Nuestra Señora del Carmen**. Then: walkers: fork L up **Calle Zamora**, veer L and then R to **Plaza Nuñez Granes** and ahead along **Calle Conde Patilla** to the **Plaza de España** and the *ayuntamiento*. Cyclists: fork R into **Calle Cervantes** to the end, turn L up **Calle General Mole** and immediately R (**Calle General Aranda**) to **Plaza de España**.

From there (**Plaza de España**) go back through **Calle Conde Patilla**, turn R into **Calle José Antonio** to the **Iglesia de Santa María**. From the **Plaza de Onesimo Redondo** (on its northwest side) go down **Calle Aguadores**.

a) Walkers: *this is the old (formerly well-waymarked) route and is very quiet, fairly shady (in the mornings) and is easy to follow*. Continue (*not well-waymarked*) and turn fourth R down some steps into **Calle Estación**. Turn R at the bottom towards an old railway station (*marshalling yard behind has been made into a park, with seats*) and continue past it. When the tarmac road bends R KSO ahead on a *camino de tierra*. 1km after the station KSO ahead at a junction by a farm and 1km later, when the *camino de tierra* bends L by a small house, continue ahead alongside a disused railway line on a small but clear and obviously well-used FP. This does a detour away from the track from time to time but then returns. *River below to L is the Órbigo.*

Just after the railway marker 289/6 the FP widens out and goes downhill towards the road which comes from under the railway line (from the R). Continue on a *camino de tierra* coming from your L from a bridge over **Río Órbigo** and continue on it to LH side of the road. When it comes to an end (*where a line of telegraph poles crosses the road*) cross over and continue on the *camino de tierra* on RH side (*first yellow arrow here*).

b) Cyclists: *the walker's route described above is NOT suitable for bikes so* turn first R out of the **Calle Aguadores** into **Calle Sancti Spiritu** which becomes the **Calle del Perú** and then runs into the **Carretera de Acubilla**. KSO along it and you will go under the railway bridge referred to in a) above, veering R.

Both: when this road begins to veer L (1km from the railway) by a lay-by, fork R uphill, veering L to a level crossing. This is the **Teso del Peñón**, *the area where, it is thought (and based on evidence from aerial photographs), that the Roman* mansio *Brigeco was located.* Fork L uphill on the other side and KSO(L) ahead when another track joins from your R. KSO at a junction, go over another level crossing, go under the motorway, KSO ahead and then turn R opposite the cemetery into

8.5km Villabrázaro 710m (677.5)

Large bar at entrance to village (has pilgrim book and does simple food), unmarked shop in main street (RH side), fountain in centre of village. Simple refugio for those with pilgrim credencial. Sello in the ayuntamiento. Plaque informs you that the village was a mansio on the Vía de la Plata in Roman times.

Go through the village on the main street and out again on the other side on a very minor tarred road. KSO for 4.5km. At a junction KSO ahead, ignoring turns, to

8.5km Maire de Castroponce 748m (686)

KSO through the village and KSO at the end on a minor road ahead, leading to a bridge over the **Río Órbigo**.

3km Puente de la Vizana (689)

Original bridge of Roman origin but with later additions and alterations. Boundary of provinces of Zamora and León. Picnic area with trees, campsite. Hostal Puente La Vizana has rooms and bar/rte (tel: 987.69.20.63). From here to La Bañeza the landscape becomes much greener, though there is not necessarily more shade to walk in.

The path from here formerly took you through the fields but it is nearly always waterlogged so now you KSO on the road until you reach

3km Alija del Infantado 740m (692)

Bars, shop, farmácia, bank (+CD), small basic refugio above Hogar del Pensionista – ask in tourist office (which also has sello).

Iglesia San Estéban (thirteenth–fourteenth centuries), Iglesia de San Verísimo (twelfth–sixteenth centuries), Castillo-Palacio (first–sixth centuries), Fuente de Mendaña. Fuente de San Ignacio of Roman origin, with water with medicinal properties (digestion, obesity, kidney problems), Rincón de la Judería (former Jewish quarter) with a lot of bodegas (on top of hill near fountain). Small ermita on LH side of road at entrance to village by children's playground was formerly in private hands but is now owned by a fundación that is constructing leisure and sports facilities there for the village. Ermita del Cristo at end of village on R and on hill at end, above it, Cruz de Peregrino (with Santiago sword).

KSO to the end of the village (*worth climbing up, L, to Fuente de San Ignacio to drink cool water, fill bottle and have a good view*). When the road veers R the old waymarking took you straight ahead on a track to LH side of the road, roughly // to it and rather overgrown. You will find it easier, however, to continue on the road for 2km (not much traffic) to the turn-off, to the L, to

3km La Nora del Río (695)

Small village wedged in between the rivers Jamuz and Órbigo. Unmarked bar in centre.

Here you have a choice, whether you are on foot or on a mountain bike:

a) KSO ahead on road and stay on it, passing through the villages of **Genestacio** *(4km, bar)*, **Quintana del Marco** (2km), **Villanueva de Jamuz** *(3km, bar in Hogar del Pensionista)*, and **Santa Elena de Jamuz** (4km). *This route is sparsely waymarked, is very easy to follow and there is not a lot of traffic.*

KSO on the road, climbing up after leaving Santa Elena. When you reach a large grain silo (now a scrap yard) on your L turn R over a railway bridge, veering L, and continue down **Calle Santa Elena** (not marked at the start), a long street. At a junction turn L (opposite house no. 35) and then turn R immediately into **Calle San Julián**. *(Turn second R off here into Calle San Roque for the* refugio, *on the corner with Calle Bello Horizonte.)*

Turn first L from **Calle San Julián** into **Calle San Blas** and immediately R *into Calle Santa Lucía*, veering L downhill. KSO at a junction along **Calle Lope de Vega** to a junction with **Calle Ramón y Cajal** in **La Bañeza** (4km).

b) Turn R over a bridge, follow the road round, veering L, skirting but not entering **La Nora del Río**. *This is the route that follows the course of the original calzada romana. It was waymarked in the early 1990s but due to the reorganisation of land boundaries most of them have now disappeared. It is not hard to follow if you are attentive to the instructions given below and is an easy ride for mountain bikes.*

After crossing a bridge veer L and then turn L after RH bend, up the *camino de tierra* that follows the LH bank of the Río Órbigo to start with. KSO(L) at RH fork (leading into woods) and KSO, ignoring turns, into

2.5km Navianos de la Vega (697.5)

Two bars (not open early).

Continue on the road you entered on and KSO through the village, passing a public garden (L) and continue along **Calle de Arriba**. Fork R at the end and continue on a *camino de tierra* out into open countryside between fields.

KSO(R) at the first fork (600m) and 400m later, by a group of trees (small brick hut over to L) where the track joins from back L, pass a turning to R. Continue ahead (*village over to L in distance is Genestacio, with water tower and fort*). 200m later KSO(L) at a fork.

At a T-junction by much larger group of trees and concrete irrigation tanks turn L and then R 100m later onto a long, straight track between fields. KSO (literally). After 500m pass the first crossroad (*village to L is Quintana del Marco*) and the second one 800m later. 750m after that turn L at another T-junction, between concrete irrigation channels, and then R alongside another one. KSO (*you can see houses in San Juan de Torres ahead here*). Pass a large group of trees 100m away to R.

KSO and 1.4km later KSO at another crossroads. KSO ahead (*irrigation channel still on L. Village over to L is Villanueva de Jamuz*). 750m later cross a crossroads and KSO and then 700m afterwards reach a T-junction at a road linking San Juan de Torres and Villanueva de Jamuz (6.5km from Navianos).

Turn L towards a white building (*electricity transformer*) and 200m later turn R to cross a bridge over an irrigation channel (*first arrow here!*). Turn L and then turn R after the white building and 300m later turn L. 200m later turn R, passing large metal barn on R, to circumnavigate a hilly area on R.

At a junction with a *camino de tierra* coming from L veer R and 300m later KSO(L). 1.5km later cross a road leading (to L) to **Santa Elena de Jamuz**. KSO and 1.5km after that cross a disused railway line and 500m later go through a tunnel under a motorway. Continue straight ahead all the time and 1.3km later you will reach the N630. Turn L along it for 150m then fork L down **Calle Libertadores** (a long street). Cross the **Plaza de los Reyes Católicos**, continue (R) ahead down **Calle Juan de Mansilla** to the **Plaza Mayor** in

21.5km La Bañeza 777m, pop. 8501 (719)

All facilities. Buses to Madrid, Santiago, León, Seville and other parts of Spain.

Hostal/Rte Astur (Calle Astorga 9, tel: 987.64.04.15),

Hostal Madrid (Calle Angel Riesco 3, tel: 987.64.00.21),

Hostal Roma (Calle Astorga 56, tel: 987.64.05.89),

Pensión Astelena (Calle Lepanto 4, tel: 987.64.11.13),

Fonda Industrial (Calle Ramón y Cajal 12, tel: 987.64.10.42),

Fonda El Nistal (Calle El Salvador 15, tel: 987.64.00.69),

Pensión Bar Johnny (Calle la Fuente 18, tel: 987.64.07.26);
otherwise accommodation is on the outskirts of the town on the
NVI. Large refugio in converted school (corner of Calles San
Roque and Bello Horizonte).
Tourist office: Calle Padre Miguelez s/n.
Bike repairs: Gonzalez de la Torre, Calle Antonio Bordas 16.

Iglesia de Santa María, Iglesia de San Salvador (both are parish
churches), Capilla de Jesús Nazareno, Capilla de las Angustias.
The church of El Salvador, of Romanesque origin, is on the site of
one of the earliest pilgrim hospitals, founded in AD 932 (barely
100 years after the discovery of the tomb of St James in the location
that was to become Santiago de Compostela).

To go into the town centre and the **Plaza Mayor** turn R down **Calle
Ramón y Cajal** (and then retrace your steps to continue).

Otherwise, cross **Calle Ramón y Cajal** and continue along **Calle El
Salvador**. Continue to the end of the street (*public garden opposite*)
then turn R (**Calle Primo de Rivera**) and then immediately L into **Calle
José Marcos de Segovia**. KSO, veering L over a level crossing, and
continue ahead on **Carretera Villalis**.

At a small junction by the town exit boards (*and entrance signs for
Santiago de la Valduerna some 20m later*) fork R onto a *camino de
tierra*. KSO, ignoring turns, continue alongside railway line then fork R
up a FP to cross **Río Duerna** by a metal 'box' bridge. Continue on the
FP to L of tracks on the other side. Cross a track coming from R (under
railway lines) and KSO ahead // to them. Turn L then fork R towards
the motorway.

Turn L and then R under a bridge (underneath the motorway),
veering R on the other side. Continue ahead, turn fourth L (just before
the track you are on veers R) and then turn next R.

Continue ahead through fields (*Montes de León begin to be visible
in the distance*) for 1km to

6km Palacios de la Valduerna (725)

Bar (unmarked) on main street on L near public garden, shop, farmácia. Tower over to L is remains of fourteenth-century fortress.

Turn R after crossing the canal, L up a lane, L again then R towards the church. Turn L (**Calle Santa María**) then KSO(L) along the main street (**Calle Carretera Tabuyo**). The *ermita* is on LH side towards the end. At a fork with a sitting area and fountain turn R down a more minor road (**Calle Camino del Monte**). Fork R in front of the cemetery and KSO on a *camino de tierra* across open heathland with occasional plantations of vines.

The mountains are very clear now in the middle distance; the road away over to R all the time. The Santuario de Nuestra Señora de Castrotierra is over to L on a hilltop, the focus of an annual local pilgrimage on March 25th and, every seven years, the start of a journey on foot to Astorga, with the Virgin carried in procession on the shoulders of the participants.

KSO(L) at the first crossing. KSO ahead at the next. *Cistus trees begin*.

When you get to a 'stop' sign with a tarred road crossing diagonally (7km from Palacios de la Valduerna) turn R along it. At the next junction (600m later) KSO straight ahead on a *camino de tierra*. KSO, gradually getting nearer to and then alongside the motorway. Turn R underneath it (via a tunnel), go towards the next tunnel but then turn L along a track (in the direction of the big white Norgasa factory ahead) leading to a motorway slip-road.

Cross it, continue to RH side of the slip-road signed 'La Coruña' then turn R to an old road. Cross it and walk along it for 20m then turn R down a minor road marked 'Estación de Valderrey 0.7'. Turn L along a lane by an old-style electricity transformer tower and KSO. Approximately 1km later, after passing between two lines of poplars, you will come to the

11km Puente Valimbre (736)

Four-arch bridge of Roman origin over Río Turienzo. Restored on several occasions, most recently in 1998. Cyclists stay on N630 from here to Astorga.

Cross the bridge and veer L uphill to the road. Cross over and continue ahead on the track that goes alongside it, not always very near. Just before the top of the hill (large modern house, isolated, in front) return to the road at a 'stop' sign.

First view of Astorga cathedral from here. After this, because of motorway construction at time of writing, you have to continue on the N630 for the last 3km to Astorga.

3km Celada de la Vega (739)

Bar/mesón at junction, Hostal La Paz (tel: 987.61.52.77, rooms) further on on same side.

Continue on the road until you reach the edge of the town. Fork R into the **Plaza San Roque** and then go up the staircase into the **Calle La Bañeza** (cyclists: wait to turn R up the **Bajada del Postigo**). KSO up the **Calle La Bañeza** to the **Plaza de España**. Continue ahead via **Calle Pio Guillón**, Calle Postas and Calle Santiago, pass in front of the **Palacio de Gaudí** and reach the cathedral in

3km Astorga 899m, pop. 14,000 (742)

All facilities, RENFE, buses to Madrid, Santiago, Seville, León, Ponferrada, Villafranca del Bierzo and other parts of Spain. Tourist office near cathedral. Large refugio in centre of town and plenty of other accommodation.

A town dating from Roman times, with extensive remains of its original walls. Astorga was (and still is) the junction of two pilgrim routes, the Camino francés and the Camino mozárabe or Vía de la Plata. This explains the unusually large number of pilgrim hospitals formerly in existence (there were 22 in the Middle Ages), the last of which, the Hospital de las Cinco Llagas (the Five Wounds), burned down early in the twentieth century. Gothic cathedral with interesting choir stalls and museum, Bishop's Palace built by the Catalan architect Antonio Gaudí, with pilgrim museum on ground floor and chapel upstairs. Several other interesting churches, Baroque town hall. It is worth spending half a day here.

From Astorga those who wish to continue to Santiago now 'turn left' along the Camino francés for another 250km and in many ways this part will seem much easier. There is an extensive network of refuges, getting your pilgrim passport stamped is much simpler and you will also meet a lot of other pilgrims, though many people experience something of a shock when they leave the relative solitude of the Vía de la Plata to be plunged into the busy hustle and bustle of this much more frequented route. There are also a lot more fountains and bars on the Camino francés and once you enter Galicia the weather is usually considerably cooler as well.

The continuation from Astorga to Santiago is described in, *inter alia*, the present author's *The Way of St James: Le Puy to Santiago, a Walker's Guide* or, for cyclists, John Higginson's companion *The Way of Saint James: A cyclists guide*, both published by Cicerone Press.

Bishop's Palace, Astorga

ROUTE VIA PUEBLA DE SANABRIA AND OURENSE
(Camino sanabrés)

6.5km Granja de Moreruela 708m (643/348)

Turn L by the church (**Calle Dr González Galindo**) and KSO ahead.
KSO(R) at a fork and continue for 1.4km in open countryside. Take the
SECOND RH turn uphill. KSO for 3km (having passed two LH turns)
and then when you do not expect it, turn R. 1km later turn L at a T-
junction (*you can see the ZA123 ahead of you here*) and continue
along it, veering R downhill to a road. Turn L along it and continue to
cross the bridge over the **Río Esla** at

7km Puente Quintos (650/341)

The original route crossed the Río Esla some 500m downstream,
as you can see from the remains of the old bridge, positioned
where you will turn away from the river after your detour to cross
the present bridge.

a) Cyclists: this section is NOT suitable, even for mountain bikes, and
you should continue along the road here until **Faramontanos de
Tábara**.

b) Walkers: On other side turn L behind the crash barrier and
continue on a small FP through rocks, leading down to the shore.
Walk alongside the river till you are level with the remains of the
old bridge and then fork R steeply uphill by large cliff-like rocks
next to the river.

Go uphill (small FP, well waymarked) // to the river to start with then
veering R up to the top of the cliff ahead of you (*good view of old
bridge if you look back as you climb*). At the top turn R through trees
by a ruined house, after which a proper track starts. KSO along it.

1km later turn L at a T-junction and continue through heathland,
ploughed up in part, with a lot of *encina* trees (*and therefore quite a
lot of shade*) KSO, ignoring turns, for 1.5km then KSO(L) uphill on a
track joining from your R. KSO, ignoring turns, till you reach a junction
by the large white gate posts at the entrance to the

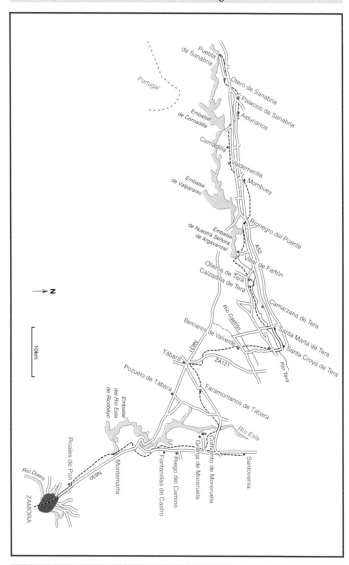

5km Finca Val de la Rosa (655/336)

Turn R and KSO for 800m, cross a tarmac road and KSO, ignoring turns. After 2km (from Finca) you will come to a T-junction: turn L here (*another tarmac road visible to R*) and KSO for 1.5km. Turn R at the next junction and KSO into

7km Faramontanos de Tábara (662/329)

Two bars (one with shop), another shop, panadería, Rte 'Porticos' in Calle del Fuente, no accommodation. Church porch good place for a rest.

Enter the village on **Calle Benavente**, KSO along it, following it round to L, KSO(R) at a fork and then turn R into **Calle Pozo**, passing a church (R) and continue on it towards small modern *ermita*. Pass to R of this down a lane, cross the ZA123 and continue ahead down a *camino de tierra*, passing a farm (L). (*NB: ANOTHER such track leaves the village // to this one, passing a large private house on its R.*)

KSO for 2.5km then turn L, 700m later turn R and KSO along the Camino through trees. Pass in front of an enclosure with farm buildings (*on your R – last arrow till Tábara*) and make sure you KSO along the line of this, straight ahead, following the wall closely: do NOT take the clear, LH fork (despite its old yellow arrows.)

Continue, past the *finca*, in a straight line, following the same line as the wall was on. The track is not very clear at first though it becomes so as you proceed and leads between fields. (*You can see the town ahead now, to L.*) Head for the LH of two large electricity pylons some 300–400m ahead of you (with town behind it). Continue ahead on a grassy tractor track. (*Not well waymarked but also not hard to follow.*)

The track goes under electricity cables and widens out. Go alongside the walled fields (on L). At a corner of the field walls, when you can see the Mozárabic tower of the **Iglesia de la Asunción** ahead, veer L and then R through field. Cross two flat concrete bridges and veer L into a wide lane leading to a T-junction in the lane 100m behind the church.

To continue: turn R.

To enter Tábara: turn L to the church and main road. (*Cross over to enter the centre of town, shops.*)

117

7.5km Tábara (669.5/321.5)

Bars, shops, bank (but no CD). Hostal Galicia (500m out of town on road to Zamora, tel: 980.59.01.36) has rooms and rte. Site of a famous monastery in Visigothic and Mozárabic periods though only a few remains and the tower are left. Two churches – eleventh-century Romanesque Iglesia de la Asunción and parish church.

To leave: retrace your steps past the church to the T-junction where you turned L to enter the town and KSO out into open countryside. When a wall on L comes to an end KSO ahead, pass under electricity cables and KSO through a fence, veering L uphill. KSO(R) when a track joins from back L and KSO(L) at a fork immediately afterwards. Some 300m later fork L towards a minor road (3km from Tábara) and cross it. *The next section is very fiddly, designed to keep you off the road, but cyclists should turn R here and continue on it for the next 2.5km, to the top of the hill.***

KSO on the other side of the road. 500m later turn R up a less prominent track // to the road (watch out carefully for waymarks on ground). KSO(L) at a fork and continue across a field. *(If you look ahead you will see the road and the white bollards of a lay-by on its L – this is where you are heading for.)* At the end, when bushes start again, veer slightly R up a small track. Cross the field ahead and skirt it to L (keeping your bearings). Then pick up the track again on the other side, veering very slightly L when another track comes from R, and then R uphill.

Veer R to walk on RH side of a double line of trees (*the original path passed between them but is now completely overgrown*) towards an old building, half brick, half stone, to the L of the road lay-by. Pass to its RH side and KSO beside it, gradually getting closer to the road.

When a track crosses, coming from L, turn R to the road and continue on an animal track on its LH side, up to the top of the hill (where the road bends R, 600m later).

**Fork L (by a 'stop' sign and vehicle access from road) down a track // to the road to begin with. KSO(R) at a fork and then KSO, gently downhill and through a wide valley. *This is a very nice section, with a fair amount of trees so there is shade to rest (though not to walk) in.* KSO, ignoring turns (two, one L and one R) for 4km.

After going up and then down a small hill turn R at a crossing of tracks. 600m later turn L at a junction and 400m after that, at a small white house, turn R. 700m later, at a crossing of similar tracks, turn L.

KSO to the road (1km). Cross it and then turn R to the village, passing a church. KSO(R) along **Calle Mayor** into the centre of

13.5km Bercianos de Valverde (683/308)

Shop, unmarked bar opposite.

Turn L in the square (with *ayuntamiento*) and continue along a lane with trees to one side. Cross a bridge over the **Río Castrón** and turn L in front of the last group of poplar plantations. *(Good place to rest before going uphill, where there is little shade.)* Turn R 250m later then L and then R again uphill past *bodegas*.

At the top a track veers R above old quarry workings. KSO(L) at a fork. KSO. KSO(R) at a fork and continue for 2km, till you cross the canal and reach the road leading into **Santa Croya**. KSO(R) along it and follow the road into the centre of the village and the *ayuntamiento*.

7km Santa Croya de Tera (690/301)

Bar, two shops, bank (no CD), farmácia, fountain. Nice green and shady public garden is also a good place for a rest.

KSO on the very long main street through the village to the end. Cross the bridge over the **Río Tera** (*swimming area on R*) and enter

1km Santa Marta de Tera (691/300)

Two bars, shop on main road in direction of Camarzana but no accommodation. Sello from priest, who lives in modern house by church. Twelfth-century Romanesque church with famous eleventh-century Santiago statue in south portal. Church open for visits Fridays, Saturdays and Sundays 10am to 1pm, 5 to 8pm or at mass times (8pm, for example); building next to church is former summer palace of Bishops of Astorga.

From the church turn L along a terrace-like road with gardens on L (between the N525 and the road you came up on; *first of blue ceramic waymarks here*). Continue downhill on a *camino de tierra*. 800m from the church fork L onto another *camino de tierra* through fields and new poplar plantations.

300m later turn L at a T-junction, veering R and then L again at the next, 400m later. Veer R, cross a concrete bridge and fork R on the other side. 1km later, at a T-junction with the river a few metres in front of you, turn R. KSO past a white building (*pump house*) and shortly afterwards you have the river to your L again.

When the *camino de tierra* bends sharp R KSO ahead here, along a line of telegraph poles and pick up another track in front of you, alongside the river.

KSO, ignoring turns, until you reach the road coming (from R) from **Camarzana de Tera**. Turn R first, towards some gravel works, then hard L to cross the bridge over the **Río Tera** at

6km La Barca (697/294)

Camping/recreation area with good swimming. Bar (summer only).

Turn hard R at the end of the bridge along a *camino de tierra* in an area marked 'La Barca – adecuación recreativa'. KSO for 1km, ignoring turns. Turn R at a T-junction and 800m later, when the *camino de tierra* veers off L, KSO ahead on a less prominent track through woods. 500m later KSO(R) along a track joining from your L, then KSO(R) along a road coming from back L (ZAP2475).

Continue on the road for 600m and just before a bridge turn R onto a *camino de tierra* running below a small hill. Pass a fountain (L) in a stone shelter by a flight of steps. Continue ahead, cross the canal and KSO, ignoring turns, to the main street in

5km Calzadilla de Tera (702/289)

Bar, shop, panadería, though the Camino does not take you through centre of village. Parish church, ermita and abandoned church of Santa Justa y Rufina.

Cross the street, turn second R towards an abandoned church (*makeshift seating in entrance*). Pass in front of it, go down a bank and then turn L on a track (you have done a 'loop' to pass the church). Cross another bridge over a canal and turn L along a *camino de tierra* beside it, behind the church. KSO alongside the canal for 2km to

2km Olleros de Tera (704/287)

Two bars, shop (unmarked) in Calle Fuente (near church).

Turn L over the canal bridge into the village, veering R, after which you have a choice:

a) *the shortest, most direct route (but NOT for cyclists) is via the Santuario de Agavanzal, but after this the track, though waymarked, is VERY overgrown until you reach the dam.* After a few metres turn R at a pink house and leave the village via the **Calle de la Agavanzal**. Cross an asphalt road (ZAP2547) and continue (the road becomes a track) to **the Santuario de Nuestra Señora de Agavanzal**, set in the fields above the LH bank of the **Río Tera**. *You can see the dam walls in the distance ahead of you by now.*

When the road ends at a T-junction near a white building carrying the letters C.H.D. and at a 'peligro' (*danger*) sign KSO on a small, rising path through the weeds. A little later (at a second 'peligro' sign) turn R on another small and rather overgrown track which slowly takes you down to the river level (ignore a steeper variant to R after about 200m) and follows the river through rich, jungle-like vegetation (might be waterlogged), then rises again to L through rocks and mossy *encinas* towards a road.

When you reach the road by the dam walls be careful as the arrows lead you R down to the river again – and straight into the water! *(They were first painted while the dam was being built and when there was still a small bridge here over the river. This was removed after completion of the dam but the arrows were not re-routed.)* Instead, turn L and L again up to the dam embankment walls (on the road).

b) KSO along the street past the church of **San Miguel**. Fork L at a junction with a covered well into **Calle Eras**. Fork R at the end onto a very minor road. *(Fountain to R outside old school building; the striped pole on the horizon is by the dam.)*

Pass some farm buildings and turn first L, passing a poplar plantation. Cross a small canal diagonally and KSO ahead, ignoring turns. When you reach a large, wide open, flat grassy area do NOT fork L down the more obvious track, despite misleading waymarks, but KSO through the grass ahead, tracking becoming clearer as you proceed, until you reach a road.

Arrows then indicate that you should cross the road, go down the bank and then veer R by a ruined building but this is extremely fiddly and more trouble than it is worth. Instead (*and especially cyclists*) it is suggested you turn R for 1km and then turn L to cross the dam walls via the road.

Both options: at the end, after crossing the dam, turn L and L again onto an asphalted *camino agricola* along the RH bank of the **Embalse de Nuestra Señora de Agavanzal** (*reservoir*) for about 3km, along the water's edge (*sandy beaches in places, good place to swim/paddle, as long as you are at least 200m away from the dam itself*) turning L by a small road bridge to

8km Villar de Farfón (712/279)

Church of San Pedro (porch is a good place for a rest), fountain at end of village. No other facilities at all.

Turn R at the church and cross the village square, then R once more to leave the village. In front of a small stone house turn L, past a new house and into a walled lane, then KSO for 3.5km. The Camino leaves on a track that must have been a very old local road and along which you (quite literally) KSO in a dead straight line (waymarks usually on the ground). To begin with it takes you through meadows which later alternate with rising, rocky terrain with brush until you arrive at the top of a hill from where you can already see **Ríonegro del Puente**. KSO downhill for another 1km, emerging into grassland. When you meet another track coming from L turn R downhill towards the old main road. At the bottom of the hill (opposite the former Hostal Maxims) turn L and KSO on a track // on L to the road, then use a small concrete track for sheep and other pedestrians crossing the river to the L of the road bridge via a collapsed but passable concrete bridge. On the other side of the river the track passes under the road bridge twice, then rises up into

6.5km Ríonegro del Puente (718.5/272.5)

Bars, shop on main street (with sello), panadería on main road. Swimming area by bridge.

Former parish church of Santiago existed until the early part of the twentieth century. Now only the tower remains (check for statue of St James in portal) and the present cemetery is on the site where the main body of the church used to be. Former hospital for pilgrims and travellers in building on RH side of main road. Santuario de Nuestra Señora de Carballada, fifteenth–eighteenth century, on the site of the original Romanesque ermita (traces in old sacristy); it belongs to the Cofradia de los Falifos (dedicated to looking after pilgrims and based in Ríonegro del Puente), one of the oldest such organisations still in existence. (Mass every evening, festival third Sunday in September.) The Palacio de Diego de Losada (diagonally across from the ayuntamiento) was restored in 1992 and is now a community centre.

Note that from Rionegro del Puente to Mombuey there is no shade at all.

Fork R up a lane // to the N525 then fork R behind the last house onto a lane, veering R towards the motorway. KSO at a crossing and turn L along a service road beside the motorway. Turn R underneath it by the SECOND underpass then L on the other side up a *camino de tierra* leading to a white industrial building ahead (to RH side of road bridge).

Pass in front of it (*the Repsol gas depot* – almacén de butano) and KSO on a track // to the N525 for 3.5km (to road KM51).

After crossing the road coming (from R) from **Santa Eulalia** (*cyclists will find it easier to use the road as far as the Hotel La Ruta*) the track goes through grass but becomes clearer as you proceed. After 1km you KSO(L) on a much more prominent track joining from R. Veer gradually back towards the main road but do NOT rejoin it at a white house opposite a junction.

When you reach the **Hotel La Ruta** (*bar/rte as well as accommodation, tel: 980.65.21.30,* panadería *opposite*) continue behind the hotel on the 'Vía de Servicio'. Continue behind the first houses in the town then continue on the pavement in

8.5km Mombuey (727/264)

All facilities. HR Rapina (tel: 980.65.21.20) on main road in village centre, but it is mainly a fonda for workers and so is often full (closed Saturdays and Sundays). Romanesque parish church of Nuestra Señora de la Asunción (restored in 1992) with thirteenth-century tower is a National Monument, its military-type construction attributed to the Templars.

After Mombuey the landscape begins to change and you enter, in spirit if not in fact, into Galicia.

Cross the road via an underpass and on the other side turn L then R (**Calle Figales**) veering R towards the **Iglesia de la Asunción**. Continue past it and then KSO(R) up **Calle Rodrigo** (a lane), which leads back to the N525. You then continue on a *cañada* alongside it for 2km, veering L to cross the motorway.

On the other side turn R 200m later and KSO. 800m later turn R at a T-junction and KSO, veering L, into the village of

4km Valdemerilla (731/264)

Church of San Lorenzo, fountain, but no other facilities.

Turn R (**Calle Principe de Asturias**), veering L into the small square (**Plaza de la Constitución**) and turn L into a lane. KSO, ignoring turns, for 3km to

3.5km Cernadilla (734/257)

Fountain.

Enter the village at the side of **Ermita del Cristo** (*Galician-style churches start from here onwards*) and fork L by an electric transformer down a street past the church (up on your L) and at the bottom of a hill (**Plaza de la Fuente**, *with fountain*). Turn L up the hill, KSO(R) at a fork and KSO for 2km to

2km San Salvador de Palazuelos (736/255)

Fountain.

Enter by the *ermita* (L) with fountain (*unusual bell-tower*). Fork L to the **Iglesia de la Transfiguración** (*its porch a good place for a rest*) and pass to L of it (**Calle Transfiguración**). Go L at a fork and continue downhill into the valley (*reservoir visible ahead – you can also see where you are going next*). Go down into the valley and then up a hill on the other side, ignoring turns. Continue ahead at a junction to a road ahead and turn R along it. Turn L (signed 'Entrepeñas 1') to the village of

4km Entrepeñas (740/251)

Embalse de Cernadilla 300–400m away to south.

Enter the village past the *ermita* (L) and continue on the road to the church (**Iglesia de la Asunción**). Pass to R of it (*fountain on L*) and fork R out of the village. Before the end (450m later) fork L onto a *camino de tierra* which becomes a walled lane, veering L.

KSO(L) at a fork uphill and, just before you reach the motorway (800m later), KSO(R) to cross the bridge, veering L on to the other side. Continue ahead, passing a football field on R, towards the church (*another Iglesia de la Asunción, with nice shady area with trees in front – yet another good place for a rest*). Continue ahead to the N525 in

3km Asturianos (743/248)

Three shops, farmácia, fountain (but no bar).

Cross the main road and go up RH side of the **Ermita del Carmen** to the end of the street then turn L, returning to the main road. *(*Cyclists: remain on road from here to Palacios de Sanabria**.)* Continue along it for 250m then turn R (road KM72) and 250m later turn L off road down a grassy track. KSO(R) at a fork then veer L towards woods (not well waymarked) and the track becomes clearer as you proceed. The path goes through oak woods, leading downhill to a section of old road. KSO along it for 50m then fork R uphill, veering R to pick up a track that goes alongside a wall and then to L of a hedge/line of trees. After a while it veers and then turns L, veering R again. Continue ahead and a track joins from back L, becoming clearer all the time. Reach the road at exit boards to

3km Palacios de Sanabria (746/245)

Two bars (one with rte), shop, bank (no CD).

Continue on the other side and pass to RH side of the church (*bars on main road, 200m to L; **cyclists turn R here*). Cross another minor road and continue on the other side, forking L onto a FP and then joining a grassy track (KSO(R)) that veers L along a line of telegraph poles.

KSO along an old walled lane (*plenty of shady trees – a very nice section*). 1.5km later, when a track joins from back R, turn L over a bridge/causeway, cobbled (large), and continue ahead on the other side. KSO.

After 800m cross a minor road and continue on a lane on the other side till you reach the road in

3km Remesal (749/242)

No facilities (but plenty of dogs).

Cross over and KSO(R) ahead then fork L and turn L round to a fountain and *lavadero*. KSO(R) ahead, veering L, then turn R and KSO ahead down a shady green lane, gently downhill.

KSO ahead in front of you all the time, the motorway getting closer and closer. When you reach a wall on L veer L under HT cables and KSO(L) ahead down a grassy lane (take LH of two parallel lanes as RH one is somewhat overgrown).

When you reach the motorway fence (no waymark) turn R alongside it and then turn L over a bridge. KSO on the other side, veering L, then go under HT cables and turn R down a walled lane. When you reach an open grassy area KSO ahead, taking a middle course, veering slightly R (as the path you want, on R, in fact, is completely overgrown) and then KSO(L) down a walled lane (overgrown for first 100m) to a fountain (the main road – N525 – is 20m ahead) in

3.5km Otero de Sanabria (752.5/238.5)

Two fountains but no other facilities. Monastery church (double-towered building outside village), parish church (note the painted wooden relief sculptures on church and sacristy doors: two of saints, a third of the seven sinners in the fiery furnace).

Wooden relief of seven sinners in the fiery furnace above south portal, parish church of Otero de Sanabria

Turn R and continue through the village to the church and then KSO to the end of the village, veering L and then R uphill by a large house in a very large garden. At the top of the hill veer L to a minor road and then turn R along it, downhill under the motorway, over a small bridge and up the other side till you reach

2.5km Triufé (755/236)

Fountain. Village still has house that was once the pilgrim hospital.

Just past the village nameboards turn L, veering R, turn L again at a T-junction and veer R past the church. Continue on a concrete road, past mainly abandoned houses, to a tarmac road. Turn L.

Cross a bridge over the motorway and turn R onto the N525. Continue along it past a hotel (on R) then cross over and turn L up the exit/slip-road leading over the **Río Tera** (*swimming area*) to a newer part of the town. Turn L uphill then turn R at a large fountain to continue up **Calle Rúa** to the historic quarter with church, *ayuntamiento, castillo* and tourist office. *A lot of old houses with armorial devices in this part of town.*

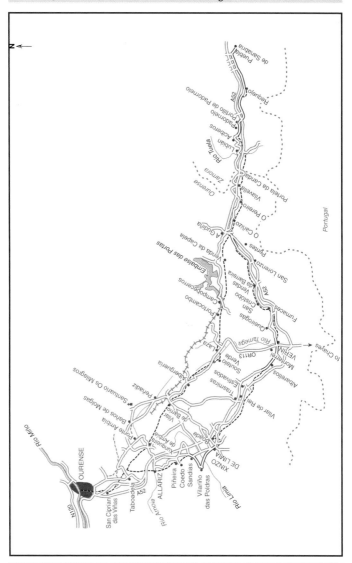

Stage and "scenery", Roman amphitheatre, Mérida

Salamanca Cathedral reflected in the Río Tormes

Tympanum of the Adoration of the Magi (San Juan del Mercado), Benavente

4km Puebla de Sanabria 960m (759/232)

All facilities, RENFE 1km above the town at top of hill (Madrid, Zamora, Ourense, Santiago), buses (from petrol station on main road 1km outside town) to Madrid, Pontevedra and various parts of Galicia. Several hotels, HS la Trucha, Ctra Vieja de Vigo (in newer part of town, tel: 980.62.00.60 and 980.62.01.50), HR Peamar, Plaza de Arrabal (tel: 980.62.01.36 and 980.62.01.07), three more hotels on main square, Hostal Galicia (cheap but nearly always full) but NO fondas or CH. Tourist office at side of ayuntamiento (open 12 to 2pm, 5 to 9pm).

Hilltop town founded in AD 569 and which formerly had a pilgrim hospital. Castle, twelfth-century church of Santa María del Azoque with Romanesque portal and Gothic vault with sculptured scallop keystones above the altar (open July to September, 10am to 1pm and 5 to 8pm except Mondays).

Facing the church turn L (**Calle Mayor**) then R into **Calle San Bernardo** and pass to RH side of **Colegio Santa María de la Vitoria** then turn R down a steep concrete lane beside the cemetery, which then becomes a walled lane. Either a) turn R onto a wider track, leading down to the road and then turn **hard L** along it or b) turn L, shorter and steeper, not so clear, to the road.

Cross an old bridge over the river and then turn L in front of the *hostal* and continue on an old road with the river below to your L, out of town, for 2km until you reach the N525.

Here arrows invite you to turn L, away from the road, but this is a fairly fiddly detour that takes you through the gap in the trees ahead L, behind the woods (to LH side), only spasmodically waymarked, and you will also have to cross a river to return to the road. Instead it is suggested that you continue (from KM88) along the *cañada* immediately below the road to the L, then slightly further way, for 1.6km until this track veers sharp L at a 'stop' sign (*opposite the road turn-off, R, to Santa Colomba*). Continue on the road (*you can see the top of the church of Santiago de Terroso ahead R by now*).

Continue on the N525 and 80m past KM91 turn R down a lane, walled at the start. KSO(L) ahead down a shady lane. At the end KSO(L) on a gravel lane leading to the Romanesque church of **Santiago de Terroso** (*note scallop shells on doors*).

Continue ahead on the road, veering L to a 'stop' sign. Cross over and go down a minor road (signposted 'Terroso 500m') beside a football field with a (modern) *cruceiro* and continue into the village.

2km Terroso (761/230)

No facilities.

KSO(R) ahead in the village (**Calle Cabecero**) veering R and then L uphill to cross a bridge over the motorway.

KSO ahead on the other side, up a lane. Just before it turns L uphill by a HT pylon fork L along a hollow lane. KSO(L) when a track joins from R. When the lane becomes overgrown take a FP above it to R. Shortly before you reach the motorway it veers L as a grassy track. Cross an open grassy space and turn L onto a *camino de tierra* to recross the motorway.

Veer R on the other side, continuing down a walled lane, turning L at a bend into the village. Turn R at the first house, KSO(R) to a fountain and then turn L (*second fountain on L, with 'aqua no tratada'*) to reach the main road opposite the **Ermita de Guadalupe** in

2.5km Requejo de Sanabria 763.5/227.5)

Shops, hotel, Rte Plaza, both on main road. Sello in ayuntamiento. Church of San Lorenzo. From here onwards you will see many houses with a *patín* (small outside stone staircase leading to balcony and/or first floor, with a landing halfway up but no banisters).

Pass to RH side of the *ermita*, in front of the *ayuntamiento (third fountain)* and KSO along **Calle Carrera**, a long street, then continuing on a minor road as far as the cemetery (L), 1.5km. Turn R and 200m later rejoin the N525 at KM95 (*two bars with rte, one on either side of road*).

Turn L and continue uphill for 3km, climbing gradually (*the 'dent' ahead of you on the skyline is the pass at the Portillo de Padornelo*).

Just past road KM98 turn L onto the old main road and stay on it. Veer R towards a gravel quarry and then KSO, veering L, R and L again and KSO(L) at a fork. When you see all three viaducts ahead of you (the N525 and both carriageways of the new A52), fork L downhill underneath them all, then KSO(R) on the level (do NOT go down to the river below), veering L in horseshoe fashion. Cross an old bridge over the river and go under the two motorway bridges again. KSO ahead uphill after that, veering R and then following the road as it zigzags up to the pass at the

6km Portillo de Padornelo 1329m (769.5/221.5)

Good views on a clear day with no haze (it can be chilly up here, even in summer).

KSO(L) ahead at a 'stop' sign and electricity mast (by a concrete hut in an enclosure). KSO(R) at a bend, down to the N525 after it emerges from a tunnel. Walk along its LH side across a bridge at the motorway and 100m later turn L down a concrete road into the village of

0.5 Padornelo (770/221)

Two fountains, two bar/shops on main road. Hotel/Rte Padornelo (tel: 980.62.01.06) by petrol station 500m later.

Continue through the village to the church and then fork R again back to the N525. Pass the petrol station and continue for 1km then turn R onto the old N525, signposted 'Hedroso 4, Lubián'. *(Cyclists continue on this old road all the way to Lubían – longer but with very little traffic and nearly all downhill.)* 300m later, at the end of the embankment wall on L, turn **hard L** downhill and then **hard R** on an old rocky track. *(Lubián visible ahead L from here; the 'dip' in the skyline now is the pass at A Canda, where you will be going tomorrow if you are on foot.)*

Small Galician-style Baroque church in Padornelo

The track leads gently downhill alongside the hill, with the valley to L. Continue to L of an irrigation channel (may be boggy in parts) and the track becomes a walled lane, descending more steeply (with stream for 200m, though plenty of 'stepping stones'). KSO(L) on a concrete lane to the *ermita* in

3.5 Aciberos (773.5/217.5)

Another small village with fountain but no other facilities. Twelve inhabitants in winter though a lot of *emigrantes* return in July and August.

Turn R and continue through the village past a fountain (*note small old building on R – this is a watermill still in working order*). Fork L at the end and KSO down a walled lane. KSO(L) at a fork, KSO(R) at a junction, following the lane downhill as it makes its way to the valley bottom. Cross a bridge over **Río Pedro**.

When the wall on R ends turn R uphill then 100m later fork L and then turn L onto a lane coming from R. KSO(L) ahead then veer round to R uphill and then turn L up another lane coming from R.

Go through a tunnel under the railway line and KSO ahead downhill. 200m later, when you come to some telephone cables, turn

hard L downhill on a similar track. Turn **hard R** 100m later onto a ridge-like walled lane. KSO(R) on a track joining from back L. Continue ahead. Keep going downhill and at the bottom turn L to cross a small bridge over the river.

KSO ahead, forking R uphill. 200m later pass the first of old derelict houses and then veer L, entering

5km Lubián (778.5/212.5)

Bars, shop but no accommodation or rte.

KSO ahead along the street. KSO(L) ahead at a fork, downhill, forking L and L again to the church. Continue past the church (L) and shop and KSO(L) at a junction; *here you will see the first of the special pilgrim marker stones by the artist Carballo and which indicate the route all through the province of Ourense. As indicated in the Introduction, there are over 100 of them altogether, all slightly different but in the same general style.*

Cyclists: continue on the old main road from here up to the pass at A Canda, though you can cycle as far as the Santuario de la Tuiza (and back) if you wish to visit this before continuing your journey.

Continue downhill towards **Río Tuelo** and then KSO(R) ahead on a concrete road signposted 'Santuario de la Tuiza 1'. Follow it downhill, over a bridge (*picnic area to L*) and under the motorway flyovers to

2km Santuario de la Virgen de la Tuiza (780.5/210.5)

This is the church of the Virgen de la Tuiza, with *romerías* four times a year; the most important one used to be on the last Sunday in September but has now been moved to August 5th, the feast of Nuestra Señora de las Nieves, when the *emigrantes* (from other parts of Spain, Europe and South America) take part. Eighteenth-century Baroque church replaces a former ermita on another site (stones brought from there) – rarely open. Fountain.

Pass between the church (L) and a barn-type building (R) and fork L ahead down a walled lane. Turn L at a junction 200m later (may be wet, though it gets drier as you advance and climb).

KSO(L) ahead, with the river to your L, veering round to reach it. *(Bridge broken at time of writing but water is shallow and quite a lot of large stones to step across.)* Cross the river and veer R on the other side by a wall to continue on another lane which becomes clearer as you proceed (*sparsely waymarked in this section*). Climb gradually more steeply, going up and down from time to time.

As you continue the trees give way to heather. *Tip of red and white transmitter mast at the pass visible ahead on skyline, with group of trees to its R: this is where you are heading for! Path becomes better and more frequently waymarked as you climb.*

Descend somewhat to cross a stream and KSO. KSO when a track joins from back L. Ford another stream (*roe deer may be visible here*) and KSO ahead. KSO(L) at a junction (that leads off to R downhill). The terrain and path is alternately somewhat overgrown and extremely clear.

About 150m later (after a junction) watch out for a LH turn uphill, up a FP. *(The track you were on up to now becomes completely overgrown and impassable shortly afterwards so if you find you can't advance you have missed the turn.)* KSO up this path and 1km later emerge onto a minor road (*leading to transmitter, L*) to the LH side of the clump of trees you saw earlier on the skyline at the

5km Portela da Canda 1262m (785.5/205.5)

A pass, forming the border of provinces of Zamora and Ourense and of the autonomous regions of Castille-León and Galicia. Fountain, picnic area under trees. Another 'Ourense waymark'. Can be chilly up here too, even in summer. Good views on a clear day.

Fork L down the track (continuation of the one you came up on), cross a road and KSO downhill on the other side. Turn R immediately onto a track that goes along RH side of the valley. After 1km KSO(L) at a fork, descending all the time. KSO(R) at a fork.

1.5km A Canda (787/204)

Village with no facilities apart from fountain.

KSO in the village, KSO(R) past the church and KSO(L) at the end by a bus shelter. Fork L along a minor road with crash barriers. 400–500m later, at a break in the crash barrier shortly before a sharp RH bend (the track goes hard L downhill here too), continue on the inside of the crash barrier (except for 'caballos', as the sign tells you: cyclists get off and push for a short distance here). 100m later fork L over a footbridge over a motorway drain and turn L downhill on an old paved track,

veering R to run // to the railway line below to L. KSO ahead, veering L
to go through a tunnel under the railway and KSO ahead on the other
side. KSO(L) ahead down a stony track, KSO(L) at a junction and KSO
ahead at a crossing, gently downhill all the time. Cross the river.

KSO uphill on the other side. KSO where a track joins from back R
and KSO(R) at a junction, veering L, and turn R to

3.5km Vilavella (790.5/200.5)

Bar, panadería and shop on main road. Hostal Porta Galega (tel:
988.42.55.93) up on N525 at petrol station. Bar/Rte 'O Carteiro'
also has rooms (tel: 988.42.55.99/42.56.48).

Turn L into the village, fork L, fork L again and continue ahead, down
a concrete lane out of the village, turning L downhill to the valley
bottom. Cross a bridge and KSO along the side of a hill. Ignore RH
turn. KSO(R) at a fork by a barn and continue along a shady walled
lane along the valley bottom.

If you come to a gateway blocked with old trees (*to keep the
animals in or out – not you!*) do not try to lift them but go round the
side and climb over a low wall.

Continue ahead on a sort of causeway to a crossing (*fountain ahead
L*) and KSO ahead. KSO, ignoring turns, till you reach

4km O Pereiro (794.5/196.5)

Pass the **Ermita de Nuestra Señora de Loreto** (pass to RH side of it)
and KSO to road. Turn L and immediately R through the village, passing
the church of **San Pedro** (*on R; Romanesque but heavily restored altar,
sacristy*).

KSO through the village, right to the end, coming to a wide, open
area and KSO(R) alongside walls, passing to R of some enormous rocks.
KSO ahead, cross the river by big stepping stones and KSO ahead in a
straight line towards the ridge ahead, where you will pick up a clear
track.

KSO ahead and continue on a green lane, shady (*look back for
good views*), then emerge on another ridge where you turn R. When
the wall stops KSO in a straight line across open heathland with VERY
large rocks, veering L, to the top of the ridge then down again to
continue alongside a wall coming from back R.

Veer R then L to another walled lane, go over a footbridge and then continue ahead to RH side of wall that veers R and then L. When it ends KSO ahead for another 100m then turn L along a 'causeway' of large stones and a 'bridge' and continue ahead towards a wall *(woods on R by now)*. Follow a track round to LH side of the woods. Follow it round to the top of a hill and a minor road. Turn L. Cross the railway line and 50m later fork L off the road onto a track leading under telephone cables. At the road KSO ahead on a *camino de tierra*.

KSO(R) at a junction by a ruined house and continue into the village of

5.5km O Cañizo (800/191)

Shop in main square near church, bar on main road outside village. Hostal Nevada at road KM127 (tel: 988.42.10.85).

KSO to the centre of the village. KSO(L) ahead then turn R and KSO(L) on the road. Continue through the village *(shop on L)* and veer R at the end. Turn L up a short street then turn L onto a walled lane. KSO at a crossing and shortly afterwards pass a *cruceiro* (L).

KSO to the N525, cross over and continue on a FP downhill *(motorway to R)* and turn L at the bottom. Continue to a road, cross over and continue on LH side and cross the motorway. Continue on the main road *(tourist office on RH side)* to the centre of

3km A Gudiña, pop. 2200 (803/188)

Small town with all facilities, taking its name from the lady (A Gudiña) who used to keep a venda (country inn) here. Refugio – ask in tourist office or Protección Civil (on RH side of main road at entry to town). Hostal Oscar (tel: 988 42.10.14) and Hotel La Madrileña (tel: 988.42.10.30) on main street in centre, Hostal Relojero (tel: 988.42.01.01) and Hostal/Bar/Rte Suizo lower down.

Halfway point along the Camino meridional between Zamora and Santiago. Baroque church of San Martiño.

At a junction (on R) with the C533 (to **Viano de Bola**) turn R and then immediately L along a street // to the main road to a square. *(For refugio go under the railway line at a junction and turn R.)*

Here there are two sets of waymarks as this is where the two routes divide: the northern, more isolated option via Laza, Vilar de Barrio and Xunqueira de Ambía and the southern one that goes through Verín, Xinzo de Limia and Allariz and contains more monuments to visit. Both

are waymarked, the northern one in its entirety, as far as Ourense, the southern route as far as the exit from Allariz and both are equally strenuous. You can, however, pass from one to the other quite easily as there are only 13km of minor road (for cyclists, for example) between Verín and Laza and 7km (also on a minor road) between Xunqueira de Ambía and Allariz. If you decide to take the southern route turn to p.147 'B. Southern Route via Verín' below.

A. Northern Route via Laza

To begin with there is quite a lot of asphalt but it is on a small, narrow road that has almost no traffic at all and that climbs high over the area known as the Sierra Seca, barren exposed hills with splendid views all round over the mountains and the reservoirs below you.

From the square in **A Gudiña** KSO(R) ahead down the street and KSO(L) ahead past a telephone transmitter. KSO(R) and join a bigger road coming from L (*good views*).

Before you reach Campobecerros you pass four of the remaining vendas (venta in Castilian) of a chain of them that formerly existed along this route, simple inns for travellers to rest, eat and sleep and frequently (like A Gudiña) named after the owner or some feature of its physical setting. Today they are just very small hamlets with hardly anyone living there – the terrain is so inhospitable that most of the population has emigrated, either to Ourense, to other parts of Spain or abroad, though many people return for their month-long summer holidays. Even the Venda da Capela, which was a hive of activity in the 1950s when the railway was built, is more or less 'dead' today, its station no longer in regular use and the majority of the RENFE housing deserted. The railway is only a single-track line (with over 100 tunnels between Puebla de Sanabria and Ourense) but it opened up Galicia to the rest of Spain – slowly – as a result. Nowadays there are plans to replace it with a high-speed line from Madrid (requiring completely new track as the present line has far too many curves for the speeds envisaged by an AVE).

KSO for 4.5km to the **Venda do Espiño de Cerdeira** (*the name refers to a 200-year old cherry tree*) and fork R through the hamlet, returning to the road at the end. KSO for 3.5km more, pass a junction and fork L 200m later into

5km Venda da Teresa (808/183)

KSO towards the hamlet and fork L on a concrete road through it. KSO(R) and exit on a walled lane, along the side of a hill (railway line below) and KSO to join the Camino coming from back R.

KSO. *Here you are high up (1088m), with splendid views on a clear day and the Embalse das Portas visible R below. The chimney that you can see on the horizon over to the R is a ventilation shaft for a canal.*

Rejoin the road coming from back R. Veer L to cross the railway line and follow the road uphill in

2km Venda da Capela (810/181)

Continue through the hamlet on a road to the end, past RENFE houses (*a line of identical buildings*), and 200m later fork L up a *camino de tierra* uphill. KSO(R) at a fork then rejoin the road 600m later and stay on it for 5km to the hamlet of the

5km Venda do Bolano (815/176)

Cyclists: KSO on road here to Campobecerros.

KSO on the road for 2km then fork L uphill on the *camino de tierra*. Continue ahead up to the top of the hill and when you start to descend and see Campobecerros in the valley below look out for a milestone-*flecha* indicating a RH turn at R angles, steeply downhill to electric cables ahead. Near the bottom turn R on a track coming from L and 150m later reach a minor road. Turn **hard L** here and follow it round into the village, passing a *lavadero* and fountain (L) and a small *ermita* on R; *note modern statue of Santiago-pilgrim/apostle in a niche over the main door (one scallop shell on his hat, two on cape, staff and gourd in his RH and book on L).*

Pass in front of the church. KSO(R) then turn L up the main street in

7km Campobecerros (822/169)

Bar/shop in street // to main one, bar/rte at top of hill on L, fountain.

At the top of the hill KSO on the road marked 'Portocambo 2.8km'. Cross a railway bridge and enter

4km Portocambo (826/165)

Turn L up the main street *(fountain on R)* and continue to the top of the hill (the pass, 1km) where there is a VERY large wooden cross at the side of the road, some 25ft/7.5m high. *This was donated by the monastery at the Santuario de los Milagros (some distance to the north west of here) and positioned there on the initiative of Don Eligio Rivas, a parish priest very active in reviving the Camino through Galicia, in memory of those pilgrims who died whilst making their way to Santiago.*

Turn L here onto a *camino de tierra* and KSO(L) ahead. KSO(R) uphill then begins a long, gradual descent on a similar track along the side of a hill, with chestnut trees to your L and good views out over the valley to your R *(this is a very nice walk in evening sunlight)*. KSO, ignoring any turns near the end, into the village of

5km As Eiras (831/160)

Picnic area with fountain and covered seating at end of village on L.

KSO on the road, downhill. Continue on the road and 500m later KSO(R) downhill at a fork. KSO, passing a roadside fountain on L (2km later). 2.5km after that, by a sharp LH bend in the road, turn R down a lane *(cyclists: dismount for a short distance or continue to Laza on road)*. Turn L at the bottom and then R and continue on a track that crosses a bridge over a river and leads to a minor road. Turn L and then fork R into

6km Laza, pop. 3000 (837/154)

Bars, shops, bank, Hostal 'A Nosa' above bar with disco (tel: 988.42.20.61), rte on main road. Refugio (ask in Protección Civil, at side of Caso do Concello).

Small town famous for it carnival. Late seventeenth-century church of San Xoán. Pilgrims coming from Portugal via Chaves and Verín (whether Portuguese or from Andalucía, Extremadura and parts of the province of Salamanca who had made a detour) joined the northern route here.

With **Casa do Concello** to your R and the church ahead R fork L down the street past **Librería Dalí**, veering L and KSO to the main road. Turn R and KSO out of the village. Turn R at a junction marked 'Vilamea/Castro', turn L over an old bridge and then return to the road.

800m later (*pilgrim stone and marker stone are on RIGHT-hand side of road here*) fork LEFT onto a minor tarmac road leading to the centre of

3km Soutelo Verde (840/151)

Bar on road at entrance, fountain in centre by very large concrete cross.

KSO ahead, forking R over a bridge and KSO(L) ahead. Cross another bridge (*ermita* to R, swimming area to L) and continue to a road. KSO(L) along it for 100m then fork R onto an unpaved road leading gently downhill.

KSO, ignoring turns. Just before the village (**Tamicelas**) pass a fountain (on L) with seats then fork L again to the church in

3km Tamicelas (843/148)

Fountain. Cyclists, even energetic ones, should continue on the road (OR110) from here to Alberguería.

Fork L uphill by church, the beginning of a steep, continuous climb up to Alberguería. Continue on a *camino de tierra* and 500m later fork R onto a track through trees. 100m later fork L uphill on a rough, rocky but clear track (*no shade*), watching out for waymarks (frequent) on the ground. *This is the Monte Requeixal – nice views as you climb.*

KSO, veering L uphill. Route flattens out briefly then turn R uphill again. KSO at a crossing. KSO(L) then KSO(R). Track continues on a ridge. *A large, single oak tree offers quite a lot of shade.*

KSO ahead, KSO(R) at a fork, veering R till you reach a minor road at the top by telephone cables. *Splendid views all round on a clear day.* Turn R along the road for 1km to

6km Alberguería (849/142) 900m

Site of former pilgrim hospital, as the village name suggests. Important cattle centre in eighteenth century with large population. Today it is almost empty but with interesting vernacular architecture if you look around. Church of Santa María, with statue of Santiago inside.

Fork L into the village and fork L again at the church. At the end turn L onto a tarmac lane and then KSO along a walled lane, veering L at a fork. Continue into open countryside, KSO(R) at a fork and then KSO(L), the track following a wall again shortly afterwards. KSO(R) at a fork, pass onto open heathland, veer R past telephone cables and KSO until you reach a minor tarred road crossing diagonally.

Continue on a track on the other side. KSO ahead at a crossing and shortly afterwards you will see another very large wooden cross on the skyline.

Reach a minor road, cross over and continue on a *camino de tierra* to

3km Cross on Monte Talariño (852/139)

Another place with splendid views on a clear day and another large wayside cross that was erected in memory of those who died on the Camino, as well as the *segadores* (reapers) from different parts of Galicia who, until well into the twentieth century, walked this way (and back) each year en route for work in the cornfields of Castille. This cross has a pile of stones around its base, added to by each pilgrim who passes.

Fork L at the cross, downhill (pass to L of it) on a grassy lane leading down to a road. Turn R along it for 500m. Just before a sharp RH bend and just after the road KM17 (OR110) fork L down a *camino de tierra* between conifers.

Shortly after LH bend (800m from road) watch out for RH right-angle turn, down to a wall. Turn R here (walled lane, often boggy) and then turn L downhill to a minor road. 300–400m later fork R downhill on a track. Turn R at the bottom on the road leading into the town.

Fork R up the old (main) road, // at first to the new one. Veer R uphill (*hórreo on L*) then veer L, following the road round on the level. Cross the (main) road and continue until you reach the main square (*with gardens and petrol station*) in

4.5km Vilar de Barrio (856.5/134.5)

Bars, fountain, shops, bank. Refugio at end of main square (ask in petrol station).

Town has scallop shell in its coat of arms. Parish church has a chapel given by the Marqués de Boveda, one of the Knights of Santiago, and whose house (still standing) was also in the town. In Vilar de Barrio you will see the first of the many hórreos (raised granaries for corn, potatoes) that are a characteristic feature of the Galician countryside.

Cyclists may like to make a detour (12km, via the road to Macedo) to the Santuario de los Milagros (services several times a day, every day, during the month of September); you can return to the route via Baños de Molgas (hostal).

Continue past the petrol station (L) into the **Avenida Sanfiz** ahead and KSO along **Rúa da Fonte** (a very long street) out of the town, passing a church (L) and fountain/*lavadero* (R). Fork L at a junction shortly afterwards and continue on the road into

2km Bóveda (858.5/132.5)

Bar, two fountains, shop.

Continue to the centre of the village, passing a church and cemetery (on R) and KSO(R) at a fork behind a fountain. KSO(L) along the street with three *hórreos* and then KSO(R) behind the OLD fountain (in stone casing) and return to the road at a junction by the shop. Turn R uphill and at a junction, as you begin to descend, KSO ahead in front down a tarred lane.

Turn L at the bottom then immediately R by a fountain and *lavadero* and at the end turn R along a minor road between fields. 300–400m later, at a crossing, turn L down a straight *camino de tierra* lined with stone posts.

KSO. Pass five crossroads, a junction, a sixth crossroads with a marble memorial cross (*to one Francisco Cid Cid*). At the seventh crossroads (the one AFTER the memorial) turn R. KSO at a crossing then 100m later turn L to a road. Turn L along it then fork R immediately up a lane behind houses in

6.5 Bobadela (865/126)

Fountain.

KSO(L) ahead at a junction. Turn R at a fork then L to the end of the village and a walled lane, veering R at a fork, L at the next one shortly afterwards and L again 100m later.

KSO(R) past an electricity transformer in the middle of woods and KSO ahead on a walled lane leading through woods. KSO till you reach a road then either continue along it for 100m then turn L at a junction or continue ahead on the other side of the road to cut the corner, THEN turn L on the road (*both options waymarked*) into the village of

2km Padroso (867/124)

Follow the road round, passing three prominent *hórreos* (*middle one dates from 1933*). KSO(R) through the village, passing a fountain (R) and KSO(R) at a fork.

At the end (tarred lane turns L) KSO along a cobbled walled lane and just after the *lavadero* (on R) turn L up another walled lane, leading uphill and continue onto open heathland.

At the top (*splendid views – again!*) cross over a track passing in front of you and continue ahead towards a large, prominent rocky outcrop.

Pass to LH side of it, go straight ahead downhill for a short distance then, veering R, pick up a track that leads down into woods, continuing on a walled lane.

Either fork R (uphill) or L ahead (*it doesn't matter as they meet up again shortly afterwards*) and go downhill. Turn L on a lane that comes from R and reach the first buildings leading to the road in the hamlet of

2km Cima da Vila (869/122)

Turn R on the road then fork R at a fountain and tall, double-sided *cruceiro*. KSO(R) to the end and after the last house continue along a walled lane leading downhill to a road 700m later. Cross over and continue downhill on the other side for 1.5km, reaching a road by the fountain/*lavadero* in

2km Quintela (871/120)

KSO on the road for 200m then turn R downhill on a more minor road (signposted 'Albergue 1km'). Pass the *refugio* (on R, next to sports centre) and a 'stop' sign at the bottom.

Continue uphill to the church (*double-sided* cruceiro *outside*) in the centre of

2km Xunqueira de Ambía (873/118)

Bars, shops, bank, refugio next to sports hall but no other accommodation. Rte Saboriño on main street near church. Bar (unmarked) at top of hill on R also does meals.

Twelfth-century Colexiata de Santa María la Real with Renaissance stalls, Baroque 'Virgen peregrina' in pilgrim outfit on side altar and sixteenth-century cloisters. Palacio Episcopal, Casa Rectoral, Museo de Arte Sacro.

Cloisters in Colexiata de Santa María

Continue uphill past the church, veering R to another square (*and another double-sided* cruceiro) and continue downhill (signposted 'Salgueiros' – this is **Calle Capitán Cortés**) then fork L down a steep hill to **Centro de Salud** (*health centre*). Go down a track to L of it (*picnic area behind*) and KSO ahead down a minor road downhill. 100m later, at a bend, KSO ahead down a track passing to RH side of a football field, leading down to a minor road.

Turn L, cross **Río Arnoya** (*swimming area to L*) and KSO (R) at a fork on the other side, uphill. 150m later fork R up a walled lane by an industrial building. KSO uphill, ignoring turns, reach a road, cross over and continue up a similar lane on the other side. Turn L on a lane coming from R then turn R along a minor road. Continue on it up to

2.5km A Pousa (875.5/115.5)

Two bars, shop. Note two large armorial devices on façade of small church (on R).

KSO on road to

1.5km Salgueiros (877/114)

No facilities.

Turn L at a junction (marked 'Ourense'). After approximately 1km pass LH turn marked 'Lamela' and 100m later turn L down a tarred lane signposted 'Gaspar' (just before a sharp RH bend). Follow it downhill and then up, returning to the road shortly before

1.5km Veirada (878.5/112.5)

No facilities.

KSO(L) at a junction at the top of a hill (marked 'Ourense'). *View of the city ahead.* Cross the railway and KSO ahead to **Ousende** (*1km, no facilities*). Continue on the road to **Penelas** (*1km, two bars*). Continue on the road and KSO through **Venda do Río** (2km) and

0.5km Pereiras (879/112)

Shop, bar/rte. Follow direction 'Ourense' all the time. 600m beyond Pereiras there is a bar on L and another one, also on L, immediately after passing under railway line, plus shop 150m later on L.

KSO at a fork (after a railway bridge) into

2km La Castellana (881/110)

Two bars. Beginning of industrial suburbs at entrance to Ourense. (Note stork's nest on disused factory chimney L.)

On entering an industrial area beyond the village fork L, staying on the main road, then at a T-junction with a 'stop' sign and large factory opposite turn L. At a fork 1km later go R (trees and traffic lights) up **Estrada de Salgeiros**; at the top the road runs into OR113 at a junction, where the variant via Verín and Xinzo de Limia joins the present route, to continue into Ourense as a single Camino. Turn R then a few metres later, opposite the entrance to **Hotel Auriense**, turn L past a double-sided *cruceiro* (on L) and then immediately R down a minor road. KSO(R) on a gravel lane, downhill, with woods to LH side.

Rejoin the road at road KM549. Pass an entrance board to **Seixalbo** and a petrol station (on R). Turn R into the first street on R (**Rúa da Santa Adega**, *sic*) and 80m later turn L down a lane towards a hill in front of you. Veer R to cross a railway line (*VERY CAREFULLY – listen as well as look out for trains*) and go down a FP to RH side of a hill.

2.5km Seixalbo/Seixalvos (883.5/107.5)

Bars, shops, buses to centre of Ourense.

To visit the recently-restored **Capilla Santa Agueda** do not cross the railway line but turn L alongside it, go under a railway bridge and then immediately turn **hard R** up a FP to the top. *Seats, good view of Ourense; large porch is good place for a rest.* Afterwards go back down the FP and turn R to pick up the Camino again.

Cross the road (after going down the FP at the side of the hill) and continue down **Rúa de Amendo**. *Sign says 'Seixalbo – nucleo rural de valor etnográfico', referring to the various interesting vernacular buildings in the district.*

At a complex *cruceiro* in **Praza Maior** (square) turn R into **Rúa Maior** and KSO into **Praza das Laxas** and then turn R (**Rúa da Igrexa**) to the church of **San Breixo** *(façade recently cleaned)*. *Parish house opposite.* Continue ahead past a church and cemetery on a small road, veering R, then fork L downhill.

(NB: Yellow/white waymarks, starting in Seixalbo, are for a DIFFERENT walk.)

KSO ahead at the bottom, joining the **Rúa de Seixalbo** (main road) at an entrance board to the city. This continues as the **Avenida de Zamora** and then the **Rúa do Progreso** *(waymarking is in the form of blue and yellow stylised conch-shell tiles set into the pavement)*, both very long streets.

Continue along Rúa do Progreso. When you reach a bridge (gardens below) go down some steps to RH side and cross diagonally R past some hot springs and fork R up **Rúa As Burgas**, passing a tourist office *(no. 12, on L)*. Turn L up **Calle de la Barrera**, leading into the **Praza Maior** then turn L ahead along the middle of three streets (facing the Casa do Concello) – the **Rúa Arcediagos** – passing a side entrance to the cathedral. Turn R into **Rúa Ceano Vivas** and then continue up **Rúa Juan de Austria** to the main entrance of the **Cathedral of San Martiño** in **Ourense**.

To continue, turn to '16km Ourense 125m (886/105)' p.158.

Pilgrim marker stone in Seixalbo, on the outskirts of Ourense

B. Southern Route via Verín

From the wayside cross (dated 1627) in the centre of **A Gudiña** (with the two sets of waymarks opposite) turn L to the N525 by the **Igrexa de San Martiño** (on your L). Cross over the main road and turn R on the other side downhill (*Bar/Rte/Hostal Suizo, Hostal Relojero and other bars 500m later*).

KSO for 2km then, having passed the entrance to a motorway sliproad on L, fork R onto a gravel track where the N525 does a sharp LH bend. 300m later turn R at a T-junction, veering R uphill to a road. 200m later fork R and R again uphill, passing a small house, and at a T-junction 800m later return to the N525 (at KM137) and turn R along it.

KSO for 2.5km, passing **Mesón Emilio** *(bar)* on R (*with useful bus shelter if raining*) and just before road KM139 turn L down a gravel track at the side of woods (*a river in wet weather*), // to the A52. Pass a bridge crossing the motorway (on L) and KSO ahead downhill. Just before you reach the bottom of the viaduct turn R towards the N525 and then L to cross an old stone bridge over **Río Riberiño**.

Then you can either a) continue uphill on the N525 (if you are cycling, for example) to a junction at the top of the hill with a bus shelter or b) turn L and go under the motorway on a FP and then veer R on the other side up a wide track that emerges, at the top of the hill, onto a tarred minor road at the entrance to the small village (*no facilities*) of

10km San Lorenzo

Do not enter the village but turn R instead and recross the motorway to reach a road junction with the N525 and a bus shelter 1km later. Turn L along the N525 and 100m later turn L through a gap in the crash barrier onto a longish section of the OLD N525, downhill. Cross a bridge over **Río Xestosa** and veer L to return to the new N525. Cross it, turn R on the other side, veering L uphill. At a T-junction at the top turn L down a forest road (the OLD N525) downhill. 300m later (after the old milestone 456) turn L downhill by a memorial to an *ingeniero de caminos* (civil engineer) who died there in a forest accident in 1927. KSO downhill to cross an old stone

6km Bridge over the Río Mente

100m later, on the other side, turn L and then fork R uphill on a clear track under a viaduct. A track joins from back R and when it nears the N525 (on your R) KSO ahead up a steep hill, // to the road to start with. It reaches a minor road by two white houses in **Navellos** 2km later. Turn R along it then KSO L by a fountain/*lavadero* up the main street, ignoring turns till you reach a fork in the village. Fork R downhill, leading to the motorway, and continue alongside it. Cross a bridge over the A52 (on L) and then turn R steeply uphill. Cross a minor tarred road at the top and continue ahead on a lane leading into the village, turning R to reach the N525 in

4km Vendas da Barreira

Shop, bakery, bars. Two bars/rte by petrol station on main road leaving town (after turn-off to Camino); HR Bar/Rte Catro Ventos at KM150.5 has rooms. Eighteenth-century Baroque church.

Cross the A52 and continue uphill on the N525 and turn R (by road KM149) onto a small woodland track steeply downhill. When you reach a T-junction with a larger *camino de tierra* turn R downhill. When you reach a small tarmac road turn L along it, downhill to the valley floor. Pass the hamlet of **Veiguiña** and cross a bridge over **Río Mente**.

KSO(L) uphill, passing a watermill (on L) and communal oven (on R). KSO(L) at the entrance to a second hamlet (**Chaira**) by a bus shelter and then fork L almost immediately and KSO through the hamlet, ignoring turns to L or R. KSO at two sets of crossroads. Turn L at a junction and then R in **Ríos** (third hamlet) up the street and at the end turn L onto a gravel lane, uphill then undulating. The track stops abruptly at the entrance to a field but then starts again 80m later on the other side as a clear track. KSO along it, ignoring turns, to the lower part of

3km San Pedro de Trasverea

Arrows indicate that you should turn L downhill into the valley, leading you in more or less straight line to **Miros** (visible ahead on the hilltop). However, if the weather is very wet you may prefer to continue past the church and the *casa do pobo* (*community centre*) to the upper part of the village, turn L on a road uphill and 500m later turn L ahead at a crossing (R to Montelso/Piornedo).

1km Miros (2km by road)

Fork R up a gravel lane opposite the *lavadero*. 1km later KSO ahead at a crossing, passing a sitting area shortly afterwards (*good views in clear weather*). At the top of the hill KSO when a track joins from back L then from back R and at a five-point crossroads turn L and KSO along a gravel lane. Pass a cemetery (on R) and descend. KSO(R) at a fork, continue ahead, ignoring turns, pass to L of a church and veer R to join the N525 in

7km Fumaces

No facilities.

Turn R along the N525 for 2.5km, forking L onto a short section of old road by two radio masts after KM158. Return to the N525 and continue on it to KM159, at the

3km Rte 'La Piscina'

Bar/rte at side of road; good views out over valley and Verín below.

Turn L off the N525 onto the OLD N525, which stays close to the new road (but not always visible), passing a picnic area and fountain 1km later. 200m after that, when you reach the new road again, turn L onto a FP behind the crash barrier to 100m (*cyclists stay on road*) to avoid the bend. Return to the road for 150m then fork L (not waymarked) onto a wide forest track. 300m later the OLD N525 joins from back R: continue ahead, gradually downhill all the time, till it veers R to join the new N525. Just BEFORE this fork L onto a sandy track and then 50m later turn L onto a *camino de tierra* leading downhill. Continue ahead on a small track at a crossing 200m later. KSO, ignoring turns and then 500m later, at a crossing, arrows indicate that you should fork R down a small FP; this takes you alongside the N525 above you for a while, then straight ahead, in a river valley (*with spectacular yellow broom in springtime*), before bringing you out at a T-junction near a farm with two large, bright orange doors, 2.5km later, where you then turn R.

However, this path is often so waterlogged as to be completely impassable so if this is the case you can continue on the track you were already on, descending gradually and veering R. After a while a track joins from back L and 1.5km (after the crossing where you continued straight ahead) another track joins from back L by the farm with the bright orange doors (*castle visible on hilltop ahead*).

100m later cross a stream and pick up the waymarks again (*the track you would otherwise have taken joins from your R here*). KSO for 300m more then turn R onto a gravel lane which veers R and then L to rejoin the N525 just before the turn-off to **Queirogás**. Turn L along the main road for 2km (*Bar/Rte Manchego and Bar/Rte Araujo opposite petrol station both have rooms*) into the centre of

8km Verín

Small town with all facilities. Buses to Ourense, Santiago, Benavente, Madrid and other parts of Spain. Several hostales and pensiones. Tourist office (and Albergue de Peregrinos) in small restored Casa del Escudo (with large coat of arms on front of building) at junction of Avenida de San Lázaro and Avenida de Vences, on other side of Río Tamega on leaving town. Verín was formerly a spa town and origin of the 'Fontenova', 'Cabreiroa' and 'Sousas' mineral waters.

Churches of La Merced (Baroque) and Santa María la Mayor in centre of town, Capilla de San Lázaro opposite tourist office.

Continue along the **Avenida Luis Espada** through the centre of town and cross **Río Tamega**. Continue along **Avenida de San Lázaro** on the other side (this is the N525) and continue for 2km until you reach **Pazos** (*shops, bars*).

Pass a turning to the hilltop **Castillo de Monterrei**. *Here you can make a detour, 3–4km each way, to the* castillo *to see the hilltop fortress village which looks out over the entire valley. This was built on the site of the Celtic Castro de Baronceli and three rings of fortifications enclosed a castle whose medieval walls you can still see, a palace, the thirteenth-century church of Santa María de Gracia and the fifteenth-century Torre de Homenaxe (a keep). The complex also contained a pilgrim hospital, which is now being restored for use as a* refugio, *and is nowadays the site of a* parador *(luxury hotel).*

Continue on the N525 for 5km more to

7km Albarellos de Monterrei

HS Bar/Rte San Xurxo at KM171 at entrance has rooms. Shops, bars, rte, bank. Church of Santiago, with statue of Santiago Peregrino on south wall.

Turn L off the N525 at KM172 (first yellow arrows here) into the village along **Rúa do Progreso** (not named at the start). Towards the end turn R opposite **Bar O'Campo** and then L in front of **Casa do Concello**. 100m later fork R down a lane through allotments, alongside **Río Rubín** back to the N525 at KM173. Cross over and go down a minor road marked 'Enfesta'.

3km Enfesta/Infesta

A long, straggling village with no facilities.

Continue through the village on **Rúa San Vicente**, then **Rúa do Progreso**, forking L later on. At a T-junction (not waymarked) turn L uphill (**Rúa de Madrid**) then immediately R by a fountain uphill. 300m later turn **hard R** on a rough forestry track uphill. 200m later cross over a bigger track crossing diagonally and KSO ahead on the other side, continuously uphill. 800m later cross another forest road and KSO on the other side, veering L uphill, till you reach the (new) N525 600m later.

Cross over and KSO ahead along a road marked 'Cualedro'. 300m later TURN (not fork) R onto a section of old road. 500m later fork L down a grassy/sandy lane and KSO (*often flooded in places but granite slabs down centre act as stepping stones*). KSO(R) at LH junction. Continue along a walled lane as you approach the village, cross a flat stone bridge over a small river (*fountain on other side on L*) and veer R and then L up a concrete lane into

3km Rebordondo

No facilities.

Turn R at house no. 106, up the main street through the village, R again at no. 86 then KSO on a minor tarred road uphill out of the village, forking L by a bus shelter (on R). At the end of the village, by the last house, the road becomes a sandy track. KSO(L) at fork, over open rocky heathland. After 300m fork R uphill then turn L after 200m more. The path leads uphill and another track joins from back L. KSO on the level, turning R in order to turn L over a road bridge over the motorway in the village of

3km Peñaverde

No facilities.

100m after crossing the bridge and just before you reach a bigger junction, turn R down a street. KSO(R) at a junction, KSO ahead at a crossing, descending gradually. The tarmac stops at the last house and the road continues as a walled lane, still downhill all the time (*a very nice descent in good weather*).

KSO(R) at a turn and 1km later an old tarred road joins from back R. 100m later KSO(L) ahead on a grassy lane (*motorway visible over to R*). The track becomes a walled lane, winding its way down to the valley floor. 1km later cross a small river, KSO up a similar lane on the other side and 200m later cross a wide grassy bridge (for animals) over the motorway.

Turn L on the other side then immediately R onto a walled lane leading to a section of the OLD N525 400m later. KSO(L) along it and 1km (after bridge) it veers R to join the NEW N525 at the entrance to

4km Viladerrei

Bar/Rte Cesar, another bar, bank.

KSO on the N525 to

1.5km Trasmiras

Shops, bars, rte, bank.

Continue through the village (very long) on the main road and turn L opposite the church onto the road marked 'Chamusiño 4, Faramontaos 5'. 500m later, just after a lane leading to the cemetery chapel and just before a bridge over the motorway, turn R down a dead straight gravel track. *This is the first of three, leading through an area which was formerly the biggest lake in Spain until a canal was cut to drain it; nowadays it is used for large-scale potato growing.*

KSO (literally) for 2km then take the FIFTH LH turn, leading under the motorway. Turn R immediately on the other side on a track alongside the A52, also dead straight. KSO for 2km. *Be careful, however, as at the time of writing there was a 30m long and 2m high pile of rubble completely blocking the track just before the first crossroads, followed by a 10m wide cavity full of water: pass to R in the field to circumvent these obstacles.*

Turn R at a T-junction (fourth crossing), past a covered picnic area, to the village of

4km Zos

No facilities.

KSO(R) at a junction at the entrance to the village, turn L and then L again in the centre, to the end. Turn L again opposite a stone wall made of large stones and then L again (no waymarking). 200m later at a road coming from a motorway bridge turn R. Then turn R down a third dead straight gravel track and KSO for 2km. Take the fourth RH turn towards a large warehouse marked 'Patatas Paz' and then turn L 100m later, veering R to the N525.

From here cyclists may like to turn L along the main road as the waymarked route takes you on a 2km rodeo *(detour) from here, around three sides of a square, to avoid a 500m stretch on the N525. Rejoin waymarks opposite a small house on RH side with three green doors,*** just after an unmarked lane to R, forking L down a minor road along the banks of Río Limia.*

Cross the N525, KSO ahead on an old tarmac road, cross a bridge over **Río Limia**, go under the motorway and turn L on the other side towards the village of

3km Boade

No facilities.

KSO ahead at a crossroads at the entrance to the village, go uphill ahead, veer R and then L uphill, fork L then TURN L and continue to the end of the village. Stay on the road, go over the motorway and KSO to the N525***. Cross over and continue diagonally ahead (fork L) down a tarred lane which follows the **Río Limia** for 2km. At a second bridge over the river turn R and immediately L along **Rúa Rosalia de Castro**. This leads to a junction with the **Avenida de Madrid**; turn (first) L here, down **Rúa de Lepanto** into the centre of

4km Xinzo de Limia

Small town with all facilities. Buses to Ourense, Santiago, Benavente, Madrid. Three hostales/rte: Orly, Buenos Aires, Limia. HS Nazaira, Fonda Vila.

Parish church of Santa Mariña has freestanding statue of San Roque Peregrino on RH side of chancel archway inside building and capital of a face above giant scallop shell to R of west portals outside.

Continue down **Rúa de Lepanto**, cross **Praza de Obispo Idacio** and the **Rúa Dous de Maio**, continue down **Rúa da Constitución** (not marked at start) then fork R down **Rúa Santa Mariña** (a small, curving street). Pass the church, turn L and then R (still on Rúa Santa Mariña) and continue ahead to the far end of a large grassy *plaza; white statue of warrior in garden is one of the typical Xinzo de Limia* entroido *(carnival) figures.*

Reach a road junction and fork L here along the C531, the **Avenida de Celanova**, marked 'Celanova' and 'Vilar de Santos'.

KSO (*there is no option but to use the road here as the surrounding area is full of gravel pits*). After 3km cross the **Canal da Lagoa de Antela**. Hardly any waymarks till you reach

4.5km Vilariño das Poldras

Purple notice at entrance to village says 'Miliarios', indicating a site to R of road.

Continue ahead on the road then turn R uphill at a bend onto a very small tarred road, passing a small church on L (*porch for rest!*) and sports ground (on R).

Veer R uphill through an older part of the village. Join a slightly bigger road coming from back L and KSO for 1km into

1km Couso de Limia

Small shop, bar, fountain, sign 'Albergue de Peregrinos 1km'.

KSO on the road then EITHER fork L 100m before a junction with traffic lights onto a small tarmac road, rejoining the N525 at KM205, OR continue to the lights and then turn L along the N525 in

3km Sandías

Bar on N525, bank, shop, farmácia. Church of San Estevo.

Continue on the road (N525) to

3.5km Piñeira de Arcos

Bar/Rte Novaiño 800m before village on N525.

Continue on the road then turn L, 100m after crossing **Río Piñeira**, up a minor tarmac road marked 'Coedo 2'. Pass from the *concello* of Sandías to that of Allariz (signboards) and continue with the river to LH side of the road, passing through the hamlet of **As Peras** and then immediately into that of

2km Coedo

Turn R by the first house after the entrance board into a sandy walled lane downhill. KSO for 1.5km and at the end it becomes tarred just before a T-junction in

1.5km Torneiros

Turn L onto a very minor road. Veer R at a fork and KSO(R) at a fountain and two *hórreos*. 100m later, at a bend uphill, a milestone post indicates a RH turn along a clear, sandy, walled lane but later the arrows disappear. Instead, continue ahead uphill onto high, open heathland. Turn R at the first bus shelter then, just before a second one, at a junction with the old N525, turn L downhill on a small tarmac road signposted 'San Salvador' into the hamlet of

2km San Salvador

Small chapel dedicated to San Salvador.

When the tarmac stops, in front of houses, KSO straight ahead down an old cobbled lane, gently downhill all the time, along the side of the valley. *This is a very nice section, with good views.* KSO, ignoring turns, down to a crossing of walled lanes in

2km Paicordero

Another hamlet with no facilities.

The tarmac starts again here. KSO ahead, following the road downhill and ignoring turns, entering the town via the **Rúa de Paicordero**. Cross the **Rúa Emilia Pardo Bazán** (*turn R uphill here if you want to go to Xunqueira de Ambía*) and continue on the other side up the paved **Rúa do Hospital**, passing the church of **San Pedro** (on R). At the end continue along **Rúa da Cruz** to the **Praza Maior** and the church of **Santiago** in

Correoira (walled lane) between San Salvador and Allariz

2km Allariz

Small historic hilltop town with shops, bars, rte, bank. Hostal Alarico on main street and Hostales Limia, O Mirador and Villa de Allariz on N525 at KM216. Tourist office by road bridge over river at entrance to town.

Romanesque churches of Santiago and San Estevo both have statues of San Roque Peregrino inside, church of San Pedro, sanctuary chapel of San Beito, church of Santa María de Vilanova (church of the Knights of Malta), Convento de Santa Clara with small museum of religious art. Mozárabic church of San Martiño de Pazó 2km from town. Museo Galego do Xoguete (toy museum).

Turn L along RH side of the church of Santiago into **Rúa de Vilanova**, veering R. Pass between the church of Santa María de Vilanova (R) and a football ground (L) and cross the twelfth-century **Ponte de Vilanova** over the **Río Arnoia**.

KSO ahead on other side and 200m later KSO(R) ahead at a junction. Reach the N525 at KM217, by the Allaruz factory, and continue ahead on the other side. Go under the A52 (motorway) and turn L on the other side (this *lugar* is **Roiroz**). Turn L but then KSO on

the road marked 'Santa Mariña de Augas Santas 4.8', even though the
waymarking indicates that you should turn R there, as at time of writing
the yellow arrows stop at the end of the village and the route is not
waymarked any further.

You should therefore continue on the road to **Santa Mariña de
Augas Santas** (6.5km from Allariz). Continue beyond it on the same
road till you reach a T-junction 2.5km later. Turn L here into **Pereiras**
(2km), where you will pick up the waymarks on the northern route
coming from Laza and Xunqueira de Ambía (*turn to '0.5km Pereiras
(879/112)' p.145*). These will take you into the centre of

16km Ourense 125m, pop. 96,000 (886/105)

All facilities, RENFE (Madrid, Barcelona, Santiago, La Coruña,
Zamora), buses to Santiago, Madrid and other parts of Spain.
Plenty of accommodation in all price brackets. Refugio (no
kitchen) is up on the hill above the cathedral in part of the
Convento San Francisco (it shares the building with an art gallery;
for opening times and contact see details on door or ask in tourist
office, Rúa As Burgas 12, when open). Bike repairs: Pazo de
Bicicletas, Avenida de Zamora 2.

The largest town on the route between Zamora and Santiago,
situated on the Río Miño. Ourense takes its name from the Roman
Aquae Urientes, its hot springs still in use today at 'As Burgas' near
the market. Renamed Sedes Auriensis in the fourth century and
residence of the Suebian kings in the sixth and seventh centuries.
Ourense's many places of interest include the Romanesque
Cathedral of San Martín, with thirteenth-century Portico del
Paraíso (which includes a seated statue of Santiago), an echo of
Maestro Mateo's Portico de la Gloría in the cathedral in Santiago,
and various Renaissance and Baroque side chapels. It also has the
fourteenth-century church of San Francisco (with interesting
cloisters) and the Baroque churches of A Trinidade, Santo
Domingo, Santa María la Madre (on the site of the first cathedral)
and Santa Eufemia, as well as the Praza Maior, and the Ponte Vella,
the Roman/medieval bridge over the Río Miño.

After visiting the cathedral turn L at the exit to retrace your steps
and in front of the church of **Santa Eufemia** turn R into **Rúa
Valentín Lamas Carvalal** and then continue along pedestrianised

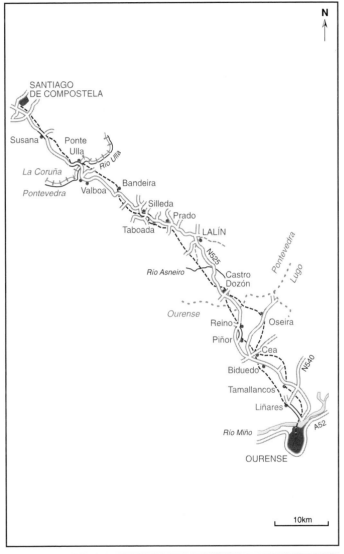

N

SANTIAGO
DE COMPOSTELA

Susana   Ponte
              Ulla
                     Río Ulla

La Coruña

Pontevedra   Bandeira
              Valboa
                        Silleda
                      Prado
              Taboada   LALÍN

                                    Pontevedra
                              N525   *Lugo*

                          Castro
       Río Asneiro   Dozón

              Ourense

                     Reino   Oseira
                     Piñor
                              Cea
                                          N540
                     Biduedo

                   Tamallancos

                        Liñares
                                        A52
       Río Miño

                        OURENSE

                                    10km

Rúa do Paseo. Cross **Rúa Cardenal Quiroga Palacios** and **Rúa Capitán Eloy** then turn L down **Rúa Concello**. Cross **Rúa Papa Juan XXIII** and continue downhill, passing to RH side of a park, to **Praza Concepción Arenal**. Veer R to cross **Avenida de la Habana**, pass in front of the church and *colegio* of **Don Bosco** and cross the **Río Miño** by the **Ponte Vella**.

KSO on the **Avenida das Caldas** on the other side. *At the junction with the Avenida de Santiago a pilgrim stone once more indicates two possibilities, both of them waymarked, both of them equally urban to start with and both of them described here. Variant (A) goes via Quintela, Liñares and Mandrás and may be easier for cyclists. (B) is the one which turns R here to pass through Cudeiro and Viduedo (see 'Route B' below) but both meet up again at Casas Novas, 2km before Cea.*

Route A (via Quintela)

Continue ahead (L) up Avenida das Caldas to the railway station. KSO(L) there and follow the direction Vigo/Pontevedra (**Rúa Eulogio Gomez Franqueira**) for about 600m. When the main road veers off L (*bus station on other side of roundabout*) KSO on the now smaller Rúa Eulogio Gomez Franqueira until it bends round to R to pass under the railway line. KSO ahead there (stay to LH side of the railway line) and KSO on the N120 for 2km to

3km Quintela (889/102)

Bars, rte, fountain on R by public garden.

Fork R (marked 'Castro de Beira') opposite **Bodegas Arnoya** (*a wine factory*), just after road KM573. KSO on the road and 800m later KSO(L) at a fork, marked 'Costiña de Cañedo/Castro de Beira', downhill (*on the course of an old Roman road*). 300m later go under a railway bridge, narrow and longer than normal – *EXTREMELY carefully (and quickly), listening out for vehicles as well as watching as the road on the other side is used like a race track by cars coming downhill towards you, despite humps*. KSO uphill, continuously, for 1.5km to

3km Castro de Beira (892/99)

Cross the road at the top of the hill and KSO past a bar/rte (on L) and continue ahead on a *camino de tierra*. KSO for 2km, ignoring turns, till you come to a (tarred) minor road coming from R (*buildings to either*

Prophets in Pórtico del Paraíso, Cathedral of San Martín, Ourense

Ermita de Santiago, Casar de Cáceres

side). KSO ahead (**Carretera Cabeança Amoeiro**). *Eucalyptus trees (in bulk) begin here.* 300m later enter

1.5km Liñares (893.5/97.5)

No facilities. Main part of village over to L.

KSO on the road and KSO at a crossing (signposted 'Amoeiro') then 500m later fork R up a track, by a wall to start with, which then veers L to a minor road. Cross over and continue on a tarred lane ahead into

1.5km Reguengos (895/96)

No facilities here either.

Continue through the village and KSO at the end on a walled lane. Continue to the road (with a 'stop' sign) and KSO on the other side down a grassy lane. KSO straight ahead, ignoring turns, till you reach a minor road at a bend in it.

KSO(L) ahead on it for 1.5km then continue on a walled lane leading gradually downhill. Cross a grassy track and KSO on another (narrow) walled lane, widening out as you go. Then KSO till you reach the humpback bridge over the **Río Barbantiño** in

3.5km Ponte Mandrás (818.5/92.5)

Fountain, bar on road.

Cross the bridge and continue through the village, veering L to pass the fountain (on R) and then KSO(L) uphill ahead to a road. Turn R along it for 60m (*bar on R*) then KSO ahead on a walled lane (*which must have been the old 'main' road as it still has much of its original paving*). KSO at a crossing and KSO, ignoring turns to L and R till you reach

1.5km Pulledo (900/91)

KSO(L) along the road for 500m to a junction with a bigger minor road and then turn R. Continue on it to the N525 at

1km Casas Novas (901/90)

Bar O Campo (with sello), shops. Here Routes A and B join up. To continue, turn to '2km Casas Novas' p.164.

Route B

Continue up **Avenida Caldas** after crossing the **Ponte Vella** and then turn R up **Avenida Santiago**, uphill. 1.5km later, by a petrol station on R, turn R down a small tarred road, the **Camiño Real**, and 100m later fork R downhill, short-cutting a bend in the N525. *(Red and white balises of other waymarked routes are also to be found in this area, from the outskirts of Ourense.)* Cross it after a bend and continue up **Camiño Real de Cudeiro** on the other side and KSO at a bend up to the *plaza* in

2.5km Soutelo

Note pazo on R, with fine coat of arms.

Continue ahead, on **Camiño Real de Soutelo**, then veering L on **Camiño Real de Cudeiro Sur**, steeply uphill all the time. *Church of San Pedro, with small plaza, has a modern cruceiro with sculpture of Santiago Peregrino on its shaft (stick in RH, book in LH, scallops on lapels).*

Reach the road *(two bars)* and then KSO on the other side on **Camiño Real de Cudeiro Norte** then 100m later turn R onto the **Camiño de Costa** *(both parts paved)*, winding its way uphill *(cyclists get off and push!)*. *Modern ermita and cruceiro on top of hill to R.* Pass a *lavadero* and fountain and KSO.

1km Miña de Chaín

Picnic area, information boards, fountain with very clear water.

Continue ahead, still uphill, on a sandy track. *(Lane bends sharp R here to the hamlet of Pavadura, 300m away.)* Blue waymark signs from here onwards. KSO(L) ahead, ignoring turns, to a T-junction in **Sartédigos**. Turn L there onto a minor road and 100m before a 'stop' sign on the main road *(Convento de las Clarísas Reparadoras visible 350m ahead)* turn R onto a *camino de tierra* and then a walled lane. Return to the road for 50m (to skirt houses on your R) and then fork R onto another *camino de tierra*.

KSO(L) on a grassy walled lane 100m later *(RH fork leads to Fonte do Santo)*. KSO for 300m (ahead) then, after a tarmac section starts, turn L at a T-junction. Pass below a hill on R with huge rock formations (this is **Outeiros de Forca**). KSO at a junction, on a sandy lane (level for a change), with woods to either side.

1km later reach another local road (*another hamlet, bus shelter*), cross it and KSO ahead on a sandy lane. KSO downhill for 1.5km to the N525. Turn L and then 50m later fork R up a minor road. Continue to the village of

2.5km Tamallancos

Bank, bar, farmácia on main road.

Turn L to the N525 for a bar, otherwise KSO for 1km, ignoring turns, to

1km Bouzas

Park/bandstand, bar/tabacos, picnic area.

Continue to the N525, cross over and fork L down a *camino de tierra* past an electricity transformer and farm. 100m later turn R and then turn L, veering R downhill. 400m later KSO ahead on a grassy lane, passing to LH side of a *matadero* (*slaughterhouse*). KSO to and through the hamlet of **Sobreira**, veering L.

Continue downhill. When the road bends R KSO down a lane, cross a minor road and continue on the other side, taking RH of two fenced lanes below fields, downhill. 80m later cross an old paved stone bridge over **Río Barbantíno** (*note scrolls at each end*). KSO and 500m later reach

2km Faramontaos

Village that was formerly attached to the monastery at Oseira, with a pilgrim hospital.

KSO ahead uphill and when the road bends R KSO(L) ahead up a walled lane, more or less // to the N525 above you to your R. Emerge by a farm at **Ermida**. Cross a minor road and KSO ahead up another walled lane, uphill still, // to the N525. At the top of the hill the lane becomes asphalted, passing between houses. Join a road coming from back L and continue for 100m more into

Monastery of Oseira

2km Viduedo

Shop, bar.

Fork R past the church for the bar on the N525. Otherwise KSO(L) ahead (*fountain*) and turn L. Reach the N525, turn L, cross over (*ignore three yellows arrows painted on this road, pointing in reverse, backwards into the village*) and at road KM258 (150m later) fork R down a walled lane. Continue ahead alongside the road for a short distance then KSO(L) onto a lane, downhill. Cross a main road 200m later, KSO, join a lane coming from back R and KSO(R) at fork. Reach another minor road and KSO, gradually uphill (*shady*). At a T-junction turn L (lane may be very muddy), past a *lavadero*, cross a minor road and then turn R in the village to continue. (*Turn L to N525 for a bar, with* sello.)

2km Casas Novas

Cross the road (N525) and turn L into the older part of the village. Continue to the end and KSO(L) on a lane that continues (*old-style paving*) through woods.

KSO at a crossing. Pass a simple *cruceiro* where another track joins from back R and continue to the road.

Cross over, continue along **Rúa do Matadoiro**, passing to L of school buildings and turn L (still Rúa do Matadoiro). Turn L opposite house no. 9 for a *refugio* (42 places). Otherwise KSO ahead uphill to

2km Cea (903/88)

Bars, shops, refugio and several bakeries, as Cea is famous for its bread (Pan de Cea). Parish church in centre and Santuario de Nuestra Señora de la Saleta in field to north of village.

There are two routes out of Cea, (A) going to Castro Dozón via the Cistercian monastery at Oseira, and (B) going there directly ('por el monte'), both of them about the same length. Read the text that follows before you make up your mind, however, not so much for the routes as such but in terms of where you may want to sleep and the distances you want to cover in each of the three or four days remaining from here to Santiago. Cyclists: unless you want to visit the monastery you will find the direct route easier. For a description of Route B turn to 'Route B (LH route) direct to Castro Dozón' p.169.

Route A (RH route) via Oseira

Continue on **Rúa do Matadoiro** to a small square with *hórreo* in the middle. Turn R into **Rúa Bacelo** and continue up to **Praza Maior** (*bell-tower with fountains,* ayuntamiento).

With your back to the *ayuntamiento* continue R ahead up the street to RH side of the **Carniceria Segundo Ventura**, cross the road to Ourense and continue up **Rúa Lozairo** ahead (marked 'Campo de futbol' and 'Piscinas municipales') to the top of the hill. Turn R along a boundary fence and R again (*ignore yellow arrows pointing LEFT for Route A*) and then turn L at the end of the road. 100m later fork R onto a wide walled lane.

KSO, ignoring turns to R and L. (*Short section may be boggy but look for stone FP to LH side by wall.*) Plenty of shade. (*You will also see the yellow and white flashes of another walk – like the French-style* balises; *both sets indicate practically the same itinerary in this section but stick to the yellow ARROWS for security.*)

After 2–3km KSO(L) at a fork with a small pumphouse visible ahead (*similar to one you passed earlier on LH side of Camino*). KSO, ignoring turns to L or R, and about 1km later, at a crossing in open, rocky heathland, KSO ahead, following alongside a wall to L, towards woods ahead, where you will find a clear track (alongside a wall). 200m later reach a minor road. Turn L along it for 300m to the hamlet of

4.5km Silvaboa (907.5/83.5)

Fountain.

Fork L past the first houses and veer R uphill at the last (ruined) house, up an old, paved road, keeping to the wall on L. When the wall takes a sharp bend to L KSO for 100m more, straight ahead, and rejoin the road. Turn L uphill. 1km later reach a bigger minor road in

2km Pieles (909.5/81.5)

Fountain.

Turn R and KSO on the road and 500m later KSO(L) at a fork signposted 'Oseira'. Pass a church (*on L, dated 1789, big porch*) and cemetery and KSO on the road. Pass a monumental fountain on R, cross a bridge over **Río Oseira** and enter the village of

3km Oseira (912.5/78.5)

Bars, campsite by river.

Cistercian monastery built at different periods between twelfth and eighteenth centuries, a National Monument since 1923 and sometimes referred to the as 'Escorial of the North' due to its sumptuous reconstruction following a fire in 1552 which left only the church. Most of what is to be seen today (three cloisters, chapter house with curiously twisted columns, plateresque portals) comes from the transition between late Gothic and Renaissance style, often in an interesting mixture. Church contains Baroque altarpiece with carving of Santiago Peregrino by Gambini. Guided visits available.

Santiago on trumeau in Pórtico del Paraíso, Cathedral of San Martín, Ourense

Turn L up the main street. To visit the monastery turn L. To continue KSO(R) up a hill and then turn **hard R** at a fountain/*lavadero* up a steep hill, passing a wayside cross (on R). Veer R up the hill alongside a wall (to L), climbing all the time and keeping the wall to your L. Reach a minor road. KSO on the other side up a steep rocky lane. When it levels out a bit KSO(L) on a walled lane.

At the top another walled lane joins from back L. KSO, more or less on the level, for 300–400m more till you veer R to a minor road. Turn L downhill. Some 300m later, cyclists: KSO on road, walkers: look out for LH turn downhill (a short-cut) alongside a wall on R, leading back to the road in the hamlet of **Mirallos**. Turn L on the road, continue past a junction and 300m later turn R onto a second walled lane on R, downhill, veering to L and then R between walls. At a T-junction turn R onto a wider walled lane downhill, cross a bridge over a stream and turn **hard L**, uphill again, ignoring turns, till you reach a wide track at a crossing.

Continue ahead until you reach a minor road by a bus stop in the hamlet of **Vilarello**. Cross the road and continue down a tarred lane on the other side, turning R past an *hórreo* 60m later. Fork L between houses at a second *hórreo* then veer L and then R to the end of the village. *(Two more hórreos on R.)* KSO on lane.

Cross a bridge over a small river and follow a road round uphill (*village to R with church is Carballeidiña*). KSO at junction, KSO at RH one, veering L to the hamlet of

4.5km Outeiro (917-74)

Turn R uphill between houses and KSO(R) ahead up a walled lane. KSO up the valley, ignoring turns. 1km later, at the top, KSO(L) at a fork, after which the lane undulates. KSO(L) at a fork ignoring any turnings, and KSO till you reach a minor road in

2km Gouxa (919-72)

Bar (marked 'tabacos'). First village on the route in the province of Pontevedra. Note *galpón*, a long, low covered building with pillars, used to protect those attending the ferias (agricultural fairs) held here and elsewhere in the area; there are very few left now, apart from this one and another in Bouzas (on the RH route out of Ourense).

Turn L on the road then turn R in the middle of the village between houses, passing behind a bar on a lane leading to a minor road. Cross over and KSO down a walled lane (may be wet for a short section), veering L. KSO till you reach a minor road at a simple *cruceiro* then KSO(L) on it, ahead. 100m later fork R up a walled lane (just before a village on L with a tiny church) and then turn L at a junction of similar lanes 150m. Continue to the street in the hamlet of **Vidueiro**, turn R, fork R at a *lavadero*, turn L at the end and then R onto a walled lane by a building made of breeze blocks (*N525 visible – and audible – away to L now*) and KSO(R) at a fork.

KSOL(L), KSO(L) again, pass a *cruceiro* (R) and at a junction shortly afterwards KSO(L) at a fork, towards TV masts that you can see on the skyline and towards the N525, passing to RH side of a very long (and very smelly!) stable building.

Cross the N525, pass to a section of old road and turn R along it to avoid a dangerous bend. Then continue on LH side of the N525 for 1.25km to Castro Dozón. Pass **Casa de Concello** (on R) and cross to RH side by a public garden with a bandstand. (To continue, turn to '4km Castro Dozón (923/68)' p.170.)

Route B (LH route) direct to Castro Dozón

Continue out of the village (of Cea) on the road, passing **Santuario de Nuestra Señora de la Saleta** on your L, and continue on the road to the village of

2km Cotelas

Shop, bar, fountain.

KSO in the village when the road bends R and in 200m fork R down a small tarred road which becomes a *camino de tierra*, downhill all the time. 800m later join a road coming from back L, cross **Ponte Mirela** and 200m later, to short-cut a bend, take the SECOND LH turning up a steep grassy track and return to the road 500m later. KSO ahead, uphill, passing a fountain and *lavadero*, for 500m to

2km Piñor

Shop, bar, farmácia.

KSO through the village on the road, running straight on into **Albarrona** (fountain by a *lavadero*), uphill all the time. KSO for 1km more to

1.5km Arenteiro

Two bars. Capela da Nosa Senhora das Neves e Peregrina, a Baroque building restored in 1974.

KSO on the road passing the **Capela** on R (*covered sitting area, good place for a rest*) downhill for 1km to

1km Ponte

No facilities.

Cross a bridge over the river and continue uphill for 200m on the other side then, at a sharp bend, turn R up a grassy lane (short-cut for the bend) bringing you back to the road. Cross it and continue uphill on a concrete lane on the other side, veering R. Turn R, then L, pass to L of buildings and emerge on the road (N525) by a placename board for **O Reino**. Cross over and turn L (signposted 'Moire' and 'Capela da Milagrosa').

For the chapel: (*on hill, picnic area, good views*) KSO ahead for 100m then backtrack to continue.

To continue: after turning L off the road turn R IMMEDIATELY, passing to LH side of a house, cross a lane and KSO up a walled lane for 1km and reach the N525 again in

1.5km Carballeda

Igrexa da Santa María on R.

Turn L along the N525 then shortly after road KM270 turn L and immediately take RH of two forks on L, leading downhill. When the track starts to climb take the middle of three tracks ahead, up a walled lane with rocky heathland to either side, then veer R. When the wall stops veer L and then R to the top of the hill, veer R, join a track coming from back L and then turn L onto a minor road. KSO for 700m then, at LH bend, KSO ahead up a rough track uphill, to RH side of the road, veering R to become a clearer track as you proceed, then walled. Follow it as it undulates and KSO(L) at a fork, join a walled lane coming from back L then turn L at a junction. Veer L and then R uphill, through open heathland with occasional plantations of young trees. 1.5km later reach a T-junction at the top of a hill (*splendid views on a clear day*).

Turn R here and 400m later turn L and then immediately R. KSO at a crossing then KSO(L) at a fork. KSO. KSO(R) at a fork 800m later then KSO(L) shortly afterwards at the next fork. Continue downhill. Join a track coming from back L then a ROAD coming from back L, continue to the N525 and turn L along it in

4km Castro Dozón (923/68)

Two bars, two shops, farmácia. No accommodation. Twelfth-century church of San Pedro.

Fork R off the road by a square with a bandstand and pass to RH side of the church. KSO(L) uphill at a *cruceiro*. 300–400m later reach a junction at the side of the N525 (which is 80m away on your L).

Veer (do not TURN) L as if going to the main road but then, when you are 2–3m away from it, fork R onto a wide earth track above it (on its RH side). KSO(L) at a fork 150m later. Continue downhill towards the N525 (after this has done a bend), veering R, then turn R and then L 50m later onto a sunken lane. KSO(L) at a fork and continue close to, but out of sight of, the N525. Return to it at KM278 and cross over to continue on its LH side. 500m later, at a small junction at the top of the hill, cross back to RH side and continue on a section of old road, 'hide and seek' style, returning to the N525 just before the church of **Santo Domingo** (*note Oseira coat of arms above main door*) in

1km Santo Domingo (924/67)

Bar.

KSO on the road. 500m later, at a bend (just before KM280), fork L up an unpaved road. 800m later, when it levels out, fork L again down a *camino de tierra*. KSO into

5km Puxallos (929/62)

No facilities. Small ermita dedicated to San Roque on R.

KSO along the road on a ridge and at a crossing 200m later KSO downhill. KSO(L) at a junction 800m later, KSO(L) at the next one then at a crossing turn R downhill. *(This is a very nice section on a clear day, with good views.)*

When you come to a T-junction at the bottom, with a very minor road, turn L into

2km Pontenoufe (931/60)

No facilities.

Turn R in the village, downhill, to cross a bridge over a small river and at a junction by a tunnel turn R on an earth road, veering R. 200m later turn **hard L** up a hollow concrete lane, winding its way uphill. KSO(L) at a fork and emerge on a minor road near the top of a hill.

Turn R uphill // to a bigger road below L. Fork R then KSO(L) ahead and turn L at a church and continue to the road in

2km Xestas (933/58)

Bar on road.

Cross over and KSO ahead down a lane through the village. Turn R by house no. 60 and KSO, ignoring turns till you reach a very minor road coming from R. KSO(L) along it and at a junction with signposting ('Medelos, Botos') KSO ahead on a minor road: *magnificent chestnut trees.*

KSO, ignoring turns, till you reach a road in

2.5km Botos de Abaixo (935.5/55.5)

Turn L and L again for FF.CC Mouriscade (this is Lalín railway station). Bar/rte and shop. Lalín (all facilities) is 4km away (uphill) on road to R if you want to sleep there (its hostales and fondas are nearly all in the centre of town).

To continue: turn L on the road (*bar on L*) and 80m later turn R downhill on a small road, cross the river and KSO uphill, forking L at a *lavadero*. KSO uphill again, KSO(R) at a fork and continue to

0.5km Botos de Arriba (936/55)

KSO past a *cruceiro (double-sided)* in the square and continue on the road. KSO(R) at a fork and KSO, ignoring turns, till you come to a T-junction with a less minor road. Cross over and continue down LH side of two grassy lanes, becoming walled. KSO for 1km ignoring turns till you reach a very minor road. Cross over and KSO. 200m later reach a bigger minor road and turn R. Continue on the road into the village of

6km Donsión (942/49)

Elaborate cruceiro with figures on base and shaft as well. Fountain.

Follow the road round to R past a fountain and a Baroque church, very large for the size of the village. Continue ahead. Fork L (signposted 'Campo' and 'Fondevila') and fork R at the next junction. Continue ahead on a stony lane leading downhill through woods. KSO(R) at a fork and KSO.

Take either fork at a junction (they meet up), turn R at a T-junction and turn L to cross a bridge over the river. KSO(L) ahead on the other side for 600m, ignoring turns, and reach the N525 just before road KM295.

Cross over and KSO on a lane between banks to

1.5km A Laxe (943.5-47.5)

Fountain.

Cross a very minor road and continue ahead, crossing the river by a *lavadero* and then fork L, veering R uphill (the main road is very close by now). Continue ahead behind houses and return to the road opposite house no. 7.

Cross over to LH side and 150m later, by a bar, either (*both options waymarked*):

a) KSO on the road (*option b rejoins it later*), or

b) fork L down a lane signposted 'Campo'. KSO, pass a *lavadero* (L) and continue down a grassy lane, veering L (you are // to the main road by now). Cross a track and KSO up a small lane alongside a hedge on L, widening out. KSO, ignoring turns, pass a high stone wall (on R) and a factory (on L) and reach a minor road at a T-junction. Cross over and continue along a minor road ahead, // to the N525 (only 60–70m away). Cross a minor road, continue behind buildings and return to the N525 in

1.5km Prado (945/46)

Bar, shops.

Continue ahead on the road (pavement) then 500m later, by a building with a bell-tower on top, turn L down a lane (*100m before Bar/Rte 'O Afilador' which also has rooms*) and then turn R, continuing ahead on a walled lane, // to the main road some 200m away. Cross a minor road, KSO and when you reach a second minor road 1.5km later, turn R to reach a section of the OLD N525 in

2km Boralla (947/44)

KSO along it, ignoring turns, for 1km till it veers R to cross the nineteenth-century bridge over the **Río Deza**. *Cyclists: KSO here to rejoin the N525.*

Fork L down a grassy lane (boggy in wet weather) downhill, passing under a railway viaduct (*the Río Deza is in a gorge below to R by now*). 200m later cross the

1.5km Ponte Taboada (948.5/42.5)

Tenth-century bridge over the Río Deza, in very good condition, with original medieval paved surface dating from AD 912, high above the river for a bridge of this type.

Continue on a paved FP on the other side, leading up to the street in

0.5km Taboada (949/42)

Turn R and KSO(R) uphill (*note REAL scallop shells accompanying waymarks in this area*). At the top, by houses, turn L and at a T-junction (*N525 ahead across fields*) turn L at another minor road. 300–400m later reach a T-junction (*note engravings on wall on R*) and continue ahead up a lane, // to the main road but at a distance. At the top turn R up a gravel track, R again and then L on a section of old road, returning to the N525 opposite the Romanesque parish church of **Santiago**, *with a painting of Santiago Matamoros in Baroque altarpiece inside and a modern statue of Santiago Peregrino in a corner of the paved sitting area outside.*

Turn L past a picnic/recreation area and continue on the N525 for 2.5km more (keep on LH side, a slip road, when the main road goes under a bridge) into

2.5km Silleda (951.5/39.5)

Small town with all facilities. Hotel/Rte Ramos (Calle San Isidoro, tel: 986.58.12.12), Café-Bar Toxa (on main road, tel: 986.58.01.11) and Bar Fernandez (Calle San Isidoro) all have rooms.

Continue through the town on the main road and turn L down the second street after the *ayuntamiento* (**Rúa Escuadro Toriz**, signposted 'Escuadro' and 'Somoza') and turn R into a lane behind an industrial building. (*Here, as elsewhere, the Camino is simply playing 'hide and seek' with the N525, to avoid walking on the main road.*) Return to it after 500m, go down a tarred lane for 150m and return to the road again, then turn L down a walled lane just before KM304. KSO along this, ignoring turns, to a road fork. Here you can either:

a) KSO ahead here on the old route, much quieter, continuing ahead on a track to RH side of a substantial house, following a wall through woods till you reach a minor road, near a factory, where you turn L; or

b) fork R uphill to a section of the OLD N525 by the *báscula pública* then turn L down a minor road opposite the **Centro Funerario** past a large factory (now on your R).

Continue down this minor road through the hamlet of **Margaride**. At the end, opposite a football field, fork R down a lane then turn L immediately onto a track through woods. KSO at a crossing, KSO(L) at a fork and KSO(R) till you reach a minor road. Turn L and immediately R through woods again. KSO(R) at a fork, veering L. Turn L down a *camino de tierra* by a depot for 'pensioned-off' buses, pass behind a factory and KSO, ignoring turns. Cross a bridge over the river and turn L at a T-junction on the other side, turning R 80m later on a minor road returning you to the N525.

Cross over and KSO ahead on a minor road, ignoring turns, for 1km. At a junction by a farm on R (AFTER the crossing with a bus shelter) fork (but do not TURN) R along a minor road 200m later, then R downhill, fork L uphill and at the top KSO(R) to the main road. Turn L up it into

6km Bandeira (957.5/33.5)

Small town with all facilities which originally had a Hospital de Peregrinos. Hostal/Rte Conder Rey (tel: 986.58.53.53), Hostal/Rte O Portón, Casa Cuiña (a fonda) on main road and Hotel Vitoriño (tel: 986.58.53.30) all have rooms.

KSO on the main street and at the end turn R down a minor road signposted 'Dornelas/Piñeiro/Cira', leading downhill to a bridge over the river. KSO(L) ahead on the other side. Turn R at a junction then L shortly afterwards, veering R. KSO(R) twice and continue on a minor road with houses at intervals. Cross three minor roads and then, at a farm, where the tarmac stops and a lane veers R, KSO(L) ahead to R of buildings, continuing straight ahead downhill. Pass to RH side of some vines where a lane veers L, down a gravel lane through woods down to a minor road. Turn L, KSO(L) at a fork. Turn R 400m later at a T-junction with a minor road.

KSO and turn L onto the road into the village of

4km Dornelas (961.5/29.5)

Fountain. Romanesque church with rounded apse (typical of many in this area).

KSO past the church, KSO(L) at the first T-junction and KSO(R) at the second onto a bigger minor road. KSO(L) twice (at two T-junctions) and KSO on a minor road. Turn L at the next junction then 50m before you reach the N525 turn R down a shady lane through woods.

From here you can make a detour to visit the Pazo de Oca, one of the largest and most palatial manor houses in Galicia, with its own

chapel, lakes and landscaped gardens; continue up to the N525 and turn R onto it at KM315, continue along it for 2km and turn L beside Hostal América onto a minor road into a thickly wooded valley with the Pazo de Oca at the bottom.

Otherwise: KSO(L) at a fork and KSO(R) at the next fork, uphill. *(N525 over to L all the time, audible as well as visible.)*   Turn R at a T-junction then turn L at the next junction and KSO(L) at the next. KSO at a crossing. Reach a road by a very long farm building (*view of Pico Sacro from here*) and KSO(R) along the road to a junction opposite a sawmill

4.5km Carballeida (966/25)

A lot of very large blue as well as white (wild) hydrangeas in this area.

KSO down the road opposite (signposted 'Castro') and KSO to

1km Seixo (967/24)

Bar/shop.

KSO through the village and turn R on a road ahead, downhill for 500m, then fork L, veering R down to a crossing and turn L (down a very minor road). Continue steadily downhill, ignoring turns till you reach (on your R) the

2km Santuario de Gundián (969/22)

Fountain. Small chapel in a park with a pavilion and sitting/picnic area; good (shady) place for a rest.

To continue: turn L on the road (when coming from above) or from the Santuario KSO ahead out of the site and continue downhill on a minor road, ignoring turns, for 1.5km till you reach the old bridge over the **Río Ulla**.

This river forms the boundary between the provinces of Pontevedra and La Coruña (which you are now entering). There are several impressive pazos in this area, which is also reputed for its good-quality aguardiente (a type of brandy).

1.5km Ponte Ulla (970.5/20.5)

Bars, shops, rte. Bar Flamingo has rooms.

Turn R and cross a bridge and then turn L towards a viaduct but before it turn R up a newly-paved walkway then fork L to the side of a substantial house up an old paved road under pergolas of vines. *(Notice in* gallego *– which you should heed as well as read – says 'Ollo con os cans' – 'Beware of the dogs'.)* Turn L at the top under an old wooden footbridge. *(The building to your L is the Pazo de Vista Alegre.)*

KSO(L) on a lane coming from R for 150m to the N525 just below KM322.

Cross over and continue on LH side for 500m then fork L on a short section of old road. Pass behind a bar/rte, continue on a short *camino de tierra* to **Talleres Rendo** *(car repairs)* and cross the N5252 and turn **hard R** on the other side. Turn L under the railway line and L again on the other side up a forest road.

Turn L and then immediately R at the top of a hill, then turn R again up a forest road, veering L, and then turn L uphill. KSO, ignore LH turn, KSO at a crossing and KSO(L) at RH junction. When the road comes to an end shortly afterwards KSO ahead on a track. KSO at a crossing and continue through woods. At the end of another gravelled road KSO(R) ahead on a track through woods. After 500m (from the first road) reach a minor road and turn L to the

4.5km Capilla de Santiaguiño (975/16)

Chapel dedicated to Santiago, built in 1696 and restored in 2000. Fountain with statue of Santiago Peregrino in niche above it. (NB: VERY aggressive small dog in house opposite at time of writing.)

Pass to RH side of the chapel and KSO on a gravel lane through woods, more or less level, then rising gradually for 2km, ignoring turnings. Pass a large modern house and reach a T-junction with a minor road. *Here the Pico Sacro (550m) is some 500m away from you, clearly visible ahead, with the ninth-century Ermita de San Sebastián just below the top; turn R to visit and then retrace your steps. This is the place where, according to legend, the bad Reina Lupa (Wolf Queen) lived and who intentionally misled the two disciples seeking a final resting place for the body of St James, sending them to a place she knew to be full of wild bulls that she hoped would kill them all. Instead, however, these animals all calmed down miraculously when the disciples arrived and let them pass unhindered and, as a result, so the story goes, the queen was converted to Christianity.*

Fountain with Santiago sculpture, next to Capilla de Santiaguiño

Turn L and continue to a crossroads with a TV mast. KSO and 100m later, by a *cruceiro*, turn R by a more minor road. KSO at a crossing (church over to L) and at the next crossing (this is Ardois/Lestedo) there is a choice of waymarks (ahead or L) though they meet up again before the railway.

KSO ahead, ignoring turns till you pass under a railway line. Turn R along a gravel lane on the other side. 150m later, when this bends R, KSO ahead on a track. Cross the end of a gravel road and KSO, through woods (the N525 is quite close, over to L, by now). KSO at a crossing, after which the track narrows and veers L down to the main road.

Cross over to a section of old road and fork L down a *camino de tierra* // to the road. Cross a humpback bridge over the river (*another aggressive dog at house on the other side*) and KSO ahead. Cross a road and KSO behind a mineral-water factory, returning to the road by a sawmill just before the entrance to

7.5km Susana (982/8.5)

Bars, supermarket, farmácia. City buses into Santiago.

Continue on LH side of the N525 then fork L onto a minor road (signposted 'Marrozos') at the side of the petrol station. KSO(R) at the first junction, turn L at the second and KSO(R) down a lane under pergolas of vines at the third. Reach a minor road, cross it, go through a tunnel under the N525 and KSO ahead on the other side. KSO(L) on a very minor road downhill, cross a bridge over a small river, turn L at a T-junction and then turn R up a bigger minor road uphill. 200m later, by house no. 46, turn L up a gravel lane, turn L on a minor road at the top and 100m later turn L to cross a bridge over the railway. *(This area is the Lugar da Cañoteira de Marrozos.)* Turn L at the end then 200m later, in a dip, turn L again, veering R uphill.

KSO, ignoring turns, to a T-junction and turn R (*cruceiro* on R) by a fountain/*lavadero* in **Aldrei**. Turn L at a T-junction, go under the railway again (**Rúa do Carballade de Aldrei**) and turn R on the other side (this *lugar* is **Vixoi**). Turn L down an unpaved road, KSO ahead at a crossing, turn R 150m later and then L downhill, leading to

4.5km Capilla de Santa Lucia (987/4)

Small church dating from 1829. Seats, trees, good place for a (final) rest.

Turn R in front of the church and continue on the walkway *(cyclists stay on road, turning R)*. Cross a road bridge, KSO on the road then KSO ahead on the middle of three lanes (more pergolas). KSO ahead at a crossing by a *cruceiro*, cross a minor road by an electricity transformer and continue ahead on a *camino de tierra*, ignoring turns. Pass under the motorway and continue ahead, on a very minor road between fields. KSO(R) over the railway again and continue on **Rúa Camiño Real de Angrois** *(bar on L)*. KSO to the end of this (very long) street to a crossroads at the **Cruceiro do Sar** (with *cruceiro*). *Bar and bar/shop on R.*

Cross the road (**Rúa do Sardiño**) and KSO(R) ahead down a cobbled lane (**Calzada do Sar**), with a first view of Santiago Cathedral. At a junction at the bottom KSO(R) along **Rúa da Fonte do Sar**, entering the Sar district of Santiago *(bars, shops)*.

Cross a bridge over **Río Sar** and turn L (**Campo do Sar**) to visit the church and cloisters of

3km Colexiata de Santa María do Sar (990/1)

Twelfth-century Romanesque collegiate church with inclined internal pillars and very fine cloisters, part of a monastery originally founded in 1136.

Continue ahead (**Calle do Sar**), pass under the railway line and continue uphill via *the Rúa do Sar de Afora*, **Rúa Castron Douro**, **Patio de Madres**, **Rúa da Virxe da Cerca** and the **Porta de Mazarelos**, the only surviving entry gate of the seven the city originally had. Continue along the **Praza da Universidade**, **Calle Caldería**, **Costa de Xelmírez** and the **Praza de Praterías** to the cathedral in

1km Santiago de Compostela 264m, pop. 80,000 (991/0)

All facilities, RENFE, buses to Madrid, Barcelona, Seville and many other parts of Spain. Plenty of accommodation and in all price ranges. Two campsites: one on the main road to La Coruña, the other at As Cancelas (on outskirts). There are many places to eat in Santiago but for somewhere cheap, filling and with plenty of choice go to the Café-Rte Casa Manolo, now in the Plaza Cervantes. Tourist office: 43 Rúa do Vilar (near cathedral).

The most important of the many places of interest in Santiago (all in the old town) is the cathedral, part Romanesque, part Baroque, with its magnificent Portico de la Gloria and façade giving onto the Plaza del Obradoiro. Raised up behind the main altar is the seated statue of St James the apostle to whom it is customary to give the traditional abrazo (hug) when visiting the cathedral for the first time (and which people you encountered along the Camino may have asked you to do on their behalf). The cathedral also houses what is probably the world's biggest censer (incense burner), the famous 'Botafumeiro'. It is made of silver and weighs nearly 80kg, requiring a team of eight men and a system of pulleys to set it in motion after mass, swinging at ceiling level from one end of the transept to the other. Guidebooks (in English) are available from the bookshops in the Rúa do Vilar (near the cathedral) or in the new town (such as Follas Novas, Calle Montero Ríos 37). There are also many interesting churches, the Museo de las Peregrinaciones, the Museo do Pobo Galego as well as many large-scale temporary exhibitions. Try to spend two or three days in Santiago as there is much to see and do.

If you have time two pilgrim destinations outside the city are worth visiting. Padrón is the place where the boat bringing St James to Galicia in AD 44 is believed to have arrived and also contains the museum of Rosalía de Castro, the nineteenth-century Galician poet; it can be reached easily by bus (some 20km) from Santiago bus station. Finisterre, the end of the known world in former times and the end of the route for many pilgrims in centuries gone by, can also be reached by bus (95km) from Santiago bus station. If you prefer, however, you can continue there on foot, a three-day journey (for walkers only) described in Appendix A.

Santiago Peregrino arrives in Compostela… (author)

APPENDIX A

SANTIAGO TO FINISTERRE

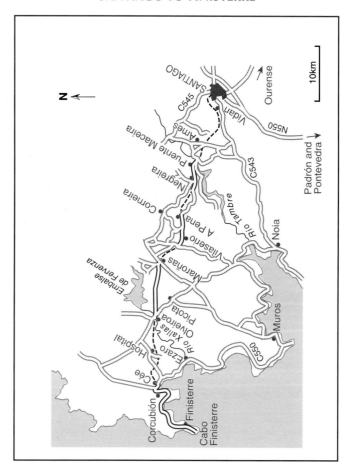

Finisterre ('Fisterra' in Galician) was the end of the known world until Columbus altered things, and was the final destination of many of the pilgrims who made the journey to Santiago in centuries gone by. There are various explanations as to how this continuation came about (one such is that it was based on a pre-Christian route to the pagan temple of Ara Solis in Finisterre, erected to honour the sun) but it is also known that a pilgrim infrastructure existed, with 'hospitals' in Cée, Corcubión, Finisterre itself and elsewhere. There are also several pilgrim references along the way: a *cruceiro* with a figure of Santiago in Trasmonte, the church of Santiago in Olveiroa with a statue of St James, a probable pilgrim *hospital* in the place of that name (apart from those already mentioned in Cée and Corcubión), the church of Santiago at Ameixenda 2km south of Cée with a relic reputed to be of one of St James's fingers, a large statue of San Roque in pilgrim gear in the church of San Marcos in Corcubión, a statue of St James in the church of Santa María das Areas in Finisterre with a cemetery chapel that formerly belonged to its pilgrim hospital, and two references to San Roque in placenames: the *encrucijada* or *alto de San Roque* at the top of the hill leaving Corcubión and the San Roque area at the entrance to Finisterre. And after pilgrim accounts of their journeys along the Camino francés, the route that those in the past most frequently wrote about was the continuation to Finisterre-Muxía. These accounts came from various European countries and were in several different languages, including the seventeenth-century Italian Domenico Laffi, four times a pilgrim to Santiago, who describes his visit to the church of Santa María das Areas 2km before the 'end of the earth' itself.

It is still possible to walk there avoiding main roads but, although numbers have increased quite a lot in the last few years, at present only a very small percentage of those who make the pilgrimage to Santiago continue on to Finisterre. This has no doubt been in part due to lack of information and route-finding difficulties but now that the entire route has been re-waymarked those who feel their journey would be incomplete without continuing to the 'end' will find it much easier to do so. Pilgrims in past centuries also continued to the Santuario de Nuestra Señora de la Barca in Muxía, 22km further up the Atlantic coast, to the north of Finisterre. This route has been waymarked recently but is not described here. Anyone interested in walking this continuation will find a short guide to it (in Spanish) in a supplement (no. 47) to the February 1996 issue of *Peregrino* magazine and in the Xunta de Galicia's booklet *Camino de Santiago en Galicia: Camino de Fisterra-Muxía,* available from their Oficina del Camino in the Avenida de Coruña (near the Santa Susanna park).

You may have to be more alert to route-finding than you probably needed to be on the Vía de la Plata but continuing to the coast on foot is definitely worth the effort. Finisterre is the real end of the journey, both in the physical sense and the religious and historical one. You will pass a number of interesting small churches, *pazos* (large Galician country houses) and old bridges along the way, apart from the now familiar *hórreos,* and the scenery is often beautiful. It is very peaceful and, as there are still relatively few walkers, the route is quite different from the often *autopista*-like Camino francés before Santiago in July and August, though the area is more densely populated than many along the Vía de la Plata. It does rain a lot in this part of Spain and it is often misty in the mornings but, if you 'turned left' in Astorga rather than continuing on via Puebla de Sanabria and Ourense, you will have the opportunity to see something of the real Galicia, away from the big towns.

Cathedral, Santiago de Compostela (author)

Allow *three days* to walk to Finisterre, with possible overnight stops in Negreira and Olveiroa, where a new *refugio* has is now open. The actual walking is not hard but there are a lot of climbs and descents. The route is waymarked with the familiar yellow arrows and they lead you from the first one, by the Carballeira de San Lourenzo in Santiago, all the way to the town of Finisterre. Watch out carefully, however, as in the past the route to Finisterre was waymarked in BOTH directions (there and back as well). The route is also marked with concrete bollards with both the blue and yellow stylised ceramic star familiar from parts of other Caminos (and whose rays indicate the direction you should take). Some of them also indicate the distance remaining to Finisterre while others give the number of kilometres left to reach Muxía.

Some maps are available in Santiago bookshops, such as the 1:250,000 map of Galicia (published by the Xunta de Galicia) and the relevant sheets (*hojas*) of the IGN's 1:25,000 series of the Mapa Topográfico Nacional de España: 94-IV (Santiago), 94-III (Negreira), 94-I (A Baña), 93-II (Mazaricos), 93-I (Brens), 92-II (Corcubión) and 92-IV (Fisterra). For the Finisterre-Muxía section you will need 67-IV (Touriñan) and 67-II (Muxía) (*hojas* 93-1, 93-2 and 92-2).

Accommodation is readily available in Negreira, Cée, Corcubión and Finisterre itself but there is a long gap (approximately 50km) between Negreira and Cée, though a *refugio* is now open in Olveiroa too, as well as the brand new one in the centre of Finisterre.

Food: you will pass some shops and bars along the way but it is better to take at least some reserve supplies with you.

Fisterrana: this is a certificate of pilgrimage given by the Concello (town hall) in Finisterre to those who have completed the route and have had their *credenciales* (pilgrim passports) (from the route they walked prior to Santiago) stamped at intervals along the way. You can make enquiries about this in the *refugio* in Finisterre.

THE ROUTE

From the **Praza do Obradoiro** in Santiago and with your back to the cathedral, pass in front of the **Hostal de la Reyes Católicos** (on your R), down the slope in front of its garage (*this is the Costa do Cristo*), go down some steps and along the **Calle de las Huertas** ahead. Veer R at the end into **Campo de las Huertas**, continue ahead down **Calle del Cruceiro del Gayo** (the first of two streets in front of you) and then along the **Rúa da Poza de Bar** (unnamed at the start); this then becomes the **Calle de San Lorenzo**.

At the **Carballeira de San Lourenzo** (*a small, shady park with seats, a fountain and a lot of old oak trees*) there is the first yellow arrow. Here you can either:

a) KSO ahead to visit the (former Franciscan monastery) church of **San Lourenzo de Trasouto** (*normal visiting hours Tuesdays and Thursdays 11am to 1pm, 4.30 to 6.30pm, otherwise open at mass times*) then retrace your steps, crossing **Carballeira** diagonally alongside the monastery wall and veering L to pick up the Camino ahead, or

b) turn R immediately (coming from the cathedral) down the **Roblada de San Lourenzo** (signposted 'Sanatorio'). Shortly afterwards veer L down a cement road (**Corredoira dos Muiños**) leading you downhill to cross a bridge over **Río Sarela** in the hamlet of

1km Ponte Sarela

The first house by the bridge has a sign 'Parroquia de San Fructuoso, Lugar de Puente Sarela' (the old buildings by the bridge were tanneries and the mills used to power them). From here for the next 7km to Ventosa, in order to avoid the main road, the route is extremely fiddly, with constant changes of direction.

Turn L on other side of the bridge, fork L at the bottom of two lanes, gently uphill, and cross the stream by small stone footbridge and stepping stones. KSO(L) at a fork shortly afterwards and KSO at a crossing and continue on a grassy track uphill through meadow. KSO(R) up a FP between hedges (passing to RH side of an electricity pylon) and join one wider track coming from R then two more, veering L to reach a minor road (*2km after Ponte Sarela*). Turn L downhill and 300m later on turn R onto a tarred lane uphill, which continues as a walled lane. KSO(L) at a fork. At another junction 400m later, despite OLD arrows to L, turn RIGHT here. KSO(L) at a fork and KSO(R) at the next.

KSO(R) on a track coming from back L, KSO(R) at a fork then turn L downhill at a staggered crossing (*all this section is through eucalyptus woods*) and then turn L at a crossing at the bottom 250m later. Turn R onto a minor road 60m later and L 80m later at a junction. KSO(R) at a turn, turn L at a junction 100m later, KSO(L) on an unpaved road 100m after that then turn L onto an earth track. Veer R to a minor road and turn L downhill to a road junction by a bus shelter and long *hórreo* in

2km Pineiro

Turn R. Fork L at a fork in the hamlet, veering R then L down an earth road, following it round to L. Just before you reach a minor road turn R on a smaller road uphill which becomes a lane. Turn L 300m later then immediately fork R into woods (*1.5km after Piñeiro*). KSO, ignoring turns and climbing gradually. At a T-junction on a level turn L. Reach a minor road and turn R then turn L onto a track 200m later, passing a yellow gas post with '102' on top. After this the track becomes a FP for a while, straight ahead downhill, then you join a wider track coming from L and forking R ahead downhill again to a road. KSO along it.

At a junction turn L and immediately R by a bus shelter and *cruceiro* down a lane, turn L and L again at the bottom to a T-junction with a sports centre on L. Turn R along the road and cross

3.5km Bridge over Río Roxos

Picnic area on other side.

Fork L uphill. Turn R at a fork (road becomes an earth track) and then turn R into woods, veering L and then R and turning L at a T-junction in **Portela**. After 150m reach a road at the entrance (on L) to **Roxos** (*this is the Alto do Vento*) and boundary of Concello de Ames (that is, turn L to Santiago). *Bar*/mesón *opposite*. Turn R downhill into

1.5km Ventosa

Turn R by a bus shelter and KSO, veering L downhill on an old road. Cross the road again (by another bus shelter) and KSO on the other side under pergolas. Pass between buildings, turn R and then turn R again in front of a huge electricity pylon. Turn L onto a very minor road then immediately L on a bigger one, then 100m later at a junction (*shop on L*) KSO ahead down into

2km Augapesada

Mesón on R. Medieval bridge (recently restored), picnic area.

Continue downhill to a junction. Turn L (signposted 'Bertamirans 3') then turn R up a small concrete road uphill (*bar 50m further on, on L after turn*) which becomes a forest track. KSO at a crossing (*two handy seats on R*), continuously uphill.

When you reach a minor road (to L) turn R (*a third seat on R shortly afterwards*). KSO, passing a fourth seat and fifth (on L) just before the road (on L). Turn R here and continue on a track uphill. Return to the road by a sixth seat and TV mast and turn R uphill along it. Pass a second TV mast and 200m later on R (by a sign 'Trasmonte-Santa María') pass a fountain. 200m later begin to go downhill and enter

2km Carballo

Continue on the road, passing a wayside cross on a wall (R) and KSO at a junction in

1km Trasmonte

Baroque church of Santa María and cruceiro (with figure of Santiago) to L. Bar/shop.

Continue on the road, passing through **Reino** and **Burgeiros**. KSO on the road, turn L at a junction and reach

2km Ponte Maceira

Bar/rte. Picturesque village in two parts with stone bridge (five main arches) over the Río Tambre, constructed late fifteenth/early sixteenth centuries and restored in medieval style in the eighteenth. Chapel of San Blas and large neo-medieval pazo on other side of bridge and several stone houses with armorial devices. (Romanesque church of Santa María de Portor 1km to north – tower visible from here.)

Turn R over a bridge, turn L uphill at the end and 200m later fork L downhill and then turn L down a minor road, // to the river, veering R.

Continue on a track straight ahead, past fields and through woods, then under the arch of a nineteenth-century bridge (**Ponte Maceira Nova**, *bar on other side*) and along the riverside, then alongside a road (below it to L). Return to the road (after 1km) by a car dealer in

2km Barca

KSO on the road for 600m, then fork L (signposted 'Logrosa') past some industrial buildings, uphill, ignoring turns to R or L. KSO(L) ahead to

1.5km Chancela

Pass the entrance gates (L) to the large **Pazo de Chancela** (*also known as Pazo de Capitán – watch out for VERY large, loose dogs here*) and KSO ahead, ignoring turns, following the road down to a 'stop' sign. Turn L, pass the large statue of a pilgrim (L) then pass a second statue (*of Minerva and the bulls*) and a fountain, veering R uphill (**Avenida de Santiago**).

1.5km Negreira

Small town with all facilities. A *refugio* is now open in the town centre here. Hostal Mezquito (Rúa do Carmen 2, in centre) has rooms.

Turn L (signposted 'Campo de Feria') down the **Carreira de San Mauro** and continue to the bottom, passing under an archway linking the **Capilla del Carmen y Santa María** on R and the **Pazo de Cotón** (*a medieval fortress restored in the seventeenth century*) on L. (*Modern statue on R is of the* emigrante/segadora *figure, with a boy pulling at his father's trousers through a window and mother and child seated.*)

Cross a bridge over **Río Barcala** and at a fork turn L uphill and 200m later, at the next fork, bear R, marked 'Negreira-Iglesia', then turn R at a *cruceiro* to the eighteenth-century church of **San Xulián**. Turn L up some steps and R along a lane, continuing straight ahead onto a tarred lane, on the level. When this bends hard R downhill KSO(L) ahead on RH of two // grassy lanes on L, still on the level, then climbing gently, through eucalyptus woods, with the road away to R below. Pass a concrete (public services) building on R and KSO, reaching the road (CP56031) 200m later. KSO on the road (uphill) for 500m, passing a turning to **Cobas** (R) and turn R opposite a shop and bus shelter in

2km Zas/Xas

KSO along the lane, passing small *ermita* (R), KSO(R) at a fork, KSO(L) at the next fork and 100m later KSO(R) again. After the last house turn L on LH of two grassy walled lanes.

KSO(L) at a junction and KSO when a track joins from back L. KSO(R) at a fork, then KSO(L) immediately afterwards on a track coming from back L; KSO, then 200m later turn L. Reach a main road 100m from the road (L) in **Camiño real** (*bar on road*) and turn R along an earth lane. 300m later turn L down a walled lane. At a junction 300m later KSO ahead then KSO(L) at the next. Cross a minor road 150m later and continue ahead on the other side on what looks like a FP but is, in fact, a walled lane. *(This is a very old, historic route, completely overgrown and impassable till the late 1990s, becoming wider as you proceed, // to the 'main' road all the time.)* Cross another very minor road and KSO ahead, in a straight line all the time.

KSO when a track joins from back L, veering R and almost immediately turn L, again in a straight line ahead, // to the road. Turn L at a crossing 150m later. KSO(R) ahead when a track joins from back L, becoming a walled lane leading downhill. KSO(L) ahead when a track joins from back R and continue to a very minor road in

4.5km Rapote

Cross over and continue on a concrete lane ahead, turn L and then R through the village to continue ahead at the end down a sunken walled lane downhill, ignoring turns, till you reach the bottom. Turn R then KSO(L) uphill on a walled lane, ignoring turns till you reach a minor road in

2km Peña/A Pena

Bar on road (turn L, R and L by first house; simple meals).

Otherwise (to continue) continue ahead, KSO(R) ahead below a church and turn L at a *cruceiro* uphill then turn L again to the road and turn R. KSO (this is **Porto Camiño**, a pass) for 400m on the road then just after a turning to **Xallas** (on L) turn R onto a track and then immediately L ahead (on the third from L of the four tracks in front of you) by a concrete water tank. KSO(L) at a fork and continue downhill, ignoring turns. Cross a stream, veer R and then L uphill again and at a T-junction turn L. Return to the road and turn R. 2km later, just before a sharp LH bend, turn L down a walled lane into

4.5km Vilaserio

Bar on R.

Fork (not turn) R downhill behind the bar and turn L on the road. Pass a turning (L) to **Pesadoira** and KSO on the road, veering L up to a crossroads and turn R into

2km Cornado

Turn L in the village then 150m later fork L uphill on an earth road. At a fork KSO(L) ahead till you reach a road (CP5604 KM18). KSO for 300m then turn L down a lane. KSO, ignoring turns, gently uphill.

At the top (marker stone 50,266) KSO ahead, gradually downhill, then 150m later fork L at a fork uphill. At a T-junction 250m after that turn R and fork L at a fork after another 250m. *(Shell and 'Maroñas' on one side of marker stone, 'Neria' and shell on other.)* KSO at a crossing, KSO at the next, cross a bridge over the river and enter

4km Maroñas

Shop on road, bar.

Turn L in the centre of the village, following the road round and turn L at the end, continuing on the lane to a T-junction, then turn L at a *cruceiro* in the centre of

1km Santa Mariña

Twelfth-century Romanesque church.

Continue to L and turn R along a lane to the 'main' road. Turn L and continue on the road for 500m (*two bars on R: first one is Casa Vitoriano, simple meals)* then turn R uphill (signposted 'Bon Xesús and Guiema'). Continue on the road for 3km to two scarcely separated hamlets and turn L in the first one (**Bon Xesús**). KSO uphill into the second (**Vilar de Xastro**, with simple *cruceiro* on LH side of road) and turn R when you get there, veering L, then fork L up a track along RH shoulder of **Monte Aro** (555m), climbing steadily (*good views as you go on a clear day*). KSO at a crossing 100m later, veering L (*views out over* embalse *when track levels out*) and veering R, to a junction 500m after that. Turn R then 100m later turn L, downhill, on an unpaved road. Continue downhill. Partway down turn **hard** L. Veer R at the bottom into

2km Lago

Turn L and continue out of the village on a very minor road. 300m later turn L at a T-junction.

Continue on the road for 400m and turn R downhill by a bus shelter. KSO(R) at a junction then KSO(L) ahead at a fork. *(Sudden view of line of 20–30 modern windmills on the horizon ahead.)* 700m later turn R then 250m later turn L. KSO on the road till you reach the small church of

3km San Cristovo de Corzón

Continue on the road, past the church with separate bell-tower, a *cruceiro* and cemetery, then 100m later turn L. KSO, ignoring turns. Cross a bridge over the small river and KSO.

Reach the 'main' road in **Mallón**. Cross a bridge over **Río Xallas** (*and enter Concello de Dumbría, leaving the Concello de Mazaricos*) in

1.5km Ponte Olveira

KSO(L) at a fork 100m after the bridge. KSO for 2km, passing a *farmácia* (L) and turning to **Santiago Olveira** (R). KSO and then opposite road KM22, fork L down a minor road into

2km Olveiroa

(Not to be confused with Olveira, another village nearby.) Village with several hórreos and interesting examples of vernacular architecture, church of Santiago with statue of St James and a refugio. Bar Mueriños 50m off route to R uphill. Refugio.

KSO through the village and 500m later turn L by a *lavadero*, crossing a small river then, at a junction by a telephone pylon, FORK L up a small concrete road (near the 'main' road) uphill. 300m later fork R onto a *camino de tierra*. When you reach telephone cables fork L up another track. *(This is a very nice section, apart from the two large, belching carbide factories on the skyline, the first of which is just outside the village of Hospital. The Camino undulates on a wide track high up, with the mountains all around and the Río Hospital below you to the L.)*

Descend fairly rapidly, cross a stone footbridge over the river and continue on a FP on the other side, veering L alongside the river, then veering R to a junction with another FP at marker stone 32,066. Turn R uphill to a wider track and turn R. KSO at a junction when a track joins from back L. Fork R downhill into

Unusual rock formations near Logoso   (author)

3.5km Logoso

KSO(R) and then KSO(L) uphill at the end of the hamlet and continue on a wide, undulating track, high up, across the shoulder of the mountain. Reach the top of the hill (*and a view of the carbide factory ahead, L*) and turn R onto the unpaved road in

1km Hospital

A village likely, given its name, to have had a pilgrim hospital here in centuries gone by though no evidence remains.

Turn L immediately and L again onto the road by KM27 (P340A) towards the factory. (*Bar Casteliño on L at top of hill does sandwiches.*) Turn R onto an old minor road at marker stone 29,353, veering R to the 'main' road by the factory and 100m later cross it. Here there is a double marker stone and you can either:

a) turn R for the direct continuation to Muxía (27km, missing out Finisterre); *this option is not described here but a very brief outline is given in the small guide published by the Xunta de Galicia (see Introduction);* or

b)   turn L to continue directly to Finisterre.

For option b) turn L and KSO on the road for 600m then turn R onto a track which becomes an old walled lane; *this is the old Camino real, the beginning of 9km of drove road leading through the mountains to Cée, more or less in a straight line, and with splendid views all round on a clear day.* Pass marker stone 27,967 and KSO. KSO(L) at a fork 100m later. Cross the main road (cruceiro *in middle*) and KSO on the other side. Pass marker stone 26,285 and KSO. Veer gradually L and KSO on the wide Camino with open vistas to all sides, 'roof of the world' style. Descend gradually, reach a T-junction 1km later and turn R. KSO then turn L downhill 400m after that and 100m later reach

5.5km Santuario de Nosa Señora das Neves

Small church in shady grounds (nice place for a rest), restored in 1997. The Fonte Santa, a fountain below the road to the L by the cruceiro, is well known for its curative properties. A romería takes place here annually, on December 8th.

Turn R below the church, veering L then R uphill, ignoring turns. Reach marker stone 23,508 and KSO(R) uphill. KSO, KSO(L) at a fork. *(Plantations of eucalyptus trees to either side.)* Pass RH turn and 100m later reach a junction at marker stone 21,878. Turn L and 50m later KSO(R) at LH turn. 200m later pass the church of

2.5km San Pedro Mártir

Small chapel set in a field, with its own fonte santa (water reputedly cures rheumatism, painful feet and verrucas), focus of local pilgrimage and another good place for a rest. Turn R to visit then retrace your steps.

KSO, ignoring turns. Pass marker stone 19,356 (ignore turning to R) and KSO.

First view of sea ahead and Cape Finisterre, Monte-de-Gozo style, after which you descend, gradually.

At a fork with a paved section to R and earth track to L, KSO(L), descending steadily. Veer R, turn L and descend steeply. *(View of another belching factory below, in Cée.)* Reach a minor road at marker stone 16,918 and turn L. Turn **hard R** immediately, downhill, R again at the bottom to a *cruceiro* and KSO(R), after a 'stop' sign, along the 'main' road in

4.5km Cée

Coastal town with all facilities. Hostal Galicia (on road to Corcubión). Hospedaje Crego (in Avenida Finisterra) is inexpensive. Church of Nosa Señora de Xunqueira (with Gothic section). 2km to south, in hamlet of Ameixenda on coast, church of Santiago has a relic reputed to be one of the saint's fingers.

Turn R and KSO for 500m, fork L downhill (signposted 'Casa do Concello, Centro de Saude') then turn L, cross the street and go down some steps/slope to **Rúa Rosalia de Castro**. From there you can either:

a) make you way down to the waterfront and KSO along it for 1km to Corcubión (across on the other side of the bay) then go up the slope*** (L) to the main road; or

b) to visit the town: turn R into **Rúa Rosalia de Castro** and KSO. Cross the square (**Praza da Constitución**, *trees, seats*) from one end to the other then turn L and then R, passing between a church (R) and **Casa do Concello** (L). Turn L, crossing a grassed area with trees, cross a canal and reach the waterfront. Continue along it and when the road starts to go uphill*** cross over and 200m later fork R up a steep concrete street at the entrance board for Corcubión. *(However, when the Paseo maritimo is completed you will then have the further option of continuing along the waterfront here.)*

KSO uphill, KSO(L) at a fork (the **Calle Rafael Juan** but not named at the start) and then continue along it when it becomes **Calle Antonio Porrúa**, passing the **Capilla del Pilar** (1931) and a fountain (L) to a small square (**Plaza de Castelao**, *seats, trees, taxi rank*) and leave by the top LH corner (**Paseo de San Marcos**) veering L to the thirteenth-century church of **San Marcos** *(large statue of San Roque in pilgrim gear in niche in RH wall)* in

1.5km Corcubión

All facilities. Bar Sirena has rooms.

Facing the church door turn **hard R** up some steps and up the street ahead (**Calle San Marcos** – *note houses with armorial devices)* to another square (**Campo de Rollo**). KSO along its LH edge, continue ahead, forking R at the first fork and L at the second, up **Camino de Vilar**, and follow the road as it zigzags uphill. KSO at a crossing and then veer L towards the main road at the top. Cross over and continue on an old road on the other side (*marker stone 12,468, sports pitch, trees, shady place for a rest,* cruceiro *and fountain on LH side – the* **Fonte de Vilar**). At a junction KSO ahead down a FP (*this is the* **Encrucijada de San Roque***, main road is the C552*). Continue along a boundary wall (with fountain) on R, downhill, down a grassy lane, descending gradually. Return to the road 500m later in the hamlet of

2km Amarela

KSO on the road for 400m till it bends sharp L then cross over and KSO(R) on a section of old road. 80m later turn R down a wide grassy lane, reaching the road again 100m later near the sea. Turn R and KSO on the road into

1.5km Estorde

Nice beach, campsite (Camping Ruta Finisterre – shuts October), Hostal Playa de Estorde, bars.

KSO on the road for 1km to

1km Sardiñeiro

Another nice beach; shops, bars.

Just BEFORE you enter the village watch out for arrows and turn L down a lane by a block of flats at the town entry nameboard. This short-cuts a bend and then returns to the road. Cross over and fork L down **Rúa do Mestre Barrera** and return to the road by **Pensión Nicola** (L). 200m later, by house no. 31, turn R up **Rúa do San Xoan** (signposted to 'Praia do Rostro' and church) then fork L immediately uphill (**Rúa de Fisterra**). At a T-junction 200m after the last house turn L up a grassy walled lane uphill through eucalyptus woods.

KSO at a crossing 600m later and at another, and shortly afterwards emerge with a view out to sea and 'the end of the world' on the second hill ahead of you. Veer R to return to the road just past a lay-by with a picnic area. Cross over and continue ahead downhill and then up (*steep FP to L midway, leading to quiet secluded beach 50m below you*) and return to the road after a bend (300m later).

350m after that (at marker stone 6484) fork L down the **Corredoira de Don Camilo**, *named after the Nobel prize-winning Galician novelist José Camilo Cela. This is a paved* paseo *that runs alongside the sea for 2km, tarmac at first, leading down to and then along the Praia de Langosteira. It continues all the way to the entrance to the town of Finisterre (2km), ending at a viewpoint with a* cruceiro; cafés and chiringuitos *(snack bars) at points along it in summer. Or, if you want, and if the tide is suitable, you can walk along the beach itself (seawater good for tired, sore, blistered feet).*

When you get to the end of the *corredoira* (this area is known as **San Roque**) go up the slope to a wayside cross and *mirador* (*viewpoint*) and continue on LH side of the road. KSO down **Calle Santa Catalina**, veering R downhill into the centre of town (port to your L).

4km Finisterre

Small fishing port with all facilities. Refugio, 20+ places. Several hostales and pensiones, including Hospedaje Lopez in centre of town and Casa Velay. From the town of Finisterre it is a further 3km to the lighthouse ('el faro') and the real 'end of the earth'.

To walk there: cross the street and continue ahead up **Rúa Real** (refugio *on LH corner*) to **Plaza de la Constitución** then straight on down **Calle Plaza** to **Plaza de Ara Solis**. Turn R and then turn L in front of **Capilla de Nuestra Señora del Buen Suceso** (*note house with armorial device, cross and sundial to R*). Continue along **Calle Ara Solis**, veering R uphill. Cross **Calle Manuel Lago Paris** and continue uphill to join the C552 coming from back R and reach the church of

1km Santa María das Areas

Twelfth-century parish church of 'Saint Mary of the Sands', Romanesque in part, with statue of St James. Gothic cruceiro, chapel which was formerly a pilgrim hospital and which had its own Porta Santa in jubilee years. Open 10am to 1pm, 3 to 7pm.

Continue for 2km more on the road to the lighthouse (*fountain – Fonte Cabanas – on R, halfway along). A rocky outcrop known as the 'Piedras Santas', a possible focus of pre-Christian worship, is apparently to be found on the north shore of the peninsula.*

Hospedaje O Semáforo (in former observatory and morse radio station) with rooms and rte (tel: 981.72.58.69), Bar O Refugio. Bronze

sculpture of pair of broken boots on rocks behind lighthouse. As the weather is often misty until about midday in this part of Spain you may well have better views from here in the late afternoon and evening.

Return to Santiago

By bus (from the long, low building in the port) – three or four journeys a day, the last one leaving at 4pm Mondays to Saturdays (6pm Sundays and holidays). Journey time 2½-3 hours, though the service is not always direct and you may have to change in Vimianzo to connect with another bus. Space permitting, it is also possible to take one or two bikes. If you want to check return times before you leave Santiago you can ring the bus company (Transportes Finisterre/Arriva) on tel: 981.56.29.24.

The continuation from Finisterre to Muxía begins from the port and leads through **Escaselas**, **Hermedesuxo de Abaixo**, **San Salvador**, **Denle**, **Castromiñán**, **Canosa**, **Lires**, **Vaosilveiro**, **Frixe**, **Guismonde**, **Morquintián**, **Vilela** and **Xurarantes** to **Muxía**.

APPENDIX B

SUMMARY OF SANTIAGO AND PILGRIM REFERENCES

(a) Seville to Astorga

Seville 1. Cathedral a) Puerta de San Miguel has carving of Santiago Peregrino b) Capilla de Santiago has painting of *St James the Great at the battle of Clavijo* by Juan de Roelas, 1609, on R as well as stained-glass window of Battle of Clavijo. 2. Hospital de la Caridad has statue of San Roque with scallops and staff in chapel, on RH side of main altarpiece.

Almadén de la Plata formerly had church dedicated to Santiago.

Calera de León Conventual de Santiago, monastery of Order of Santiago founded by Pelay Pérez in 1275, master of Order of Santiago a) Painting behind high altar in monastery church of Nuestra Señora de la Asunción depicts knights carrying banner of Order of Santiago in battle against Moors b) Stained glass of apse contains swords of Santiago.

Monasterio de Nuestra Señora de Tentudía Belonged to Order of Santiago. Italian tiled altarpiece in RH Santiago chapel with Santiago Matamoros.

Fuente de Cantos Church of Nuestra Señora de la Granada has statue of San Roque inside on R and statue of Santiago Apóstol (with shells on each lapel) on altar *mayor*.

Calzadilla de los Barros Town coat of arms contains scallop shell and sword of Santiago.

Zafra 1. Hospital de Santiago (now mental hospital), founded by los Condes de Feria in 1457. 2. Colegiata de Nuestra Señora de la Candelaria has statue of Santiago Apóstol to upper R of main altar. 3. Arco del Cubo, Campo de Rosario, has equestrian Santiago bas-relief.

Los Santos de Maimona 1. Town coat of arms with Cruz de Santiago. 2. Palacio de la Encomienda (command headquarters of military Order of Santiago) is now *ayuntamiento*. 3. Church of Nuestra Señora de los

Angeles has a) Puerta del Perdón and b) lion with sword of Santiago above door. Town formerly belonged to Knights of Santiago and had five *ermitas*, including one from 1504 onwards dedicated to Santiago.

Villafranca de los Barros Church of Santa María del Valle has a) much shell decoration inside: shells on collars around pillars of south porch, south nave and around south nave portal b) statue of San Roque with very large scallop shell, staff and big leg wound in south porch c) Santiago Apóstol with book and shell in main altarpiece on RH side, centre, of main altarpiece. (Town also belonged to Knights of Santiago.)

Almendralejo Another town reconquored from Moors by Order of Santiago (1241). 1. Church of Purificación de Nuestra Señora has escutcheon incorporating scallop and sword of Santiago in apse. 2. Capilla de Santiago. 3. Church of San Roque in western suburbs.

Torremegía Palacio del Marquesado de Torremegía has ring of huge scallops around Renaissance main portal.

Mérida 1. Church of Santa María (church of last Master of the Order of Santiago) has escutcheon incorporating scallops and cross of Santiago on west door. 2. Church of Santa Eulalia has stone bas-relief of Santiago Peregrino with hat and staff on pulpit.

Aljucén Church of San Andrés (inside) has Santiago crosses on all its pedestals.

Casas de Don Antonio 1. Ermita de Nuestra Señora del Pilar at exit to village has two depictions of Santiago a) relief sculpture of Santiago Apóstol, with hat, on altarpiece and b) tiny statue of Santiago Matamoros on prancing horse, taken on annual *romería* on May 1st to: 2. Ermita de Casa de Santiago Bencaliz (which has very small Roman bridge behind it).

Cáceres 1. Town coat of arms includes sword of Santiago, scallop shells. 2. Escutcheon of sword of Santiago and scallop shells on façade of a) Palacio de Hernando de Ovando, Plaza Santa María and b) in cloister in Casa de Lorenzo de Ulloa, Calle Ancha. 3. Iglesia de Santiago a) bas-relief of pilgrim with staff, scrip, hat, shell above north portal (first pilgrim figure on journey) b) collars of scallop shells encircle north portal pillars c) Baroque main altarpiece has huge Santiago Matamoros at Clavijo d) south chapel has wooden chairs with scallop shells on back e) stained glass in apse contains sword of

Santiago. 4. Iglesia de Santa María a) relief sculpture of Santiago Matamoros in main altarpiece (sixteenth century, possibly by Roque Balduque) b) wooden sculpture of Santiago Peregrino.

Casar de Cáceres 1. Iglesia de la Asunción in centre of village has Baroque wood painted Santiago on LH side of main altarpiece with fine Santiago Peregrino complete with staff, gourd, hat and scallop. Modern but inverted black scallop in grille of southwest chapel. 2. Ermita de Santiago, at end of village, has modern Santiago Matamoros with giant sword above altar.

Cañaveral Sixteenth-century Ermita de San Roque.

Galisteo Church of Santa María has scallops in groups of five in decorative ironwork in north portal.

Carcaboso Modern church of Santiago Apóstol with glass roundel of Santiago Matamoros above west door.

Plasencia 1. New Cathedral: Santiago Peregrino on main altarpiece (bottom R). 2. Old Cathedral: scallop shell decoration on pillars in its cloisters. 3. Old Cathedral museum has eighteenth-century statue of Santiago Apóstol. 4. Sculpture of Santiago Peregrino in town walls.

Aldeanueva del Camino San Servando, one of its two parish churches, has modern tiled Santiago panel above high altar.

Baños de Montemayor A *casa-hospital* belonging to *ayuntamiento* in Plaza de la Alberguería existed here until nineteenth century.

Valverde de Valdelacasa 1. Iglesia de Santiago. 2. Calle Camino de Santiago. 3. Remains of former hospital, 1704 in lintel, with Santiago cross in coat of arms.

Fuenterrobles de Salvatierra Formerly had both *ermita* and hospital dedicated to Santiago; latter was demolished in 1770 due to bad condition. Was also Santiago fountain in area, near Sierra de Tanda.

Pico de la Dueña now topped by sword of Santiago.

Salamanca 1. Twelfth-century brick church of Santiago by Roman bridge with sword of Santiago in escutcheon on west front. 2. Old Cathedral a) Talavera chapel: shield with scallop shells b) Salas Capitalinas: statue of Santiago Apóstol with book, dressed in white c) Santa Catalina chapel: statue of San Roque d) Anaya chapel has marble bas-relief of Santiago Peregrino on base of tomb of Don Gutiérrez de

Monroy and tiny alabaster bas-relief of heavily bearded Santiago with other apostles along base of alabaster tomb of Bishop Anaya. 3. New Cathedral: painted wood statue of Santiago Apóstol in north aisle of Capilla de Santiago. 4. Convento de Sancti Spiritu, its church associated with the Order of Santiago: a) Santiago Matamoros in pediment of north portal b) Santiago Matamoros in pediment of south portal with medallion of head of Santiago Peregrino L, above south portal c) painted Santiago Matamoros in centre of main altarpiece d) stone Santiago Apóstol in north aisle. 5. Colegio Arzobispo Fonseca (Irish College): medallion of Santiago Matamoros above main portal and frieze of scallop shells. 6. Corner of Calle Cervantes and Calle Rabanal: shell escutcheon. 7. Convento de las Dueñas: medallion of San Roque and shell motifs in lower cloister. 8. University – Patio de las Escuelas: shell decoration in ironwork of main doorway. 9. Casa de las Conchas, civilian residence so named for its shell-covered facade, built *c.* 1490 by Dr Rodrigo Arias Talavera Maldonado, knight of the Order of the Knights of Santiago in Salamanca. 10. Museum has statue with attributes of Santiago Apóstol with shell on hat.

Calzada de Valdunciel Statue of Santiago Peregrino in church of Santa Elena, in sandals and with no hat.

Villanueva de Campeán Calle de Santiago.

Zamora 1. Twelfth-century Romanesque church of Santiago del Burgo has painted bas-relief of Santiago Matamoros above painted wooden statue of Santiago Apóstol with staff and book on main altarpiece. 2. Second Santiago church, outside town walls, tiny Romanesque Ermita de Santiago de los Caballeros. 3. Church of San Claudio de Olivares has statue of San Roque Peregrino. 4. Cathedral: gilded statue of Santiago Peregrino with hat, scallop, gourd and staff in niche on RH side of chancel. 5. Cathedral museum: painting of head of Santiago on RH side of predella of wall-mounted San Ildefonso altarpiece.

Castrotorafe Ruins of Castillo, seat of Order of the Knights of Santiago.

Benavente Former Hospital de la Piedad has pilgrim doorknocker and scallops incorporated into arms of founder on main facade. Modern church of Santiago in suburbs.

Alija del Infantado Modern Cruz del Orden de Santiago on hill high to R above village at exit.

La Bañeza Hospital donated to church of El Salvador in 932 for pilgrims and other needy.

(b) Tábara to Santiago

Santa Marta de Tera Santiago Peregrino statue in LH portal of south door.

Pumarejo de Tera Church dedicated to Santiago.

Olleros de Tera Formerly had pilgrim hospital.

Rionegro del Puente 1. Former pilgrim hospital (building still exists). 2. Former church of Santiago (only tower left) is now cemetery chapel. 3. Cofradía de los Falifos, oldest such organisation devoted to looking after pilgrims, still functioning.

Triufé House that was formerly pilgrim hospital still standing.

Terros Church dedicated to Santiago.

Campobecerros Church dedicated to Santiago with modern statue of Santiago pilgrim/apostle in niche over front door and representation of Santiago Matamoros inside building.

Laza Church contains depictions of Virgen del Rosario, Santiago and San Roque Peregrino on main altarpiece.

Albergería Site of former pilgrim hospital. Statue of Santiago inside church of Santa María.

Vilar de Barrio Scallop shell in town coat of arms.

Xunqueira de Ambía 'Virgen Peregrina' in Baroque pilgrim outfit on side altar of twelfth-century church.

Ourense Pórtico del Paraíso in cathedral has seated statue of Santiago, against pillar; sword in RH, open book in LH, with text facing viewer, no hat, three scallop shells at base of column.

Albarellos de Monterrei Church with statue of Santiago Peregrino on south wall.

Monterrey Ruins of eighteenth-century pilgrim hospital in hilltop castle complex.

Xinzo de Limia Romanesque church of Santa Mariña has a) freestanding statue of San Roque on LH side of chancel arch b) capital of a face above giant scallop to RH side of west portal.

Piñeira de Arcos Modern *cruceiro* with statue of Santiago Peregrino on shaft.

Allariz Church dedicated to Santiago. Both this and church of San Estevo have statues of San Roque Peregrino inside.

Faramontaos Village formerly had pilgrim hospital.

Oseira Formerly had pilgrim hospital. Monastery church of Santa María la Real has Baroque altarpiece with painting of Santiago Peregrino.

Puxallos Ermita de San Roque.

Taboada Church of Santiago has a) painting of Santiago Matamoros in Baroque altarpiece inside building b) modern statue of Santiago Peregrino in sitting area outside.

Bandeira Formerly had pilgrim hospital.

Capilla de Santiaguiño (between Ponte Ulla and Susana) 1. Chapel dedicated to Santiago, built 1696, restored 2000. 2. Fountain with statue of Santiago Peregrino in niche above it.

Santiago de Compostela Life-size brass statue of St James seated up behind main altar.

APPENDIX C

SUGGESTIONS FOR FURTHER READING

General

Donald Atwood and C.R. John, *Penguin Dictionary of Saints*, 3rd ed., Harmondsworth: Penguin, 1995.

Nancy Louise Frey, *Pilgrim Stories*, Berkley and Los Angeles: University of California Press, 1998. This refers specifically to the experiences of modern pilgrims along the road to Santiago de Compostela, before, during and after making their pilgrimage, but the questions raised confront any modern pilgrim on a route where the journey itself, rather than the destination, is the real issue at stake.

Martin Robinson, *Sacred Places, Pilgrim Paths: an anthology of pilgrimage*, London: Fount, 1997. An anthology reflecting the experiences of pilgrims through the ages, dealing with places of pilgrimage, preparation for the journey, the journey itself, the inner journey, worship on the way and on arrival and the questions raised once the pilgrimage is over.

The Way of a Pilgrim, trans. R.M. French, London: Triangle, 1995. First published in English in 1930 this book was written by an unknown Russian pilgrim in the nineteenth century, telling the story of his wanderings from one holy place to another in Russia and Siberia in search of the way of prayer.

Vía de la Plata

Actas. Congreso sobre o Camiño Xacobeo na Provincia de Ourense, Xunta de Galicia (Consellería de Cultura, Dirección Xeral de Promoción do Camiño de Santiago), 1995. Collection of papers (in Spanish) given at a conference in 1993 on the history, geography and tradition of the Camino de Santiago in the province of Ourense.

María Cuenda and Darío Izquierdo, *La Virgen María en las Rutas Jacobeas. Ruta meridional – Vía de la Plata*. 1999. One of a set of three volumes (the other two deal with the Camino francés and the Camino portugués) that examines representations in art and architecture of the Virgen Mary along the Vía de la Plata, many of them linked with the theme and portrayals of St James. Contains excellent photographs.

Salvador Llopis, *Por Salamanca también pasa el Camino de Santiago*, Salamanca, 1965, reprinted 1998: Fuenterroble de Salvatierra (Salamanca), Asociación de Amigos del Camino de Santiago 'Vía de la Plata'. As its title indicates, this book describes the route in the province of Salamanca, including variants. Originally published in 1965 but reprinted in 1998 by the 'Amigos' in Fuenterroble de Salvatierra.

Eligio Rivas, *Camino meridional de Santiago, continuación de la Vía de la Plata*, Xunta de Galicia. History of the places the route goes through in the Galician section.

La Ruta de la Plata a pie y en bicicleta: monumentos, gastronomía, refugios, etapas, Madrid: El País Aguilar, 2000. Practical guide to the route but only from Mérida to Astorga. Contains very good maps and information on the Roman aspects of the route (roads, bridges, history) but very little on the Vía de la Plata as a pilgrimage route.

La Ruta de la Plata, Camino mozárabe de Santiago, Bilbao: Sua Edizoak, 1996. A guide to the route for motorists but with background information and photographs of interest to all types of pilgrim.

La Ruta de la Plata de Sevilla a Gijón, León: Ediciones Lancia, 1993. Guide to the history of the route and its monuments, with good photographs.

La Ruta de la Plata: Guía práctica del viajero, Madrid: Editorial Everest, 1994. Another guide to the route for motorists but with background material and photographs of interest to all types of pilgrim.

José Sendín Blázquez, *Calzada y Camino de Santiago – Vía de la Plata – Historia, Mito, Leyenda*, Zamora: Fundación Ramos de Castro, 1992. As its title suggests, this is a collection of writings pertaining to the local history, myths and legends surrounding the southern route to Santiago.

José Sendín Blázquez, *Mitos y leyendas del Camino de Santiago del Sur*, Plasencia: Ediciones Lancia, 1996. A further collection of history, myths and legends about people and places along the Vía de la Plata.

APPENDIX D

USEFUL ADDRESSES

Confraternity of Saint James
27 Blackfriars Rd,
London SE1 8NY   tel: (020) 7928 9988
Web http:// www.csj.org.uk Email:office@csj.org.uk

Amigos del Camino de Santiago de Sevilla: Vía de la Plata
Calle Paraíso de Santa Eufémia 27
41940 Tomares
(Sevilla) tel: 95.415.44.85

This is the address (but NOT an office you can visit) from which to obtain the special 'Vía de la Plata' credencial.

Asociación de Amigos del Camino de Santiago 'Vía de la Plata'
Calle La Fuente 14
37769 Fuenterroble de Salvatierra
(Salamanca)   tel: 923.15.10.83

Federación Asociaciones Amigos del Camino de Santiago
'Vía de la Plata'
Calle Santa Clara 33
49002 Zamora

Bookshops in Santiago

Librería Egeria, Plaza de la Inmaculada 5, 15704 Santiago de Compostela. Up-market religious bookshop.

Librería San Pablo, Rúa do Vilar 39, 15705 Santiago de Compostela. Religious/general bookshop.

Librería Encontros, Rúa do Vilar 68, 15705 Santiago de Compostela. General bookshop.

Librería Gali, Rúa do Vilar 66, 15705 Santiago de Compostela. General bookshop.

Follas Novas, Montero Ríos 37, 15706 Santiago de Compostela. University/general bookshop.

Abraxos Libros, Montero Ríos 50, 15706 Santiago de Compostela. University/general bookshop.

Other

Manfred Zentgraf – Verlagsbuchhandel, D-97332 Volkach/Main, In den Böden 38,Germany.
Walking books. Specialises in pilgrim guides.

APPENDIX E

GLOSSARY

One or two linguistic hints may help to equate the Galician words to the Castilian ('Spanish') ones you probably already know (Galician is sometimes described as 'Portuguese with Castilian spelling'). For example:
– dropping intervocalic consonants (*media/meia, salud/saude, arena/area*)
– e = ei (*crucero/cruceiro*)
– ue = o (*puerta/porta, puerta/porta*)
– j = x (*junta/xunta, Jesús/Xesús*)
Plurals of abbreviations: the letters are doubled (FF.CC = *ferrocarriles* – seen on road signs crossing railway tracks)
Words beginning with al-, a- are usually of Arabic origin (*azúcar, alcalde, algodón, albericoque, almacén, almohada*)

agua (non) potable	(not) drinking water
agua non tratada	'untreated' (chlorine-free) water
albergue	inn; also used to refer to a pilgrim refuge/hostel
alcalde	mayor
alcázar	fortress, castle
aldea	hamlet
almacén	warehouse, store
alguacil	constable, municipal employee
alto	hill, height
arcén	hard shoulder, verge
arroyo	stream, small river
ayuntamiento	town hall
barrio	suburb, district
bascula pública	public weighbridge

bodega	wine cellar, tavern; also used to describe a storage place for wine and other items located in hillsides elsewhere, in the open countryside
cafetería	a café that also serves snacks (not a self-service restaurant for hot meals)
callejón	alley, passageway
calzada	(paved) road, causeway
camino	track, path
camino de tierra	earth road/track
cañada	widest category cattle track, drover's road
cancela	outer door/gate; wrought-iron/lattice gate
capilla	chapel
carretera	(main) road, highway
Casa Consistorial	town hall in small places
Casa do Concello	town hall in small places (in Galicia)
casa huéspedes (CH)	guesthouse
casco antiguo	historic quarter (of a town)
cierren la puerta	'close the gate'
cigüena	stork
circunvalación	by-pass, ring road
colegiata/colexiata	collegiate church
cordel	middle category of old cattle/drover's road
corredoira	walled lane (Galicia)
cortefuego(s)	firebreak (in forest)
cortijo	farm, farmhouse (in the south)
coto de caza	hunting/game preserve
coto de pesca	fishing preserve
cruceiro	wayside cross
¡cuidad con el perro!	beware of the dog
dehesa	estate; pastureland
depósito de agua	water tower
desvío	detour, diversion (on roads)

embalse	dam, reservoir
encina	holm oak (an evergreen variety)
ermita	originally a hermitage but nowadays frequently used to describe a small church or chapel
estanco	kiosk (selling tobacco, stamps)
estrada	main road, highway (Galicia)
finca	smallholding
fonda	guesthouse, inn
frontón	pelota court
fuente	fountain, spring
gallego	Galician
gasolinera	petrol station
'la general'	'main road' (= *carretera general*)
hogar del pensionista	bar/social club for senior citizens
hórreo	(raised) granary
hospedaje	a *fonda* (in Galicia)
hospedería	inn, hostelry
hostal	hotel (less expensive than a *hotel*)
humilladero	cross or statue often placed at entrance or exit to village and used for devotional purposes
igrexia/eirexa	church (Galician)
jacobeo/xacobeo (adj.)	of St James
jara	cistus (bush)
latifundio	(very) large estate
lavadero	outdoor washing-place, (public) wash-house
lugar	small collection of houses (a subdivision of a *pueblo*)
merendero	picnic area, refreshment stall
meseta	plateau, tableland
mesón	restaurant (often simple, with period decor)
minifundio	smallholding, very small farm
molino/muiño	mill

mosteiro	monastery (Galician)
nave	nave (in church); hangar, industrial building
¡ojo al perro!	beware of the dog! (Castilian)
ollo o can	beware of the dog! (Galician)
palmero	pilgrim who has been to Jerusalem
panadería	bakery
pantano	marsh, swamp (natural); reservoir, dam (artificial)
pasadero	causeway, stepping stones (in river)
paseo	stroll, walk; avenue
paso canadiense	cattle grid
peregrino	pilgrim
perros sueltos	loose dogs (not tied up)
plaza de toros	bull ring
presa	dam; weir, barrage
posada	inn (simpler than a *fonda*)
praia fluvial	swimming area (in river)
pueblo	village, small town
puente	bridge
puerta	door, gateway
puerto	mountain pass; port
repetidor	TV mast, transmitter, antenna
rollo	stone wayside cross, often at junctions; raised up and may be highly decorated
rodeo	roundabout or indirect route
romería	pilgrimage to a local shrine
romero	pilgrim (originally one who had been to Rome)
rúa	street (Galician)
santuario	church where, originally, relics of a saint were believed to be kept
sellar	to (rubber) stamp
sello	stamp, seal

senda	(small) path, track
señal	waymark, signal
tapas	light snack taken with drinks in a bar
travesía	cross-street, short street which joins two others
ultramarinos	grocer's shop
vega	fertile plain, lowland area, valley (often found in placenames)
venta/venda	country inn (in former times)
vereda	smallest category of cattle/drover's road
villa	small town

For pilgrims who attend mass and who would like to be able to join in at least once during the service the Lord's Prayer is given below in Spanish:

Padre nuestro, que estás en el cielo,
santificado sea tu Nombre;
venga a nosotros tu reino;
hágase tu voluntad en la tierra como en el cielo.
Danos hoy nuestro pan de cada día;
perdona nuestras ofensas,
como también nosotros perdonamos
a los que nos ofenden;
no nos dejes caer en la tentación,
y líbranos del mal.

APPENDIX F

INDEX OF PRINCIPAL PLACENAMES

APPENDIX G

INDEX OF MAPS USED IN THIS BOOK

APPENDIXES

LISTING OF CICERONE GUIDES

NORTHERN ENGLAND
LONG DISTANCE TRAILS

THE DALES WAY

THE ISLE OF MAN COASTAL PATH

THE PENNINE WAY

THE ALTERNATIVE COAST TO COAST

NORTHERN COAST-TO-COAST WALK

THE RELATIVE HILLS OF BRITAIN

MOUNTAINS ENGLAND & WALES VOL 1 WALES. VOL 2 ENGLAND.

CYCLING

BORDER COUNTRY BIKE ROUTES

THE CHESHIRE CYCLE WAY

THE CUMBRIA CYCLE WAY

THE DANUBE CYCLE WAY

LANDS END TO JOHN O'GROATS CYCLE GUIDE

ON THE RUFFSTUFF - 84 Bike Rides in Nth Engl'd

RURAL RIDES No.1 WEST SURREY

RURAL RIDES No.1 EAST SURREY

SOUTH LAKELAND CYCLE RIDES

THE WAY OF ST JAMES Le Puy to Santiago - Cyclist's

LAKE DISTRICT AND MORCOMBE BAY

CONISTON COPPER MINES

CUMBRIA WAY & ALLERDALE RAMBLE

THE CHRONICLES OF MILNTHORPE

THE EDEN WAY

FROM FELL AND FIELD

KENDAL - A SOCIAL HISTORY

A LAKE DISTRICT ANGLER''S GUIDE

LAKELAND TOWNS

LAKELAND VILLAGES

LAKELAND PANORAMAS

THE LOST RESORT?

SCRAMBLES IN THE LAKE DISTRICT

MORE SCRAMBLES IN THE LAKE DISTRICT

SHORT WALKS IN LAKELAND
Book 1: SOUTH

Book 2: NORTH

Book 3: WEST

ROCKY RAMBLER'S WILD WALKS

RAIN OR SHINE

ROADS AND TRACKS OF THE LAKE DISTRICT

THE TARNS OF LAKELAND Vol 1: West

THE TARNS OF LAKELAND Vol 2: East

WALKING ROUND THE LAKES

WALKS SILVERDALE/ARNSIDE

WINTER CLIMBS IN LAKE DISTRICT

NORTH-WEST ENGLAND

WALKING IN CHESHIRE

FAMILY WALKS IN FOREST OF BOWLAND

WALKING IN THE FOREST OF BOWLAND

LANCASTER CANAL WALKS

WALKER'S GUIDE TO LANCASTER CANAL

CANAL WALKS VOL 1: NORTH

NORTH-WEST ENGLAND

WALKS FROM THE LEEDS-LIVERPOOL CANAL

THE RIBBLE WAY

WALKS IN RIBBLE COUNTRY

WALKING IN LANCASHIRE

WALKS ON THE WEST PENNINE MOORS

WALKS IN LANCASHIRE WITCH COUNTRY

HADRIAN'S WALL
Vol 1 : The Wall Walk

Vol 2 : Wall Country Walks

WALKS FROM THE LEEDS-LIVERPOOL CANAL

NORTH YORKS MOORS

THE REIVER'S WAY

THE TEESDALE WAY

WALKING IN COUNTY DURHAM

WALKING IN THE NORTH PENNINES

WALKING IN NORTHUMBERLAND

WALKING IN THE WOLDS

WALKS IN THE NORTH YORK MOORS Books 1 and 2

WALKS IN THE YORKSHIRE DALES Books 1,2 and 3

WALKS IN DALES COUNTRY

WATERFALL WALKS - TEESDALE & HIGH PENNINES

THE YORKSHIRE DALES

YORKSHIRE DALES ANGLER'S GUIDE

THE PEAK DISTRICT

STAR FAMILY WALKS PEAK DISTRICT/Sth YORKS

HIGH PEAK WALKS

WEEKEND WALKS IN THE PEAK DISTRICT

WHITE PEAK WALKS
Vol.1 Northern Dales

Vol.2 Southern Dales

WHITE PEAK WAY

WALKING IN PEAKLAND

WALKING IN SHERWOOD FORES

WALKING IN STAFFORDSHIRE

THE VIKING WAY

WALES AND WELSH BORDERS

ANGLESEY COAST WALKS

ASCENT OF SNOWDON

THE BRECON BEACONS

CLWYD ROCK

HEREFORD & THE WYE VALLEY

HILLWALKING IN SNOWDONIA

HILLWALKING IN WALES Vol.1

HILLWALKING IN WALES Vol.2

LLEYN PENINSULA COASTAL PATH

WALKING OFFA'S DYKE PATH

THE PEMBROKESHIRE COASTAL PATH

THE RIDGES OF SNOWDONIA

SARN HELEN

SCRAMBLES IN SNOWDONIA

SEVERN WALKS

THE SHROPSHIRE HILLS

THE SHROPSHIRE WAY

SPIRIT PATHS OF WALES

WALKING DOWN THE WYE

A WELSH COAST TO COAST WALK

WELSH WINTER CLIMBS

LISTING OF CICERONE GUIDES

THE MIDLANDS

CANAL WALKS VOL 2: MIDLANDS

THE COTSWOLD WAY

COTSWOLD WALKS Book 1: North

COTSWOLD WALKS Book 2: Central

COTSWOLD WALKS Book 3: South

THE GRAND UNION CANAL WALK

HEART OF ENGLAND WALKS

WALKING IN OXFORDSHIRE

WALKING IN WARWICKSHIRE

WALKING IN WORCESTERSHIRE

WEST MIDLANDS ROCK

SOUTH AND SOUTH-WEST ENGLAND

WALKING IN BEDFORDSHIRE

WALKING IN BUCKINGHAMSHIRE

CHANNEL ISLAND WALKS

CORNISH ROCK

WALKING IN CORNWALL

WALKING IN THE CHILTERNS

WALKING ON DARTMOOR

WALKING IN DEVON

WALKING IN DORSET

CANAL WALKS VOL 3: SOUTH

EXMOOR & THE QUANTOCKS

THE GREATER RIDGEWAY

WALKING IN HAMPSHIRE

THE ISLE OF WIGHT

THE KENNET & AVON WALK

THE LEA VALLEY WALK

LONDON THEME WALKS

THE NORTH DOWNS WAY

THE SOUTH DOWNS WAY

THE ISLES OF SCILLY

THE SOUTHERN COAST TO COAST

SOUTH WEST WAY
Vol.1 Mineh'd to Penz.

Vol.2 Penz. to Poole

WALKING IN SOMERSET

WALKING IN SUSSEX

THE THAMES PATH

TWO MOORS WAY

WALKS IN KENT Book 1

WALKS IN KENT Book 2

THE WEALDWAY & VANGUARD WAY

SCOTLAND

WALKING IN THE ISLE OF ARRAN

THE BORDER COUNTRY - A WALKERS GUIDE

BORDER COUNTRY CYCLE ROUTES

BORDER PUBS & INNS - A WALKERS' GUIDE

CAIRNGORMS, Winter Climbs 5th Edition

CENTRAL HIGHLANDS 6 LONG DISTANCE WALKS

WALKING THE GALLOWAY HILLS

WALKING IN THE HEBRIDES

NORTH TO THE CAPE

THE ISLAND OF RHUM

THE ISLE OF SKYE A Walker's Guide

WALKS IN THE LAMMERMUIRS

WALKING IN THE LOWTHER HILLS

THE SCOTTISH GLENS SERIES

  1 - CAIRNGORM GLENS

  2 - ATHOLL GLENS

  3 - GLENS OF RANNOCH

  4 - GLENS OF TROSSACH

  5 - GLENS OF ARGYLL

  6 - THE GREAT GLEN

  7 - THE ANGUS GLENS

  8 - KNOYDART TO MORVERN

  9 - THE GLENS OF ROSS-SHIRE

SCOTTISH RAILWAY WALKS

SCRAMBLES IN LOCHABER

SCRAMBLES IN SKYE

SKI TOURING IN SCOTLAND

THE SPEYSIDE WAY

TORRIDON - A Walker's Guide

WALKS FROM THE WEST HIGHLAND RAILWAY

THE WEST HIGHLAND WAY

WINTER CLIMBS NEVIS & GLENCOE

IRELAND

IRISH COASTAL WALKS

THE IRISH COAST TO COAST

THE MOUNTAINS OF IRELAND

WALKING AND TREKKING IN THE ALPS

WALKING IN THE ALPS

100 HUT WALKS IN THE ALPS

CHAMONIX to ZERMATT

GRAND TOUR OF MONTE ROSA Vol. 1 and Vol.2

TOUR OF MONT BLANC

FRANCE, BELGIUM AND LUXEMBOURG

WALKING IN THE ARDENNES

ROCK CLIMBS BELGIUM & LUX.

THE BRITTANY COASTAL PATH

CHAMONIX - MONT BLANC Walking Guide

WALKING IN THE CEVENNES

CORSICAN HIGH LEVEL ROUTE: GR20

THE ECRINS NATIONAL PARK

WALKING THE FRENCH ALPS: GR5

WALKING THE FRENCH GORGES

FRENCH ROCK

WALKING IN THE HAUTE SAVOIE

WALKING IN THE LANGUEDOC

TOUR OF THE OISANS: GR54

WALKING IN PROVENCE

THE PYRENEAN TRAIL: GR10

THE TOUR OF THE QUEYRAS

ROBERT LOUIS STEVENSON TRAIL

WALKING IN TARENTAISE & BEAUFORTAIN ALPS

ROCK CLIMBS IN THE VERDON

TOUR OF THE VANOISE

WALKS IN VOLCANO COUNTRY

FRANCE/SPAIN

ROCK CLIMBS IN THE PYRENEES

WALKS & CLIMBS IN THE PYRENEES

THE WAY OF ST JAMES Le Puy to Santiago - Walker's

THE WAY OF ST JAMES Le Puy to Santiago - Cyclist's

SPAIN AND PORTUGAL

WALKING IN THE ALGARVE

ANDALUSIAN ROCK CLIMBS

BIRDWATCHING IN MALLORCA

219

LISTING OF CICERONE GUIDES

COSTA BLANCA ROCK

COSTA BLANCA WALKS VOL 1

COSTA BLANCA WALKS VOL 2

WALKING IN MALLORCA

ROCK CLIMBS IN MAJORCA, IBIZA & TENERIFE

WALKING IN MADEIRA

THE MOUNTAINS OF CENTRAL SPAIN

THE SPANISH PYRENEES GR11 2nd Ed.

WALKING IN THE SIERRA NEVADA

WALKS & CLIMBS IN THE PICOS DE EUROPA

VIA DE LA PLATA

SWITZERLAND

ALPINE PASS ROUTE, SWITZERLAND

THE BERNESE ALPS A Walking Guide

CENTRAL SWITZERLAND

THE JURA: HIGH ROUTE & SKI TRAVERSES

WALKING IN TICINO, SWITZERLAND

THE VALAIS, SWITZERLAND. A Walking Guide

GERMANY, AUSTRIA AND EASTERN EUROPE

MOUNTAIN WALKING IN AUSTRIA

WALKING IN THE BAVARIAN ALPS

WALKING IN THE BLACK FOREST

THE DANUBE CYCLE WAY

GERMANY'S ROMANTIC ROAD

WALKING IN THE HARZ MOUNTAINS

KING LUDWIG WAY

KLETTERSTEIG Northern Limestone Alps

WALKING THE RIVER RHINE TRAIL

THE MOUNTAINS OF ROMANIA

WALKING IN THE SALZKAMMERGUT

HUT-TO-HUT IN THE STUBAI ALPS

THE HIGH TATRAS

SCANDANAVIA

WALKING IN NORWAY

ST OLAV'S WAY

ITALY AND SLOVENIA

ALTA VIA - HIGH LEVEL WALKS DOLOMITES

CENTRAL APENNINES OF ITALY

WALKING CENTRAL ITALIAN ALPS

WALKING IN THE DOLOMITES

SHORTER WALKS IN THE DOLOMITES

WALKING ITALY'S GRAN PARADISO

LONG DISTANCE WALKS IN ITALY'S GRAN PARADISO

ITALIAN ROCK

WALKS IN THE JULIAN ALPS

WALKING IN SICILY

WALKING IN TUSCANY

VIA FERRATA SCRAMBLES IN THE DOLOMITES

OTHER MEDITERRANEAN COUNTRIES

THE ATLAS MOUNTAINS

WALKING IN CYPRUS

CRETE - THE WHITE MOUNTAINS

THE MOUNTAINS OF GREECE

JORDAN - Walks, Treks, Caves etc.

THE MOUNTAINS OF TURKEY

TREKS & CLIMBS WADI RUM JORDAN

CLIMBS & TREKS IN THE ALA DAG

WALKING IN PALESTINE

HIMALAYA

ADVENTURE TREKS IN NEPAL

ANNAPURNA - A TREKKER'S GUIDE

EVEREST - A TREKKERS' GUIDE

GARHWAL & KUMAON - A Trekker's Guide

KANGCHENJUNGA - A Trekker's Guide

LANGTANG, GOSAINKUND & HELAMBU Trekkers Guide

MANASLU - A trekker's guide

OTHER COUNTRIES

MOUNTAIN WALKING IN AFRICA - KENYA

OZ ROCK – AUSTRALIAN CRAGS

WALKING IN BRITISH COLUMBIA

TREKKING IN THE CAUCASUS

GRAND CANYON & AMERICAN SOUTH WEST

ROCK CLIMBS IN HONG KONG

ADVENTURE TREKS WEST NORTH AMERICA

CLASSIC TRAMPS IN NEW ZEALAND

TECHNIQUES AND EDUCATION

SNOW & ICE TECHNIQUES

ROPE TECHNIQUES

THE BOOK OF THE BIVVY

THE HILLWALKER'S MANUAL

THE TREKKER'S HANDBOOK

THE ADVENTURE ALTERNATIVE

BEYOND ADVENTURE

FAR HORIZONS - ADVENTURE TRAVEL FOR ALL

MOUNTAIN WEATHER

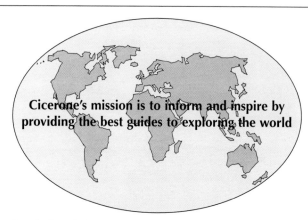

Cicerone's mission is to inform and inspire by providing the best guides to exploring the world

CICERONE